YOUR PERSONAL
HOROSCOPE
2024

JOSEPH POLANSKY

YOUR PERSONAL HOROSCOPE 2024

Month-by-month forecast for every sign

Thorsons

The author is grateful to the people
of STAR ★ DATA, who truly fathered
this book and without whom it
could not have been written.

Thorsons
An imprint of HarperCollins*Publishers*
1 London Bridge Street
London SE1 9GF

www.harpercollins.co.uk

HarperCollins*Publishers*
Macken House, 39/40 Mayor Street Upper
Dublin 1, D01 C9W8, Ireland

First published by Thorsons 2023

3 5 7 9 10 8 6 4

info@stardatamedia.com

Star ★ Data asserts the moral right to be
identified as the author of this work

A catalogue record of this book is
available from the British Library

ISBN 978-0-00-858931-8

Printed and bound in the U.S.A.
by Lake Book Manufacturing, LLC

Contents

Introduction

Welcome to the fascinating and intricate world of astrology!

For thousands of years the movements of the planets and other heavenly bodies have intrigued the best minds of every generation. Life holds no greater challenge or joy than this: knowledge of ourselves and the universe we live in. Astrology is one of the keys to this knowledge.

Your Personal Horoscope 2024 gives you the fruits of astrological wisdom. In addition to general guidance on your character and the basic trends of your life, it shows you how to take advantage of planetary influences so you can make the most of the year ahead.

The section on each sign includes a Personality Profile, a look at general trends for 2024, and in-depth month-by-month forecasts. The Glossary (*page 5*) explains some of the astrological terms you may be unfamiliar with.

One of the many helpful features of this book is the 'Best' and 'Most Stressful' days listed at the beginning of each monthly forecast. Read these sections to learn which days in each month will be good overall, good for money, and good for love. Mark them on your calendar – these will be your best days. Similarly, make a note of the days that will be most stressful for you. It is best to avoid booking important meetings or taking major decisions on these days, as well as on those days when important planets in your Horoscope are retrograde (moving backwards through the zodiac).

The Major Trends section for your sign lists those days when your vitality is strong or weak, or when relationships with your co-workers or loved ones may need a bit more effort on your part. If you are going through a difficult time, take a look at the colour, metal, gem and scent listed in the 'At a Glance' section of your Personality Profile. Wearing a piece of jewellery that contains your metal and/or gem will strengthen your vitality, just as wearing clothes or decorating your room or office in the colour ruled by your sign, drinking teas made from the herbs ruled by your sign or wearing the scents associated with your sign will sustain you.

Another important virtue of this book is that it will help you to know not only yourself but those around you: your friends, co-workers, partners and/or children. Reading the Personality Profile and forecasts for their signs will provide you with an insight into their behaviour that you won't get anywhere else. You will know when to be more tolerant of them and when they are liable to be difficult or irritable.

In this edition we have included foot reflexology charts as part of the health section. So many health problems could perhaps be avoided or alleviated if we understood which organs were most vulnerable and what we could do to protect them. Though there are many natural and drug-free ways to strengthen vulnerable organs, these charts show a valid way to proceed. The vulnerable organs for the year ahead are clearly marked in the charts. It's very good to massage the whole foot on a regular basis, as the feet contain reflexes to the entire body. Try to pay special attention to the specific areas marked in the charts. If this is done diligently, health problems can be avoided. And even if they can't be completely avoided, their impact can be softened considerably.

I consider you – the reader – my personal client. By studying your Solar Horoscope I gain an awareness of what is going on in your life – what you are feeling and striving for and the challenges you face. I then do my best to address these concerns. Consider this book the next best thing to having your own personal astrologer!

It is my sincere hope that *Your Personal Horoscope 2024* will enhance the quality of your life, make things easier, illuminate the way forward, banish obscurities and make you more aware of your personal connection to the universe. Understood properly and used wisely, astrology is a great guide to knowing yourself, the people around you and the events in your life – but remember that what you do with these insights – the final result – is up to you.

A Note on the 'New Zodiac'

Recently an article was published that postulated two things: the discovery of a new constellation – Ophiuchus – making a thirteenth constellation in the heavens and thus a thirteenth sign, and the statement that because the Earth has shifted relative to the constellations in the past few thousand years, all the signs have shifted backwards by one sign. This has caused much consternation, and I have received a stream of letters, emails and phone calls from people saying things like: 'I don't want to be a Taurus, I'm happy being a Gemini', 'What's my real sign?' or 'Now that I finally understand myself, I'm not who I think I am!'

All of this is 'much ado about nothing'. The article has some partial truth to it. Yes, in two thousand years the planets have shifted relative to the constellations in the heavens. This is old news. We know this and Hindu astrologers take this into account when casting charts. This shift doesn't affect Western astrologers in North America and Europe. We use what is called a 'tropical' zodiac. This zodiac has nothing to do with the constellations in the heavens. They have the same names, but that's about it. The tropical zodiac is based on the Earth's revolution around the Sun. Imagine the circle that this orbit makes, then divide this circle by twelve and you have our zodiac. The Spring Equinox is always 0 degrees (Aries), and the Autumn Equinox is always 0 degrees Libra (180 degrees from Aries). At one time a few thousand years ago, these tropical signs coincided with the actual constellations; they were pretty much interchangeable, and it didn't matter what zodiac you used. But in the course of thousands of years the planets have shifted relative to these constellations. Here in the West it doesn't affect our practice one iota. You are still the sign you always were.

In North America and Europe there is a clear distinction between an astrological sign and a constellation in the heavens. This issue is more of a problem for Hindu astrologers. Their zodiac is based on the actual constellations – this is called the 'sidereal' zodiac. And Hindu astrologers have been accounting for this shift all the time. They keep close tabs on it. In two thousand years there is a shift of 23 degrees, and they subtract this from the Western calculations. So in their system many a Gemini would be a Taurus and this is true for all the signs. This is nothing new – it is all known and accounted for, so there is no bombshell here.

The so-called thirteenth constellation, Ophiuchus, is also not a problem for the Western astrologer. As we mentioned, our zodiac has nothing to do with the constellations. It could be more of a problem for the Hindus, but my feeling is that it's not a problem for them either. What these astronomers are calling a new constellation was probably considered a part of one of the existing constellations. I don't know this as a fact, but I presume it is so intuitively. I'm sure we will soon be getting articles by Hindu astrologers explaining this.

Glossary of Astrological Terms

Ascendant

We experience day and night because the Earth rotates on its axis once every 24 hours. It is because of this rotation that the Sun, Moon and planets seem to rise and set. The zodiac is a fixed belt (imaginary, but very real in spiritual terms) around the Earth. As the Earth rotates, the different signs of the zodiac seem to the observer to rise on the horizon. During a 24-hour period every sign of the zodiac will pass this horizon point at some time or another. The sign that is at the horizon point at any given time is called the Ascendant, or rising sign. The Ascendant is the sign denoting a person's self-image, body and self-concept – the personal ego, as opposed to the spiritual ego indicated by a person's Sun sign.

Aspects

Aspects are the angular relationships between planets, the way in which one planet stimulates or influences another. If a planet makes a harmonious aspect (connection) to another, it tends to stimulate that planet in a positive and helpful way. If, however, it makes a stressful aspect to another planet, this disrupts that planet's normal influence.

Astrological Qualities

There are three astrological qualities: *cardinal, fixed* and *mutable*. Each of the 12 signs of the zodiac falls into one of these three categories.

Cardinal Signs
Aries, Cancer, Libra and Capricorn
The cardinal quality is the active, initiating principle. Those born
   under these four signs are good at starting new projects.

Fixed Signs
Taurus, Leo, Scorpio and Aquarius
Fixed qualities include stability, persistence, endurance and
   perfectionism. People born under these four signs are good at
   seeing things through.

Mutable Signs
Gemini, Virgo, Sagittarius and Pisces
Mutable qualities are adaptability, changeability and balance. Those
   born under these four signs are creative, if not always practical.

Direct Motion

When the planets move forward through the zodiac – as they normally
do – they are said to be going 'direct'.

Grand Square

A Grand Square differs from a normal Square (usually two planets
separated by 90 degrees) in that four or more planets are involved.
When you look at the pattern in a chart you will see a whole and
complete square. This, though stressful, usually denotes a new manifestation in the life. There is much work and balancing involved in the
manifestation.

Grand Trine

A Grand Trine differs from a normal Trine (where two planets are 120 degrees apart) in that three or more planets are involved. When you look at this pattern in a chart, it takes the form of a complete triangle – a Grand Trine. Usually (but not always) it occurs in one of the four elements: Fire, Earth, Air or Water. Thus the particular element in which it occurs will be highlighted. A Grand Trine in Water is not the same as a Grand Trine in Air or Fire, etc. This is a very fortunate and happy aspect, and quite rare.

Houses

There are 12 signs of the zodiac and 12 houses of experience. The 12 signs are personality types and ways in which a given planet expresses itself; the 12 houses show 'where' in your life this expression takes place. Each house has a different area of interest. A house can become potent and important – a house of power – in different ways: if it contains the Sun, the Moon or the 'ruler' of your chart; if it contains more than one planet; or if the ruler of that house is receiving unusual stimulation from other planets.

1st House
Personal Image and Sensual Delights

2nd House
Money/Finance

3rd House
Communication and Intellectual Interests

4th House
Home and Family

5th House
Children, Fun, Games, Creativity, Speculations and Love Affairs

6th House
Health and Work

7th House
Love, Marriage and Social Activities

8th House
Transformation and Regeneration

9th House
Religion, Foreign Travel, Higher Education and Philosophy

10th House
Career

11th House
Friends, Group Activities and Fondest Wishes

12th House
Spirituality

Karma

Karma is the law of cause and effect which governs all phenomena. We are all where we find ourselves because of karma – because of actions we have performed in the past. The universe is such a balanced instrument that any act immediately sets corrective forces into motion – karma.

Long-term Planets

The planets that take a long time to move through a sign show the long-term trends in a given area of life. They are important for forecasting the prolonged view of things. Because these planets stay in one sign for so long, there are periods in the year when the faster-moving (short-term) planets will join them, further activating and enhancing the importance of a given house.

Jupiter
stays in a sign for about 1 year

Saturn
2½ years

Uranus
7 years

Neptune
14 years

Pluto
15 to 30 years

Lunar

Relating to the Moon. See also 'Phases of the Moon', below.

Natal

Literally means 'birth'. In astrology this term is used to distinguish between planetary positions that occurred at the time of a person's birth (natal) and those that are current (transiting). For example, Natal Sun refers to where the Sun was when you were born; transiting Sun refers to where the Sun's position is currently at any given moment – which usually doesn't coincide with your birth, or Natal, Sun.

Out of Bounds

The planets move through the zodiac at various angles relative to the celestial equator (if you were to draw an imaginary extension of the Earth's equator out into the universe, you would have an illustration of this celestial equator). The Sun – being the most dominant and powerful influence in the Solar system – is the measure astrologers use as a standard. The Sun never goes more than approximately 23 degrees north or south of the celestial equator. At the winter solstice the Sun reaches its maximum southern angle of orbit (declination); at the summer solstice it reaches its maximum northern angle. Any time a planet exceeds this Solar boundary – and occasionally planets do – it is said to be 'out of bounds'. This means that the planet exceeds or trespasses into strange territory – beyond the limits allowed by the Sun, the ruler of the Solar system. The planet in this condition becomes more emphasized and exceeds its authority, becoming an important influence in the forecast.

Phases of the Moon

After the full Moon, the Moon seems to shrink in size (as perceived from the Earth), gradually growing smaller until it is virtually invisible to the naked eye – at the time of the next new Moon. This is called the waning Moon phase, or the waning Moon.

After the new Moon, the Moon gradually gets bigger in size (as perceived from the Earth) until it reaches its maximum size at the time of the full Moon. This period is called the waxing Moon phase, or waxing Moon.

Retrogrades

The planets move around the Sun at different speeds. Mercury and Venus move much faster than the Earth, while Mars, Jupiter, Saturn, Uranus, Neptune and Pluto move more slowly. Thus there are times when, relative to the Earth, the planets appear to be going backwards. In reality they are always going forward, but relative to our vantage point on Earth they seem to go backwards through the zodiac for a period of time. This is called 'retrograde' motion and tends to weaken the normal influence of a given planet.

Short-term Planets

The fast-moving planets move so quickly through a sign that their effects are generally of a short-term nature. They reflect the immediate, day-to-day trends in a horoscope.

Moon
stays in a sign for only 2½ days

Mercury
20 to 30 days

Sun
30 days

Venus
approximately 1 month

Mars
approximately 2 months

T-square

A T-square differs from a Grand Square (see above) in that it is not a complete square. If you look at the pattern in a chart it appears as 'half a complete square', resembling the T-square tools used by architects and designers. If you cut a complete square in half, diagonally, you have a T-square. Many astrologers consider this more stressful than a Grand Square, as it creates tension that is difficult to resolve. T-squares bring learning experiences.

Transits

This term refers to the movements or motions of the planets at any given time. Astrologers use the word 'transit' to make the distinction between a birth, or Natal, planet (see 'Natal', above) and the planet's current movement in the heavens. For example, if at your birth Saturn was in the sign of Cancer in your 8th house, but is now moving through your 3rd house, it is said to be 'transiting' your 3rd house. Transits are one of the main tools with which astrologers forecast trends.

Aries

THE RAM

Birthdays from
21st March to
20th April

Personality Profile

ARIES AT A GLANCE

Element – Fire

Ruling Planet – Mars
  Career Planet – Saturn
  Love Planet – Venus
  Money Planet – Venus
  Planet of Fun, Entertainment, Creativity and Speculations – Sun
  Planet of Health and Work – Mercury
  Planet of Home and Family Life – Moon
  Planet of Spirituality – Neptune
  Planet of Travel, Education, Religion and Philosophy – Jupiter

Colours – carmine, red, scarlet

Colours that promote love, romance and social harmony – green, jade
  green

Colour that promotes earning power – green

Gem – amethyst

Metals – iron, steel

Scent – honeysuckle

Quality – cardinal (= activity)

Quality most needed for balance – caution

Strongest virtues – abundant physical energy, courage, honesty, independence, self-reliance

Deepest need – action

Characteristics to avoid – haste, impetuousness, over-aggression, rashness

Signs of greatest overall compatibility – Leo, Sagittarius

Signs of greatest overall incompatibility – Cancer, Libra, Capricorn

Sign most helpful to career – Capricorn

Sign most helpful for emotional support – Cancer

Sign most helpful financially – Taurus

Sign best for marriage and/or partnerships – Libra

Sign most helpful for creative projects – Leo

Best Sign to have fun with – Leo

Signs most helpful in spiritual matters – Sagittarius, Pisces

Best day of the week – Tuesday

Understanding an Aries

Aries is the activist *par excellence* of the zodiac. The Aries need for action is almost an addiction, and those who do not really understand the Aries personality would probably this hard word to describe it. In reality 'action' is the essence of the Aries psychology – the more direct, blunt and to-the-point the action, the better. When you think about it, this is the ideal psychological makeup for the warrior, the pioneer, the athlete or the manager.

Aries likes to get things done, and in their passion and zeal often lose sight of the consequences for themselves and others. Yes, they often try to be diplomatic and tactful, but it is hard for them. When they do so they feel that they are being dishonest and phoney. It is hard for them even to understand the mindset of the diplomat, the consensus builder, the front office executive. These people are involved in endless meetings, discussions, talks and negotiations – all of which seem a great waste of time when there is so much work to be done, so many real achievements to be gained. An Aries can understand, once it is explained, that talk and negotiations – the social graces – lead ultimately to better, more effective actions. The interesting thing is that an Aries is rarely malicious or spiteful – even when waging war. Aries people fight without hate for their opponents. To them it is all good-natured fun, a grand adventure, a game.

When confronted with a problem many people will say, 'Well, let's think about it, let's analyse the situation.' But not an Aries. An Aries will think, 'Something must be done. Let's get on with it.' Of course, neither response is the total answer. Sometimes action is called for, sometimes cool thought. But an Aries tends to err on the side of action.

Action and thought are radically different principles. Physical activity is the use of brute force. Thinking and deliberating require one not to use force – to be still. It is not good for the athlete to be deliberating the next move; this will only slow down his or her reaction time. The athlete must act instinctively and instantly. This is how Aries people tend to behave in life. They are quick, instinctive decision-makers and their decisions tend to be translated into action almost immediately. When their intuition is sharp and well tuned, their actions are powerful and successful. When their intuition is off, their actions can be disastrous.

Do not think this will scare an Aries. Just as a good warrior knows that in the course of combat he or she might acquire a few wounds, so too does an Aries realize – somewhere deep down – that in the course of being true to yourself you might get embroiled in a disaster or two. It is all part of the game. An Aries feels strong enough to weather any storm.

There are many Aries people who are intellectual. They make powerful and creative thinkers. But even in this realm they tend to be pioneers – outspoken and blunt. These types of Aries tend to elevate (or sublimate) their desire for physical combat in favour of intellectual, mental combat. And they are indeed powerful.

In general, Aries people have a faith in themselves that others could learn from. This basic, rock-solid faith carries them through the most tumultuous situations of life. Their courage and self-confidence make them natural leaders. Their leadership is more by way of example than by actually controlling others.

Finance

Aries people often excel as builders or estate agents. Money in and of itself is not as important as are other things – action, adventure, sport, etc. They are motivated by the need to support and be well-thought-of by their partners. Money as a way of attaining pleasure is another important motivation. Aries function best in their own businesses or as managers of their own departments within a large business or corporation. The fewer orders they have to take from higher up, the better. They also function better out in the field rather than behind a desk.

Aries people are hard workers with a lot of endurance; they can earn large sums of money due to the strength of their sheer physical energy.

Venus is their money planet, which means that Aries need to develop more of the social graces in order to realize their full earning potential. Just getting the job done – which is what an Aries excels at – is not enough to create financial success. The co-operation of others needs to be attained. Customers, clients and co-workers need to be made to feel comfortable; many people need to be treated properly in order for success to happen. When Aries people develop these abilities – or hire someone to do this for them – their financial potential is unlimited.

Career and Public Image

One would think that a pioneering type would want to break with the social and political conventions of society. But this is not so with the Aries-born. They are pioneers within conventional limits, in the sense that they like to start their own businesses within an established industry.

Capricorn is on the 10th house of career cusp of Aries' solar horoscope. Saturn is the planet that rules their life's work and professional aspirations. This tells us some interesting things about the Aries character. First off, it shows that, in order for Aries people to reach their full career potential, they need to develop some qualities that are a bit alien to their basic nature: they need to become better administrators and organizers; they need to be able to handle details better and to take a long-range view of their projects and their careers in general. No one can beat an Aries when it comes to achieving short-range objectives, but a career is long term, built over time. You cannot take a 'quickie' approach to it.

Some Aries people find it difficult to stick with a project until the end. Since they get bored quickly and are in constant pursuit of new adventures, they prefer to pass an old project or task on to somebody else in order to start something new. Those Aries who learn how to put off the search for something new until the old is completed will achieve great success in their careers and professional lives.

In general, Aries people like society to judge them on their own merits, on their real and actual achievements. A reputation acquired by 'hype' feels false to them.

Love and Relationships

In marriage and partnerships Aries like those who are more passive, gentle, tactful and diplomatic – people who have the social grace and skills they sometimes lack. Our partners always represent a hidden part of ourselves – a self that we cannot express personally.

An Aries tends to go after what he or she likes aggressively. The tendency is to jump into relationships and marriages. This is especially true if Venus is in Aries as well as the Sun. If an Aries likes you, he or she will have a hard time taking no for an answer; many attempts will be made to sweep you off your feet.

Though Aries can be exasperating in relationships – especially if they are not understood by their partners – they are never consciously or wilfully cruel or malicious. It is just that they are so independent and sure of themselves that they find it almost impossible to see somebody else's viewpoint or position. This is why an Aries needs as a partner someone with lots of social graces.

On the plus side, an Aries is honest, someone you can lean on, someone with whom you will always know where you stand. What he or she lacks in diplomacy is made up for in integrity.

Home and Domestic Life

An Aries is of course the ruler at home – the Boss. The male will tend to delegate domestic matters to the female. The female Aries will want to rule the roost. Both tend to be handy round the house. Both like large families and both believe in the sanctity and importance of the family. An Aries is a good family person, although he or she does not especially like being at home a lot, preferring instead to be roaming about.

Considering that they are by nature so combative and wilful, Aries people can be surprisingly soft, gentle and even vulnerable with their children and partners. The sign of Cancer, ruled by the Moon, is on the cusp of their solar 4th house of home and family. When the Moon is well aspected – under favourable influences – in the birth chart, an Aries will be tender towards the family and will want a family life that is nurturing and supportive. Aries likes to come home after a hard day on the battlefield of life to the understanding arms of their partner and the unconditional love and support of their family. An Aries feels that there is enough 'war' out in the world – and he or she enjoys participating in that. But when Aries comes home, comfort and nurturing are what's needed.

Horoscope for 2024

Major Trends

Last year was, for the most part, happy and prosperous. Jupiter was in your sign until May and then he moved into your money house. So it was a prosperous year. The prosperity continues in the year ahead as Jupiter is still in your money house until May 26. On May 26 Jupiter moves on into your 3rd house and stays there for the rest of the year ahead. This is a great transit for students, teachers, writers and intellectual workers, sales and marketing people. All of you will enjoy enhanced intellectual and communication abilities. Students will do well in school.

Pluto, the planet of transformation and new birth, has been moving through your 10th career house for many, many years now. So, you have been giving birth to your ideal career, your ideal life work. But as we mentioned last year, he is getting ready to move out of your career house and into your 11th house. This year he will spend a few months in your 11th house and then will move back into your 10th house. Most of the career dramas are over with, however, although those of you born late in Aries, April 17 to 19, will feel this transit most strongly. It can bring dramas in the lives of children and changes in your creative life. Those of you who have heart problems need to take more care of the heart.

Last year Saturn, your career planet, moved into Pisces your spiritual 12th house and joined Neptune in that house. This is the situation for the entire year ahead. Spirituality has been important in your life for many years now and becomes even more important in the year ahead. More on this later.

Your most important interests in the year ahead are finance until May 26; communication and intellectual interests from May 26 onwards; career, from January 1 to January 22 and from September 3 to November 20; and spirituality.

Your paths of greatest fulfilment this year are the body and image; finance until May 26; and communication and intellectual interests from May 26 on.

Health

(Please note that this is an astrological perspective on health and not a medical one. In days of yore there was no difference, both these perspectives were identical. But these days there could be quite a difference. For a medical perspective, please consult your doctor or health practitioner.)

Although some of you – those born late in the sign from April 17–19 – need to pay more attention to the heart, for most of you, health should be good this year. There are no long-term planets stressing you out. They are either making harmonious aspects to you or leaving you alone. Further, your 6th house of health is pretty much empty this year; only short-term planets will move through there for short periods of time. This I consider a positive for health as it shows that you don't need to focus overly much on it – there is no need to give it special attention. Health is good, so there is no need to fix something that isn't broken. Sure, as our regular readers know, there will be times during the year when health and energy are less easy than usual. But these times are not trends for the year, only short-term blips caused by the transiting planets. When they move away your naturally good health and energy returns.

Good though your health is, you can make it better. Give more attention to the following – the vulnerable areas of your Horoscope this year (the reflex points are shown in the chart opposite):

- The head, face and skull are always important areas for Aries. Regular head and face massage will be a great pick-me-up. You not only strengthen the given area but the entire body as well. Craniosacral therapy is also excellent for the skull. The plates in the skull are movable and need to be kept in right alignment.
- The musculature. You don't need to be a bodybuilder but you do need good muscle tone. Weak or flabby muscles can knock the spine and skeleton out of alignment, and this will cause all kinds of other problems. So vigorous physical exercise, according to your age and stage in life, seems very important.
- The adrenals. The important thing with the adrenals is to avoid anger and fear, the two emotions that stress them out.

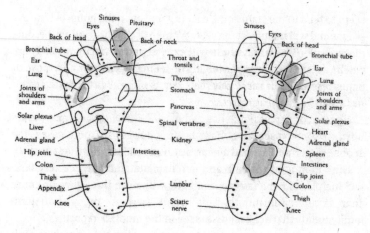

Important foot reflexology points for the year ahead

Try to massage all of the foot on a regular basis – the top of the foot as well as the bottom – but pay extra attention to the points highlighted on the chart. When you massage, be aware of 'sore spots' as these need special attention. It's also a good idea to massage the ankles and below them.

- The arms, shoulders, lungs and respiratory system. Regular arm and shoulder massage will be wonderful; Tension tends to collect in the shoulders and needs to be released.
- The small intestine.
- The heart (for those born late in Aries). The important thing with the heart is to avoid worry and anxiety, as these are the emotions that stress it out. Replace worry with faith.

Since these areas are the most vulnerable in your Horoscope, problems, if they do occur, will most likely happen there. So keeping them healthy and fit is sound preventive medicine.

Home and Family

Your 4th house of home and family is not prominent this year, it's not a house of power. This will change next year, but in the meantime this would show a stable kind of home and family year. Although things seem to tend to the status quo, a lot is going on in the home behind the scenes and will manifest next year. Women of childbearing age become more fertile. The family circle will expand and in happy ways. There will be a good fortune in the buying or selling of a home and a move or happy renovation is very likely. This year is more about preparation for next year.

A parent or parent figure has had marital challenges for many years now; in some cases, they have been widowed. In some cases, the spouse or partner has had a near-death experience or major surgery.

The Moon is your home and family planet and she is a very fast-moving planet – the fastest of all. She will move through your entire chart in any given month. This means there are many short-term family trends that are best discussed in the monthly reports.

A parent or parent figure could have moved last year, but this year it seems that moves for either of the parents or parent figures are not likely. A sibling or sibling figure is having a prosperous year, but again, a move doesn't seem likely. If he or she is single romance is likely to happen. Children and children figures in your life can feel cramped in their home but a move is not advisable. Let them use their creativity to make better use of the space that they have. Psychological or spiritual counselling would be a great help to them. Grandchildren, if you have them, or those who play that role in your life, will have a prosperous year but a move is more likely next year than this year.

Finance and Career

As we mentioned earlier, you are continuing a prosperity cycle that began last year. Jupiter in your money house expands earnings, makes assets that you already own more valuable and brings happy financial opportunities. You tend to be a risk-taker in finance and this year it seems to pay off. Speculations seem favourable. Of course, you should never do this blindly but only under intuition. Jupiter moving through your money house favours foreign investments and investments in foreign companies. Foreigners in general seem very important in your financial life. This transit favours the publishing and travel businesses, and it indicates that you are doing a lot of business-related travel this year. In April Jupiter will travel with Uranus and this can bring sudden

and unexpected financial benefit. The financial life is especially exciting in April and is very positive.

When Jupiter moves into Gemini on May 26 the transit favours
buying, selling, trading and retailing. You seem fortunate in those
activities.

Uranus has been in your money house for many years now and will
still be there for the rest of the year ahead. So, you have been making
many financial changes over the years – dramatic ones – and this
continues in the year ahead. Friends and social connections have been
helpful in finance. The tech industry and the online world in general is
important financially. If you are an investor, you have a good feeling for
these kinds of companies.

Pluto, as mentioned above, has been moving through your 10th
house of career for a long, long time. And over the past 30 years or so
your career has been completely transformed and reborn and in a
better way, more to your liking. Last year another important career
development happened as Saturn, your career planet, moved into
Pisces, your 12th house of spirituality and idealism. So, you've been
feeling a need for a more idealistic kind of career. You have the feeling
that there is more to the career than just being successful and making
money. You want something that is more idealistic, more helpful to the
world. This position would favour careers with non-profit organizations, charities, or companies involved in altruistic kinds of activities.
In many cases it might not be necessary to change the actual career,
and it might not be practical. However, you can involve yourself in
these things and further your career that way. You might become
known more for your charitable activities than for your professional
skills. In addition, important career contacts can be made as you
involve yourself in charitable causes.

Love and Social Life

Your 7th house of love is not a house of power this year, with only
short-term planets moving through there briefly. So this is not a major
focus in the year ahead. Also, most of the long-term planets are in the
Eastern sector of your Horoscope, the sector of self, meaning that your
path of personal happiness seems more important than relationships

or other people. You feel you want to get that straightened out first and then love will happen later on.

The empty 7th house tends to a status quo kind of love year. Those who are already married will tend to stay married and singles will tend to stay single. You seem OK with things as they are.

Two eclipses in the year ahead occur in your 7th house. The first is a lunar eclipse on March 25 and the second is a solar eclipse on October 2. These will tend to test the current relationship. Dirty laundry, long-suppressed grievances, tend to surface for resolution. If the relationship is basically sound it will survive and even get better. But a fundamentally unsound relationship could dissolve under the stress.

While romance is basically stable this year, friendships tend to be active. You seem friendly with money people in your life and a lot of your socializing seems business related. You like to do business with friends and like to socialize with those you do business with. Social connections, as we mentioned, are very important in your financial life.

A sibling or sibling figure finds romance this year and it could even lead to marriage. The relationships of children or children figures in your life become more stormy this year. This will be a long-term trend. Grandchildren of an appropriate age are having a quiet love and social year.

Self-improvement

As we mentioned earlier, Saturn's move into your 12th house makes the spiritual life even more important than it has already been for many years. For a good number of years Neptune has been in your 12th house, thus spirituality was very idealistic and moody. In a good mood you could see heaven and the choirs of angels and had high mystical experiences. But in a bad mood you were capable of becoming an atheist. Now with Saturn in your 12th house you are going to bring order and stability to the spiritual life. Progress will happen through daily discipline and regimes, regardless of your mood of the moment. This aspect favours a more scientific and structured approach to spirituality. Also, with Saturn in your 12th house there is a need to see practical results from your spiritual practice. It's not just about having mystical experiences. It has to improve your everyday life and your career. We discussed Saturn's move into your 12th house as it relates to your career. But another way to read this transit is that your career, your real mission, these days is your spiritual growth and practice.

Pluto is in the midst of his transition from Capricorn to Aquarius, from your 10th house to your 11th. This year he visits the 11th house twice, but next year he will be there for the long haul, for the next 30 or so years. So an alchemical process is happening in your social life and especially your friendships. Long-time friendships will get tested and new and better ones will come. Over the next 30 years or so you will be in a completely different social situation.

Month-by-month Forecasts

January

Best Days Overall: 8, 9, 16, 17, 25, 26, 27
Most Stressful Days Overall: 5, 6, 20, 10, 11, 23, 24, 30, 31
Best Days for Love: 5, 6, 8, 9, 27, 28, 30, 31
Best Days for Money: 1, 2, 8, 9, 10, 11, 18, 19, 27, 28, 29
Best Days for Career: 6, 10, 11, 14, 23

Though health and energy could be better, the month ahead is both successful and prosperous. If you feel tired, make sure to get some rest. Enhance the health with thigh massage and massage of the liver reflex point until the 14th. After the 14th back and knee massage will be wonderful for you.

You are in the midst of a yearly career peak until the 20th, so the focus is on the career this month; home and family issues can take a back seat for a while. You serve your family best by being successful in your career. The new Moon of the 11th occurs in your 10th house, making it an especially strong career day. But you will feel the effects of this new Moon well into next month, until the next new Moon. This new Moon will clarify career issues and bring you all the information you need to make a proper decision. It will also clarify issues involving parents, bosses and the government. Mars, the ruler of your Horoscope, enters your 10th house on the 5th and stays there for the rest of the month. This is another indicator of career success. You are elevated not only because of your professional skills but also because of who you are as a person.

The Sun is making very beautiful aspects to Jupiter early in the month, indicating luck in speculations and the prosperity of a child or child figure in your life. Jupiter, who has been in your money house since last year, is still there in the month ahead, signifying that great financial expansion is happening. This will go on for a few more months, until May 26.

February

Best Days Overall: 4, 5, 12, 13, 21, 22, 23
Most Stressful Days Overall: 6, 7, 19, 20, 26, 27, 28
Best Days for Love: 6, 7, 17, 26, 27, 28
Best Days for Money: 6, 7, 14, 15, 17, 18, 24, 25, 26, 27
Best Days for Career: 6, 7, 10, 19, 29

Health and energy are much improved this month as most of the short-term planetary stress has ceased for the moment. You can enhance your health even further through back and knee massage until the 4th and with ankle and calf massage from the 4th to the 23rd. You seem more open to alternative and experimental therapies from the 4th onwards too. On the 23rd, as Mercury your health planet enters your 12th house, enhance the health with foot massage and spiritual-healing techniques.

Children and children figures in your life are having a very strong social month. They seem more popular than usual. This is a strong social month for you as well but not necessarily a romantic one. The month ahead favours Platonic relationships, friendships and group activities. Being involved with friends, organizations and groups will help your bottom line as well. Though you are not in a career peak this month, you still seem very successful as Mars, your Horoscope's ruler, is still moving through your 10th house of career until the 13th. On the 19th, as the Sun enters Pisces, he starts to make wonderful aspects to your career planet. This will continue to boost your career. Your 12th house of spirituality has been very powerful for the past two years, and it becomes even more powerful after the 19th. So, this is an excellent month for those of you on the spiritual path: great progress should be made.

Finances are still very fortunate. Your financial planet, Venus, in your 11th house from the 17th onwards favours the tech and online worlds. You have been experimental in your finances for many years, and this month perhaps even more so than usual. You have rich friends and they seem to provide financial opportunities.

Singles can find romantic opportunities as they get involved with friends, groups and organizations. There are romantic opportunities to be found online and through social media. But these don't seem like serious things – more like experiments.

March

Best Days Overall: 2, 3, 11, 12, 19, 20, 21, 29, 30
Most Stressful Days Overall: 4, 5, 6, 17, 18, 24, 25, 26
Best Days for Love: 7, 8, 17, 18, 24, 25, 26, 27, 28
Best Days for Money: 4, 5, 7, 8, 13, 14, 17, 22, 23, 27, 28
Best Days for Career: 4, 5, 6, 9, 10, 17, 18, 27, 28, 29

Spirituality and the lunar eclipse of the 25th are the main headlines of the month ahead. Sixty per cent of the planetary power will be either in your 12th house or moving through there. This is a lot of power, a lot of spiritual stimulation. So again, like last month, this is a time for intense spiritual growth and for spiritual breakthroughs. The spiritual world, though invisible, is letting you know that it is around. The month ahead will be filled with all kinds of supernatural phenomena. Your dream life will be more active than usual and probably more revelatory. Your ESP abilities are greatly enhanced this month – especially from the 15th to the 17th as Neptune gets stimulated by other planets. Your intense spiritual focus will help you get through the lunar eclipse of the 25th.

This lunar eclipse occurs in your 7th house of love and will test marriages and romantic relationships. Sometimes it is not the relationship itself that is at fault; it is the fact that the spouse, partner or current love is having their own personal dramas. This complicates the relationship. The beloved's parent or parent figure may also be having personal dramas. Perhaps he or she is experiencing career changes.

With the Moon ruling your 6th house, every lunar eclipse impacts your home and family life, and this one is no different. There can be personal dramas in the lives of family members, and especially that of a parent of parent figure. Repairs might be needed in the home. Sometimes an eclipse will reveal hidden flaws in the home that you were unaware of. Thus, now you have a chance to correct these flaws.

The planetary momentum is overwhelmingly forward this month – all the planets are moving forward. So, the pace of life is quicker than usual. Progress to your goals happens more quickly. This is how you like things.

The Sun will move into your own sign on the 20th and will stay there for the rest of the month ahead. You are entering one of your yearly personal pleasure peaks. This is a time to enjoy all the pleasures of the senses and to get the body in the shape that you want. Children and children figures in your life seem very devoted to you from the 20th onwards. Job-seekers or those who hire others have great prospects from the 10th onwards; if you are looking for work job opportunities will seek you out. The same is true if you employ others: the right employee is seeking you.

April

Best Days Overall: 7, 8, 16, 17, 26, 27
Most Stressful Days Overall: 1, 2, 13, 14, 15, 21, 22, 28, 29
Best Days for Love: 7, 8, 16, 17, 21, 22, 27, 28
Best Days for Money: 7, 8, 9, 10, 16, 17, 18, 19, 27, 28
Best Days for Career: 1, 2, 5, 6, 13, 14, 23, 24, 28, 29

The main headline of this month is a very strong solar eclipse on the 8th that occurs in your own sign. This eclipse is strong for many reasons. For a start, it is a total eclipse; secondly, it occurs in your sign; and thirdly, it impacts two other planets, Mercury and Venus. So, do take it easy and relax your schedule while the eclipse is in effect. Usually this is a few days before and a few days after it happens, but sensitive people will feel an eclipse's effects up to two weeks before it happens. Each of you will get a personal cosmic message as to when to start to take it easy. Some wild or unexpected event will happen that will alert you. Since the Sun is your planet of children, children and children figures also need to take it easy. They can experience personal dramas in their lives. Both you and any children figures have a need to re-define yourselves: your image, the way that you think of yourself and the way that you want others to think of you. This will lead to wardrobe changes and changes in your presentation in the coming months. If you and/or the children figures haven't been careful in dietary matters, this eclipse can bring a detox of the body.

Since your money planet Venus is affected by this eclipse, there can be financial shake-ups and a need to make important financial changes. Course corrections are needed both in the social life and in finance. Once again, like last month your current relationship will get tested. If the relationship is basically sound it will survive and perhaps get even better, but if it is fundamentally flawed it is in danger. A parent or parent figure has financial dramas and is forced to make important changes.

The impact on Mercury shows that cars and communication equipment will get tested. Often, repairs or replacements are necessary. It would be a good idea to drive more carefully while the eclipse is in effect – in fact, better not to do any unnecessary driving, if possible. Siblings and sibling figures are also affected by this eclipse and are likely to have personal dramas. Students can experience dramas at school and sometimes they even change schools. There are changes in their educational plans.

The impact on Mercury also indicates there will be dramas in your place of work, perhaps job changes happening. Those of you who employ others can experience employee turnover in the coming months.

There will be important changes in your health regime in the coming months as well.

May

Best Days Overall: 5, 6, 13, 14, 23, 24
Most Stressful Days Overall: 11, 12, 17, 18, 19, 25, 26
Best Days for Love: 7, 8, 15, 16, 20, 21, 22, 27, 28
Best Days for Money: 7, 8, 15, 16, 26, 27, 28
Best Days for Career: 3, 4, 11, 12, 21, 22, 25, 26, 30, 31

A lot of important changes are happening this month. Mars moves into your sign on the 1st and stays there for the rest of the month ahead. Jupiter will leave your money house on the 26th and enter your 3rd house. By the 20th – and especially by the 26th – most of your important financial goals have been achieved and you can now direct attention to other things – your education, your mental development and your stock of knowledge. Jupiter's move into your 3rd house will enhance your mental and communication faculties, and the Sun's move into the 3rd house on the 20th enhances them even further.

Almost all of the planets are moving forward this month, so the pace of life is fast. Progress happens quickly, and with Mars in your own sign the pace of life is probably even quicker than we say. Health and energy are excellent this month. You have the energy of five people and are probably doing the work of five people! A good way to work off some of this extra energy is to spend more time in the gym. Avoid confrontations wherever possible and watch the temper.

The Sun and Uranus are travelling together on the 13th and 14th; for the children and children figures in your life this brings a happy romantic or social experience – much depends on their age. For you it shows a need to be more mindful on the physical plane: be careful not to be too much in a hurry. A parent or parent figure is again making important financial changes. Unexpected money can come to this person but also an unexpected expense can happen.

The month ahead is a very prosperous; you have been in a yearly financial peak since April 19. Venus remains in your money house until the 23rd. On the social level this would tend to indicate an attraction to wealthy people, the good providers and people who show love in material ways. On the material level this would indicate enhanced prosperity, which we have discussed earlier. Venus in the 3rd house after the 23rd shows earning through buying, selling and trading. The gift of the gab is not only important in your financial life but also in your romantic life. You are attracted to smart people, intellectuals, people who are easy to talk to. Romantic opportunity can happen at school or school functions, lectures, seminars and perhaps at the library or bookstore.

June

Best Days Overall: 1, 2, 9, 10, 11, 19, 20, 28, 29
Most Stressful Days Overall: 7, 8, 14, 15, 16, 21, 22
Best Days for Love: 5, 6, 14, 15, 16, 17, 26, 27, 30
Best Days for Money: 3, 4, 5, 6, 14, 16, 17, 24, 26, 27
Best Days for Career: 7, 8, 17, 18, 21, 22, 23, 26, 27

Pluto has been retrograde since May 2, signalling that the spouse, partner or current love needs to be more careful with major investments or purchases. These need a lot more research, and this will be the situation for many months to come. If surgery has been recommended to you, and it is elective, better to postpone.

The power this month is in your 3rd house of communication and intellectual interests, and it will be a very good month for students, writers, teachers, bloggers and intellectual workers. Your mental and intellectual faculties are still very enhanced, and this will be the case for many more months. Jupiter's position firmly in your 3rd house often shows someone who acquires a new car and communication equipment.

Mars is still in your first house until the 9th, so keep in mind our discussion of this last month. On the 9th Mars will move into your money house and stay there for the rest of June. This indicates a very personal focus on finance. You seem to be personally involved with this and not delegating it to others. In general, you tend to be speculative and risk-taking in finance and this month, especially from the 9th onwards, even more so than usual. Financial decisions are made very quickly, perhaps too quickly. Sleep on things before making an important decision. Mercury travels with Uranus on the 24th and 25th. It is a good idea to drive more carefully on those days, and there might be dramas at the workplace. More changes are happening in your health regime as well.

Saturn, your career planet, goes retrograde on the 29th. In the meantime, both the Sun and Venus move into your 4th house of home and family (Venus on the 17th and the Sun on the 20th). So, we have a very clear message: career issues will need time to resolve. In the meantime, focus on the home and family. With these kinds of planetary positions, it's beneficial to work on the career in a meditative and imaginative way, rather than by overt physical actions. This will set the stage for future career success when Saturn starts to move forward again. Two important planets are out of bounds this month. Mercury will be out of bounds from the 11th to the 29th and Venus will be out of bounds from the 13th to the 29th. Thus, in love and finance you're venturing outside your usual sphere. Probably there are no answers for you in the usual places and you must seek them elsewhere.

July

Best Days Overall: 7, 8, 17, 18, 25, 26
Most Stressful Days Overall: 4, 5, 6, 12, 13, 19, 20
Best Days for Love: 5, 6, 12, 13, 17, 18, 25, 26
Best Days for Money: 1, 2, 3, 5, 6, 12, 13, 17, 18, 21, 22, 25, 26, 27, 28, 29, 30
Best Days for Career: 4, 5, 6, 14, 15, 16, 19, 20, 23, 24

Many of the trends that we wrote of last month are still in effect this month, especially until the 22nd. The focus needs to be on the home and family and, more importantly, on your emotional wellness. Once you find your point of emotional harmony the career will take care of itself in due course. But with your career planet still retrograde, give it more time.

Health needs more attention this month, but there is nothing serious afoot – only short-term stress caused by the short-term planets. When your energy is less than normal pre-existing conditions can flare up and seem to be more severe. But this will pass. Until the 2nd enhance the health with right diet and emotional wellness. From the 2nd to the 25th it will be beneficial to pay more attention to the heart.

A light-hearted attitude to life will do much to improve your health. Joy itself is a powerful healing force, as you will see this month. After the 25th pay more attention to the small intestine. Right diet seems important now as well.

Finances are still good, with Mars remaining in your money house until the 20th. You still seem very focused on finance. You're spending on yourself and adopting the image of prosperity. People see you as a money person these days.

Mars will travel with Uranus on the 13th and 14th which brings a happy connection with a friend or with an organization. You seem more experimental with the body those days too, and it is probably a good idea to be more mindful on the physical plane. If you are experimenting with the body, do it in a safe kind of way.

On the 20th Mars joins Jupiter in your 3rd house. This adds to the focus on communication and intellectual activities which has been discussed in previous months.

Venus, which does double duty in your Horoscope – she is both love planet and the financial planet – is in your 4th house until the 11th. This shows that you are socializing more from home and with the family. You spend more on the home and family and perhaps earn from there as well. Family and family connections seem financially supportive. On the 11th Venus will move into your 5th house and stay there for the rest of the month ahead. This is a happy financial transit. It shows happy money, money that is earned in happy ways and which is spent on happy things. You are enjoying the wealth that you have. You spend on the children and the children figures in your life, and on fun leisure activities.

The new Moon of the 5th occurs in your 4th house. This will clarify many of your emotional issues and relations with the family.

Health and energy improve dramatically from the 22nd onwards.

August

Best Days Overall: 3, 4, 13, 14, 21, 22, 30, 31
Most Stressful Days Overall: 1, 2, 8, 9, 15, 16, 28, 29
Best Days for Love: 8, 9, 17, 18, 29
Best Days for Money: 8, 9, 17, 18, 23, 24, 25, 27, 29
Best Days for Career: 11, 12, 15, 16, 19, 20, 28, 29

A happy month ahead, Aries – enjoy! You are in the midst of a yearly personal pleasure peak. It began on July 22 and will go on until the 22nd of this month. Health and energy are excellent and there is no reason not to enjoy life. The opportunities for this will certainly come, and it's up to you to take them. This is a great month to take a vacation from your cares and worries and just enjoy life. When you emerge from this on the 22nd you'll have a whole new perspective on things.

Mercury, your health planet, is retrograde from the 4th to the 25th, so this is not a good time for medical tests or procedures. If you can, try to reschedule them for either before the retrograde or after. Of course, if there's no choice you must just do your best. Enhance the health with abdominal and chest massage this month.

Venus, which rules both love and finance in your life, will be in the sign of Virgo until the 29th. This complicates both love and finance. Venus is not happy in the sign of Virgo, and this is probably the case in both love and finance. Happily this transit is short term and passes quickly – by the 29th she moves into Libra, her own sign and house. Here, she is happy and powerful: a great signal for both love and money. Meanwhile, money is earned the old-fashioned way, through work and productive service. This is not an especially good aspect for speculations or winning the lottery.

In love the main danger is being hyper-critical. You are more of a perfectionist while Venus is in Virgo. Probably the spouse, partner or current love is also like this. Singles would be attracting these kinds of people. Perfection is your right and your ultimate destiny, but perfection is a road to be travelled, it is generally not handed to us on a plate. Work to improve your relationship every day and you will be on the road to perfection, though the ultimate destination seems far off. In life, we must enjoy the road as much as the destination.

Venus in Libra, your 7th house, shows that there are happy financial partnerships or joint ventures happening. The opportunities will certainly come. Your social connections are always important financially but this period even more so. Your social grace and charm, your ability to get on with others, are probably more important financially than your professional skills. For singles, Venus in Libra signals a happy love interest, and the person seems wealthy – well off.

The family as a whole seems more prosperous this month. The Sun's entry into Virgo on the 22nd brings prosperity for children and children figures in your life. It is also a wonderful aspect for job-seekers. You're in the mood for work and prospective employers pick up on this.

September

Best Days Overall: 1, 9, 10, 18, 19, 26, 27, 28
Most Stressful Days Overall: 4, 5, 6, 12, 13, 24, 25
Best Days for Love: 4, 5, 6, 14, 15, 23, 24
Best Days for Money: 4, 5, 6, 14, 15, 20, 21, 22, 23, 24
Best Days for Career: 7, 8, 12, 13, 16, 17, 24, 25

Venus remains in her own sign and house, Libra, until the 23rd. This is a good signal for both love and the money. For singles, it shows a happy love interest. Love is much more romantic and happy than it was last month. Your earning power is also much stronger with Venus in her own sign and house. As we mentioned last month, this can bring opportunities for partnerships or joint ventures. Of course, you don't just jump into these things, the details always matter, but the opportunities will be there. Health and energy are basically good but after the 22nd will need more watching. Enhance the health with chest massage until the 9th and abdominal massage from the 9th to the 26th. After the 26th hip massage and massage of the kidney reflex will be helpful. If health problems do arise, restore harmony with your friends, spouse, partner or current love as quickly as possible.

A lunar eclipse on the 18th is probably the main headline of the month. It occurs in your 12th house and impacts your spiritual planet, Neptune. So, important spiritual changes are going on. The dream life is likely to be hyperactive while the eclipse is in effect, but it's not advisable to pay too much attention to these things, as it will mostly be merely distorted images caused by the disturbance in the astral realm. In coming months you will be making important changes to your spiritual practice, teachers and teachings in general. Your attitudes to spirituality will also undergo important changes. Guru figures in your life will have personal dramas. There will be shake-ups and disturbances in spiritual or charitable organizations you are involved with.

This eclipse will sideswipe Jupiter, although not a direct hit. But it will force changes in your religious, philosophical and theological beliefs. This is basically a good thing as many of our beliefs need to be changed, amended or revised. Some need to be dispensed with altogether. This is usually not pleasant while it's happening, but the end result is good. It will change the way you live your life. The eclipse can also bring dramas and disturbances in your place of worship and personal dramas in the lives of worship leaders. Students at college level will change their educational plans, and sometimes even change schools. If you are involved in legal issues they will take a dramatic turn this month, one way or another.

Foreign travel is not recommended while the eclipse is in effect, and you should be more patient with family members as the eclipse can bring up all kinds of grievances and passions.

Mars, the ruler of your Horoscope, will enter your 4th house of home and family on the 5th and stay there for the rest of the month. This is an excellent time to do renovations or major repairs on the home. The lunar eclipse of the 18th could necessitate this.

October

Best Days Overall: 6, 7, 8, 15, 16, 24, 25
Most Stressful Days Overall: 1, 2, 3, 9, 10, 21, 22, 23, 29, 30
Best Days for Love: 1, 2, 3, 4, 5, 13, 14, 24, 25, 29, 30
Best Days for Money: 2, 4, 5, 11, 12, 13, 14, 17, 18, 19, 20, 24, 25, 29, 30
Best Days for Career: 4, 5, 9, 10, 13, 14, 21, 22, 23, 31

A solar eclipse on the 2nd, though not a total eclipse, still seems to have a strong impact you, so you should relax your schedule while this eclipse is in effect. This applies to children and children figures as well. Things that must be done, should be, of course, but anything that's not urgent – especially if it's stressful – is best rescheduled.

This eclipse occurs in your 7th house of love and will once again test your current relationship. The kinds of tests tend to vary. Sometimes the spouse, partner or current love is undergoing a personal crisis or drama and this is what tests the relationship. More often, old, long-buried grievances surface to be dealt with. Good relationships will survive these things, but flawed ones are in danger.

This eclipse is a direct hit on Mars, the ruler of your Horoscope, and brings a need to re-define yourself, your self-concept and the image you want to project to others. This is basically a healthy thing to do from time to time but here the events of the eclipse force it on you. The same re-definition is going on with children and children figures in your life. This will lead in the coming months to wardrobe and appearance changes.

Mercury, your health and work planet, is also impacted by this eclipse, and so there can be dramas at your place of work, perhaps job changes. Those of you who employ others will have dramas with employees and perhaps unexpected employee turnover in the coming months. The health regime will also change over the coming months, and probably in dramatic ways. This is not necessarily a bad thing. You've had a need to do this for a while and the eclipse is just forcing the issue.

Cars and communication equipment will get tested, and perhaps repairs or replacements are necessary. This not only applies to you but to children and children figures as well. Best to avoid unnecessary driving while the eclipse is in effect, but if you must drive be more mindful and defensive.

November

Best Days Overall: 3, 4, 12, 13, 20, 21, 29, 30
Most Stressful Days Overall: 5, 6, 18, 19, 25, 26, 27
Best Days for Love: 3, 4, 12, 13, 22, 23, 25, 26, 27
Best Days for Money: 3, 4, 8, 9, 12, 13, 14, 15, 16, 17, 22, 23, 26, 27
Best Days for Career: 1, 2, 5, 6, 10, 11, 18, 19, 28, 29

Saturn, your career planet, starts to move forward on the 5th; career issues are now clarified and you can begin to move forward with your career.

Venus will be out of bounds all month. This gives important information on both love and finance. You are outside your normal boundaries in both these areas of life. There are no answers for you in your natural sphere so you must search outside it. You must be a bit more daring. Sometimes this position signals that your current love, spouse or partner is also outside his or her normal boundaries and that pulls you as well. This can also be true of the money people in your life.

Mercury, too, will be out of bounds from the 7th to December 2. Thus, in health matters you also seem outside your normal boundaries. Perhaps the obligations of work also pull you outside your normal boundaries.

Health is good this month, however, and will get even better from the 21st onwards. You can enhance your health even further with a detox regime at the start of the month, and with massage of the thighs and the liver reflex from the 2nd onwards.

The planetary power this month is in the 8th house of regeneration, until the 21st. This is a great period for occult studies, deep psychological study and detox regimes of both mind and body. It is a good time to resurrect projects that you thought were dead. It is also a sexually active kind of month – whatever your age or stage in life the libido is stronger than usual.

Venus will be in Sagittarius, your 9th house, until the 11th. This is excellent for finances. It shows financial expansion and larger-than-life financial goals. Larger goals tend to prosperity even if you don't completely realize them. By nature, you are a free spender, Aries, but this month even more so than usual. On the 11th, as Venus moves into conservative Capricorn, the financial judgement improves. You regain a good down-to-earth attitude to finances. Normally you are attracted to a quick buck, but from the 11th onwards you have a more long-term perspective on wealth. Pay rises can come, perhaps bonuses as well. The authority figures in your life seem favourably disposed to your financial goals. Your good career reputation leads to financial opportunities.

The love life, too, seems happy. Singles find romantic opportunities at college or religious functions until the 11th. You are attracted to educated and refined people. You like people who can teach you, or from whom you can learn. You have the aspects of a person who falls in love with the professor or worship leader. Sometimes people at your place of warship can play Cupid. After the 11th the needs in love change a bit. You are attracted to people of power, authority and prestige, and you will be mixing with these kinds of people. The problem with this position is that you can be tempted to relationships of convenience rather than of true love.

December

Best Days Overall: 1, 9, 10, 17, 18, 28, 29
Most Stressful Days Overall: 2, 3, 4, 15, 16, 22, 23, 24, 30, 31
Best Days for Love: 2, 3, 4, 13, 14, 22, 23, 24
Best Days for Money: 2, 3, 4, 6, 11, 12, 13, 14, 22, 23, 24
Best Days for Career: 2, 3, 4, 7, 8, 15, 16, 25, 26, 30, 31

A happy and successful month ahead. Enjoy.

Mars, your Horoscope's ruling planet (and so very important in your chart), will spend the month in your 5th house of fun, children and creativity. It is a mini personal pleasure peak. Along with this, the beneficent 9th house is very strong until the 21st. This brings foreign travel for many of you. College-level students do well in their studies. Religious, theological and philosophical subjects interest you very much. The mood is optimistic.

Health and energy are excellent, especially until the 21st. After the 21st health will need more attention. As always, make sure to get enough rest. Enhance the health, like last month, with massage of the liver reflex and the thighs.

Mercury, your health planet, began to go backwards on November 25 and remains retrograde this month until the 15th. So, avoid making major, dramatic changes to the health regime or diet during this period – research these things more. And try to avoid elective kinds of medical tests or procedures. Reschedule them for after the 15th.

Job offers also need more study, and if there is no rush to accept, make sure you get all the facts.

On the 21st, as the Sun enters your 10th house, you'll begin a yearly career peak. You can safely let go of home and family issues and focus on the career. With your career planet Saturn now moving forward your career actions will be clear, confident and powerful.

Venus will be in your 10th house until the 7th and this continues the trend we saw last month about love and finance. You're still attracted to high-fliers and powerful people. There are romantic opportunities with bosses or people involved in your career. Don't confuse convenience with real love, however, but if you can have both, all the better.

If you didn't get a pay rise or bonus last month it could still happen in the month ahead. On the 7th Venus moves into your 11th house. This makes you more attracted to unconventional types of people and unconventional types of relationships. This is not an especially strong transit for marriage, but it does make for a more exciting love and social life. Friendships are unusually important in your financial life as well. Being involved with societies, group activities and organizations is not only good for your bottom line but can also lead to romance.

Taurus

THE BULL

Birthdays from
21st April to
20th May

Personality Profile

TAURUS AT A GLANCE

Element – Earth

Ruling Planet – Venus
  Career Planet – Uranus
  Love Planet – Pluto
  Money Planet – Mercury
  Planet of Health and Work – Venus
  Planet of Home and Family Life – Sun
  Planet of Spirituality – Mars
  Planet of Travel, Education, Religion and Philosophy – Saturn

Colours – earth tones, green, orange, yellow

Colours that promote love, romance and social harmony – red-violet, violet

Colours that promote earning power – yellow, yellow-orange

Gems – coral, emerald

Metal – copper

Scents – bitter almond, rose, vanilla, violet

Quality – fixed (= stability)

Quality most needed for balance – flexibility

Strongest virtues – endurance, loyalty, patience, stability,
   a harmonious disposition

Deepest needs – comfort, material ease, wealth

Characteristics to avoid – rigidity, stubbornness, tendency to be overly
   possessive and materialistic

Signs of greatest overall compatibility – Virgo, Capricorn

Signs of greatest overall incompatibility – Leo, Scorpio, Aquarius

Sign most helpful to career – Aquarius

Sign most helpful for emotional support – Leo

Sign most helpful financially – Gemini

Sign best for marriage and/or partnerships – Scorpio

Sign most helpful for creative projects – Virgo

Best Sign to have fun with – Virgo

Signs most helpful in spiritual matters – Aries, Capricorn

Best day of the week – Friday

Understanding a Taurus

Taurus is the most earthy of all the Earth signs. If you understand that Earth is more than just a physical element, that it is a psychological attitude as well, you will get a better understanding of the Taurus personality.

A Taurus has all the power of action that an Aries has. But Taurus is not satisfied with action for its own sake. Their actions must be productive, practical and wealth-producing. If Taurus cannot see a practical value in an action they will not bother taking it.

Taurus's forte lies in their power to make real their own or other people's ideas. They are generally not very inventive but they can take another's invention and perfect it, making it more practical and useful. The same is true for all projects. Taurus is not especially keen on starting new projects, but once they get involved they bring things to completion. Taurus carries everything through. They are finishers and will go the distance, so long as no unavoidable calamity intervenes.

Many people find Taurus too stubborn, conservative, fixed and immovable. This is understandable, because Taurus dislikes change – in the environment or in their routine. They even dislike changing their minds! On the other hand, this is their virtue. It is not good for a wheel's axle to waver. The axle must be fixed, stable and unmovable. Taurus is the axle of society and the heavens. Without their stability and so-called stubbornness, the wheels of the world (and especially the wheels of commerce) would not turn.

Taurus loves routine. A routine, if it is good, has many virtues. It is a fixed – and, ideally, perfect – way of taking care of things. Mistakes can happen when spontaneity comes into the equation, and mistakes cause discomfort and uneasiness – something almost unacceptable to a Taurus. Meddling with Taurus's comfort and security is a sure way to irritate and anger them.

While an Aries loves speed, a Taurus likes things slow. They are slow thinkers – but do not make the mistake of assuming they lack intelligence. On the contrary, Taurus people are very intelligent. It is just that they like to chew on ideas, to deliberate and weigh them up.

Only after due deliberation is an idea accepted or a decision taken. Taurus is slow to anger – but once aroused, take care!

Finance

Taurus is very money-conscious. Wealth is more important to them than to many other signs. Wealth to a Taurus means comfort and security. Wealth means stability. Where some zodiac signs feel that they are spiritually rich if they have ideas, talents or skills, Taurus only feels wealth when they can see and touch it. Taurus's way of thinking is, 'What good is a talent if it has not been translated into a home, furniture, car and holidays?'

These are all reasons why Taurus excels in estate agency and agricultural industries. Usually a Taurus will end up owning land. They love to feel their connection to the Earth. Material wealth began with agriculture, the tilling of the soil. Owning a piece of land was humanity's earliest form of wealth: Taurus still feels that primeval connection.

It is in the pursuit of wealth that Taurus develops intellectual and communication ability. Also, in this pursuit Taurus is forced to develop some flexibility. It is in the quest for wealth that they learn the practical value of the intellect and come to admire it. If it were not for the search for wealth and material things, Taurus people might not try to reach a higher intellect.

Some Taurus people are 'born lucky' – the type who win any gamble or speculation. This luck is due to other factors in their horoscope; it is not part of their essential nature. By nature they are not gamblers. They are hard workers and like to earn what they get. Taurus's innate conservatism makes them abhor unnecessary risks in finance and in other areas of their lives.

Career and Public Image

Being essentially down-to-earth people, simple and uncomplicated, Taurus tends to look up to those who are original, unconventional and inventive. Taurus people like their bosses to be creative and original – since they themselves are content to perfect their superiors' brainwaves. They admire people who have a wider social or political consciousness and they feel that someday (when they have all the comfort and security they need) they too would like to be involved in these big issues.

In business affairs Taurus can be very shrewd – and that makes them valuable to their employers. They are never lazy; they enjoy working and getting good results. Taurus does not like taking unnecessary risks and they do well in positions of authority, which makes them good managers and supervisors. Their managerial skills are reinforced by their natural talents for organization and handling details, their patience and thoroughness. As mentioned, through their connection with the earth, Taurus people also do well in farming and agriculture.

In general a Taurus will choose money and earning power over public esteem and prestige. A position that pays more – though it has less prestige – is preferred to a position with a lot of prestige but lower earnings. Many other signs do not feel this way, but a Taurus does, especially if there is nothing in his or her personal birth chart that modifies this. Taurus will pursue glory and prestige only if it can be shown that these things have a direct and immediate impact on their wallet.

Love and Relationships

In love, the Taurus-born likes to have and to hold. They are the marrying kind. They like commitment and they like the terms of a relationship to be clearly defined. More importantly, Taurus likes to be faithful to one lover, and they expect that lover to reciprocate this fidelity. When this doesn't happen, their whole world comes crashing down. When they are in love Taurus people are loyal, but they are also very possessive. They are capable of great fits of jealousy if they are hurt in love.

Taurus is satisfied with the simple things in a relationship. If you are involved romantically with a Taurus there is no need for lavish entertainments and constant courtship. Give them enough love, food and comfortable shelter and they will be quite content to stay home and enjoy your company. They will be loyal to you for life. Make a Taurus feel comfortable and – above all – secure in the relationship, and you will rarely have a problem.

In love, Taurus can sometimes make the mistake of trying to control their partners, which can cause great pain on both sides. The reasoning behind their actions is basically simple: Taurus people feel a sense of ownership over their partners and will want to make changes that will increase their own general comfort and security. This attitude is OK when it comes to inanimate, material things – but is dangerous when applied to people. Taurus needs to be careful and attentive to this possible trait within themselves.

Home and Domestic Life

Home and family are vitally important to Taurus. They like children. They also like a comfortable and perhaps glamorous home – something they can show off. They tend to buy heavy, ponderous furniture – usually of the best quality. This is because Taurus likes a feeling of substance in their environment. Their house is not only their home but their place of creativity and entertainment. The Taurus' home tends to be truly their castle. If they could choose, Taurus people would prefer living in the countryside to being city-dwellers. If they cannot do so during their working lives, many Taurus individuals like to holiday in or even retire to the country, away from the city and closer to the land.

At home a Taurus is like a country squire – lord (or lady) of the manor. They love to entertain lavishly, to make others feel secure in their home and to encourage others to derive the same sense of satisfaction as they do from it. If you are invited for dinner at the home of a Taurus you can expect the best food and best entertainment. Be prepared for a tour of the house and expect to see your Taurus friend exhibit a lot of pride and satisfaction in his or her possessions.

Taurus people like children but they are usually strict with them. The reason for this is they tend to treat their children – as they do most things in life – as their possessions. The positive side to this is that their children will be well cared for and well supervised. They will get every material thing they need to grow up properly. On the down side, Taurus can get too repressive with their children. If a child dares to upset the daily routine – which Taurus loves to follow – he or she will have a problem with a Taurus parent.

Horoscope for 2024

Major Trends

Uranus has been in your sign for many years now, Taurus, and will be there for some more to come. So, as we have written in past years, you are learning to deal with sudden and unexpected changes. Black swan events, in the vernacular. Yet this year, with Jupiter in your own sign until May 26, these sudden changes are actually good things, which you haven't yet recognized.

With Jupiter in your own sign, the year ahead is a happy one. You are living on a higher standard than usual. Women of childbearing age are more fertile than usual. There is more sex appeal to the image and many of you are probably dressing that way too.

On May 26 Jupiter will move into your money house, ushering in a year of prosperity. This is Taurus heaven. Pluto, your love planet, will move into the sign of Aquarius twice this year, from January 22 to September 3 and from November 20 to the end of the year. This will bring important changes to your love life. Love attitudes and needs will change. This year you are seeing only the beginnings of this but in future years you will see it more strongly. More on this later.

Your most important interests in the year ahead are the body and image, until May 26; finance from May 26 onwards; religion, philosophy, higher education and foreign travel until January 22 and from September 3 to November 20; career from January 22 to September 3 and from November 20 to the end of the year; and friends, group activities and organizations.

Your paths of greatest fulfilment in the year ahead will be spirituality; the body and image until May 26; and finance from May 26 onwards.

Health

(Please note that this is an astrological perspective on health and not a medical one. In days of yore there was no difference, both these perspectives were identical. But these days there could be quite a difference. For a medical perspective, please consult your doctor or health practitioner.)

For most of you, health should be excellent this year as the long-term planets are either in harmonious aspect or are leaving you alone. The empty 6th house is another positive indicator for health. You have no need to overly focus here as there is nothing wrong. As the saying goes, 'If it ain't broke, don't fix it.' Sure, there will be periods when health and energy are less easy than usual, but these are not trends for the year. They are only short-term blips caused by the stressful transits of short-term planets. When they pass your normal good health and energy return.

You are living the good life this year, enjoying good foods, good wines, good restaurants, etc., but there is a price tag attached. You need to watch your weight more. And, as we have mentioned, women of childbearing age are more fertile than usual.

Pluto's move into Aquarius – albeit a brief foray this year – is significant for you, Taurus. The good news is that most of you – the overwhelming majority – will not feel it this year. But those of you born early in the sign, April 20–22, will feel it strongly. It shows a need to give more attention to the heart and to your emotional wellness.

Good though your health is, you can make it better. Give more attention to the following – the vulnerable areas of your Horoscope this year (the reflex points are shown in the chart opposite):

- The neck and throat are always important for Taurus, and regular neck and throat massage should be part of your usual health regime. Tension tends to collect in the neck and needs to be released.
- The kidneys and hips. Likewise, these two areas are always important for Taurus. Regular massage of the hip reflex points will not only strengthen the kidneys and hips but the lower back as well.

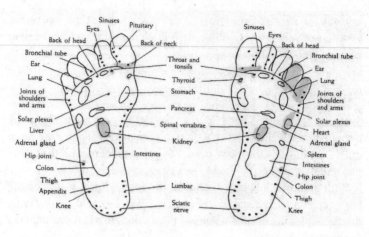

Important foot reflexology points for the year ahead

Try to massage all of the foot on a regular basis – the top of the foot as well as the bottom – but pay extra attention to the points highlighted on the chart. When you massage, be aware of 'sore spots' as these need special attention. It's also a good idea to massage the ankles and below them.

• The heart. This is only important for those Taureans born from April 20–22. The important thing with the heart is to avoid worry and anxiety, the two emotions that stress it out. Replace worry with faith. Meditation will be a great help.

Two eclipses occur in your 6th house of health this year. The first is a lunar eclipse on March 25; the second is a solar eclipse on October 2. This indicates important changes to your health regime and we will discuss it further in the monthly reports.

Your health planet Venus is a fast-moving planet and in any given year she will move through all the signs and houses of your Horoscope. Thus, there are many short-term health trends that depend on where Venus is and the kind of aspects she receives. These are best dealt with in the monthly reports.

Venus does double duty in your Horoscope. Not only is she your health planet, she is the ruler of your Horoscope. Thus, there is a vanity component to health. The state of your health dramatically impacts the personal appearance. Just stay healthy and the personal appearance will shine. Good health will do more for your looks than hosts of lotions and potions.

Home and Family

Since the 4th house is not a house of power this year, most of you, the overwhelming majority, will have a stable family year. Things will more or less continue as they have been. You seem satisfied with the status quo and have no need to make great changes here.

With the Sun ruling your 4th house, two solar eclipses in the coming year – one on April 8 and the other on October 2 – could create family dramas and bring needed repairs in the home. We will discuss this in the monthly reports.

For those of you born early in Taurus, from April 20–22, the situation is different. There can be surgical procedures or near-death kinds of experiences in the lives of parents or parent figures. There can be a need for major renovations or construction work in the home. Perhaps the problems are in the plumbing and pipes. There can be conflict between your current love and a parent or parent figure.

Because the Sun is a fast-moving planet, there are many short-term home and family trends that depend on where the Sun is and the kind of aspects he receives. These are best discussed in the monthly reports.

If you're making major repairs in the home, August 15 to August 22 is a propitious good time. If you're planning cosmetic redecorations, or to buy decorative objects for the home, July 12 to August 5 will be a good time.

One of the parent figures in your life has been restless for many years and probably has had multiple moves. Another move, a happy one, could happen in the year ahead. The other parent or parent figure seems to have a family year tending to the status quo.

Siblings and sibling figures are also having a stable home and family year. Moves are not likely. Their focus seems mostly on spirituality this year and they are having spiritual breakthroughs.

Children and children figures in your life can have multiple moves this year. They need to cultivate emotional stability. Grandchildren, if you have them, or those who play that role in your life, are having a status quo home and family year. They are, however, making important emotional and psychological progress.

Finance and Career

As we mentioned above, the year ahead is very prosperous. Until May 26, with Jupiter in your own sign, you will be living to a higher standard than usual. This transit doesn't necessarily bring extra money, but a higher standard of life. And you find that you can afford this higher standard. After May 26 Jupiter moves into your money house, expanding earnings and bringing earning opportunities. For investors this favours bonds and the bond market. All of you seem to have better access to outside money after May 26. This can be through expanded credit facilities or through outside investors. Good tax efficiency seems very important. And tax issues seem to govern many of your financial decisions. Jupiter moving through your money house is generally a sign of inheritance. But hopefully no one has to die – you could be named in someone's will or be named for some administrative position in a will or estate or otherwise profit from an estate. There could be earnings from insurance payments as well. You have a knack for seeing value where other people see only death and decay. Thus, you can profit from troubled companies or properties and play the turnaround. Sometimes people walk into a junk shop and walk out with a valuable antique.

Since Mercury is your financial planet, there are many short-term trends in finance that depend on where Mercury is and the kinds of aspects that he receives. Next to the Moon he is the fastest moving of all the planets. The short-term trends are best discussed in the monthly reports.

Mercury will be retrograde four times this year, although only three will be full-blown retrogrades. (He is retrograde on January 1 for one day only.) He will be properly retrograde from April 2–24; from August 5–26; and from November 26 to December 14. These are times to avoid major purchases or investments. Instead, you should review your financial goals and gain clarity on your finances. They are not good times for overt actions.

Uranus, your career planet, has been in your sign for many years now, showing ambition and happy career opportunities that pursue you rather than the other way around. You have the image of a successful person and dress the part. People see you this way. Jupiter, the planet of expansion and success, is travelling with your career planet early in the year, signalling career success and expansion. April, when these planetary aspects are very exact, seems especially successful. Promotions or other types of career elevation are likely. However, now that Pluto is moving into your 10th house of career this year, there are going to be many changes here over the long term. Though your career is successful in the year ahead the cosmos wants something even better for you, and in the coming years you will find it. Pluto likes to destroy and then rebuild in a new and better way. His destruction is not intended as punishment but is a necessary factor to create something new and better. You are being led, through many trials and travails, to the career of your dreams. It can get messy – a new birth is always messy – but the end result is good.

This year Pluto will be in your 10th house from January 22 to September 3 and from November 20 to the end of the year. Aside from what has been mentioned above, his positioning indicates that you further your career by social means. You socialize with high and powerful people, people who can help you careerwise. It will be beneficial to attend or host the right parties and gatherings. Your social grace and general likeability are very important to your career success.

Love and Social Life

With Uranus in your own sign for so many years now, love has been unstable. Divorce or break-ups in the past five or six years would have been unsurprising. Love is still unstable in the year ahead. Those involved romantically with a Taurus should give them as much space as possible. Taurus has a need for personal freedom these days and this is not always helpful in relationships. They can be more rebellious than usual. Taurus children are also like this.

Singles will date and have love in their lives, but marriage right now is probably not advisable.

Your love planet Pluto has been in Capricorn, your 9th house, for over 30 years. Thus, you have been conservative in love. You favour the traditional kind of relationship and perhaps attract traditional kinds of people who feel the same way. But Pluto is changing signs this year, moving from Capricorn to Aquarius. This is not yet the full-blown transit but is a harbinger of things to come. (The full-blown transit will happen next year.) Pluto's move signals a less traditional approach to love and relationships. You are becoming more experimental in this department. You are willing to try different things, to see what works best for you personally. The rule books in love will get thrown out the window. You will experiment for yourself.

Pluto's temporary move into your career house this year indicates that you will be attracted to people of high status and power. Power is a romantic turn-on. You will be mingling more with these kinds of people as well. Pluto will be at the top of your chart for many months this year, and for many years ahead. This is good for love as it shows focus; it is high on your priorities. You're paying attention here. This focus tends to bring success. If you are single, rest assured that marriage will happen in the coming years, but it is not advisable right away. There is no rush for this. Let Uranus move out of your sign first. This will happen in a few years and you'll feel it when it does.

May 26 and 27 brings a very important romantic opportunity for singles.

Self-improvement

Taureans are generally very good people, but spirituality, which you see as other-worldliness, is not your strong point. You are fundamentally down-to-earth people and do not see practicality and material focus as unspiritual. Yet, in 2023 as Jupiter moved through your 12th house, many of you embarked on a spiritual path and gained much from it. It's as if the spiritual doors opened in your mind and awakened you to higher realities. This love for spirituality continues in the year ahead. Jupiter is no longer in your 12th house, but the north node of the Moon will be there for the entire year. The north node of the Moon is not a planet but an abstract point. It is said to denote an area of life that brings great expansion and fulfilment to a person. And this is what we have in your Horoscope this year. This is a year to build on the progress that was made in 2023. One of the good things you will learn is that spirituality, properly understood, is really the most practical thing a person can do. It has immense, stupendous, practical impacts on life. For everything that happens on the material plane is merely a side-effect of spiritual forces. Change the spiritual forces, change the consciousness, and you change the physical reality.

Mars is your spiritual planet. Thus, you like to express your spiritual ideals in physical action. Activism would be your spiritual path. This favours disciplines such as karma yoga, the yoga of action. It would also favour tai chi or qi gong, each of which emphasizes physical actions. The physical and spiritual are blended together.

Neptune, which has been in your 11th house for many years now, favours involvement with spiritual groups and someone who attracts spiritual friends into the life. These kinds of friendships and involvements are part and parcel of your spiritual path.

For many years now your main spiritual lesson was to be comfortable with change: learning to embrace change and to make it your friend. This is not easy for a Taurus but by now you are getting the hang of it. This lesson is almost over with and by 2025, as Uranus leaves your sign, you will have mastered it. Uranus says to you, 'If you want me to answer your prayer you'll have to let me shake things up a little. You have to let me uproot the status quo.' All these changes you've been going through, uncomfortable though they sometimes were, were really answers to your prayers.

For more information on astrology, healing and spiritual topics, please visit my blog at www.spiritual-stories.com.

Month-by-month Forecasts

January

Best Days Overall: 1, 2, 10, 11,18, 19, 18, 29
Most Stressful Days Overall: 6, 7, 12, 13, 25, 26, 27
Best Days for Love: 2, 3, 6, 7, 8, 9, 11, 12, 19, 20, 27, 28, 31
Best Days for Money: 1, 2, 9, 10, 11, 18, 19, 21, 22, 28, 29, 30, 31
Best Days for Career: 2, 11, 12, 13, 19, 29

This will be a happy and successful month for you. Health is basically good for the overwhelming majority of you, but after the 20th will need more attention. The weight needs watching as well! You're living the good life these days and weight gain is the price we pay for it. Enhance the health by resting when you feel tired, and through massage of the liver reflex and the thighs until the 23rd. After the 23rd back and knee massage will be powerful.

Love doesn't seem a major focus this month as your 7th house is basically empty – only the Moon will move through there on the 6th and 7th. Nevertheless, the Sun will be travelling with your love planet Pluto on the 20th and 21st and can bring happy romantic opportunity for singles. This transit can also show more entertaining from home and with family members. Perhaps family is playing an important role in your love life.

The Sun's move into your 10th house on the 20th initiates a yearly career peak. Thus, much career progress will happen. The family seems supportive of your career and we don't see the usual conflict between home and career. The two areas of life blend in with each other this month. One supports the other.

Prosperity also seems strong this month. Jupiter, in your own sign, doesn't necessarily increase wealth, but it does elevate your lifestyle. You're living to a higher standard. If you have good business ideas, there are outside investors available. Also, you have good access to credit. Money can come to you through insurance payments, or perhaps via tax refunds.

Your spiritual planet, Mars, is out of bounds from the beginning of the year until the 24th, signalling that you are outside your normal boundaries in your spiritual life. Probably you are exploring teachings and practices outside your normal sphere. Perhaps exotic practices.

February

Best Days Overall: 6, 7, 14, 15, 24, 25
Most Stressful Days Overall: 1, 2, 3, 8, 9, 21, 22, 23, 29
Best Days for Love: 1, 2, 3, 6, 7, 8, 17, 26, 27, 29
Best Days for Money: 6, 7, 8, 9, 14, 15, 17, 18, 24, 25, 29
Best Days for Career: 6, 7, 8, 9, 14, 15, 16, 24, 25

The career, which is booming, is the main headline this month. Your 10th house is unusually powerful this month with half the planets either stationary there or moving through there this month. This focus is an indicator of success. The new Moon of the 9th will also occur in your 10th house, energizing the career even further. It is a super career day. This new Moon will help the career in other ways as well. For as the days progress, until the next new Moon, career issues will be clarified for you. All the information you need to make good career decisions will come to you very naturally and normally.

Health definitely needs more attention paid to it this month. As always, make sure to get enough rest. You probably won't be able to escape career obligations, but you can handle them in a more sensible way. Try to schedule in more rest periods as you pursue your career goals. Enhance the health with back and knee massage until the 17th; perhaps a visit to the chiropractor, osteopath or masseuse would be beneficial. After the 17th give more attention to the ankles and calves. Massage them regularly. Health should improve after the 19th, but still needs to be watched.

Your financial planet Mercury will be in your 10th house of career from the 4th to the 23rd. This is excellent for finance as it shows that the subject is high on your list of priorities. It also indicates that bosses and authority figures in your life are favourably disposed to your financial goals. Often this kind of transit brings a pay rise. In general, your good career reputation brings financial gain and opportunities to you.

Your love planet's position in your 10th house (until September 3) shows that likeability and social grace are just as important for success as your professional skills. It will be beneficial to attend or host career-related parties and gatherings. For singles Pluto's aspect gives a few messages. First, focus on your career and your life work and love will fall right into place. Secondly, it indicates that there are romantic opportunities with bosses, supervisors and people involved in your career. Third, it shows an attraction to successful and powerful people.

The planetary momentum is all forward this month. Events happen quickly, and there is fast progress towards your goals.

March

Best Days Overall: 6, 7, 14, 15, 24, 25
Most Stressful Days Overall: 1, 8, 19, 20, 21, 27, 28
Best Days for Love: 1, 7, 8, 14, 15, 17, 18, 24, 27, 28
Best Days for Money: 1, 4, 5, 9, 11, 13, 14, 15, 16, 19, 20, 22, 23, 30
Best Days for Career: 4, 5, 7, 8, 13, 14, 22, 23

Your 11th house of friends has been powerful for the past two years and this month it is even more powerful. So, you are very much involved with friends, group activities and trade or professional organizations. These activities are not only fun, but they help the bottom line too. They help your earnings. Children and the children figures in your life will have an excellent social month. They are making new friends and meeting new people and attending more parties and gatherings in general. If they are of appropriate age romance is also likely, though I don't see a marriage this year.

Health and energy are much improved this month and will get even better after the 23rd. You can enhance the health even further with ankle and calf massage until the 11th, and with foot massage from the 11th onwards. Spiritual-healing techniques are also more powerful from the 11th onwards.

Venus, the ruler of your Horoscope, is still in your 10th house of career until the 11th. She is very elevated in this position, and this shows what is happening with you. You are elevated and people look up to you and aspire to be like you.

Your financial planet Mercury travels with Neptune on the 16th and 17th and this indicates fabulous financial intuition. This also signals the involvement of friends in your finances. It would also show that involvement with a trade or professional organization boosts the finances.

Mercury's move into your 12th house of spirituality on the 10th also emphasizes the financial intuition.

A lunar eclipse on the 25th will bring disturbances at the workplace and perhaps job changes. These changes can be within your present situation or with a new one. It also shows a need to change your health regime, which will happen in the coming months. This eclipse will also test cars and communication equipment. Often, repairs or replacements are necessary. It is a good idea to drive more carefully while the eclipse is in effect. In fact, better to avoid unnecessary driving.

April

Best Days Overall: 1, 2, 9, 10, 18, 19, 20, 28, 29
Most Stressful Days Overall: 3, 4, 16, 17, 23, 24, 25, 30
Best Days for Love: 3, 7, 8, 11, 16, 17, 21, 23, 24, 25, 27, 28
Best Days for Money: 1, 2, 7, 8, 9, 10, 11, 12, 17, 18, 19, 26, 27
Best Days for Career: 2, 3, 4, 10, 29, 30

The powerful – very powerful – total solar eclipse of the 8th is the major headline of the month. You and family members should take it nice and easy while the eclipse is in effect.

This solar eclipse occurs in your 12th house of spirituality, bringing a dramatic change in your spiritual life, practice and attitudes. Some of these changes can be quite normal, as spiritual growth often necessitates changes in the practice. Guru figures in your life have personal dramas. There are likely to be disruptions and upheavals in charitable or spiritual organizations that you are involved with. Friends are having financial dramas and need to make important financial changes. Since this eclipse is a direct hit on Mercury, your financial planet, you too need to make very important financial changes. Your financial thinking has not been realistic, as the events of the eclipse will show. Thus, important course corrections need to happen. These changes will turn out to be very good, as you are in a year of prosperity.

Children, and children figures in your life, as well as parents and parent figures, are having personal dramas. All of you, yourself included, need to take stock and need to re-define yourselves – your image, personality, and the way that you want others to think of you. This will lead to wardrobe changes, changes of hairstyle and overall look in the coming months. Children and children figures are having their relationships tested these days. This has been going on for a long time but now the events of the eclipse exacerbate things.

There can be personal dramas in the lives of family members and perhaps repairs are needed in the home. Siblings and sibling figures should drive more carefully while the eclipse is in effect. It would be best for them to avoid unnecessary driving, but if they must do so let them drive more defensively. They too are making important financial changes.

Since Venus is also directly affected by this eclipse there can be job changes or changes in the conditions of work. Those who employ others can experience dramas in the lives of their employees, and employee turnover in the coming months.

May

Best Days Overall: 7, 8, 15, 16, 25, 26
Most Stressful Days Overall: 1, 13, 14, 20, 21, 22, 27, 28
Best Days for Love: 1, 7, 8, 9, 15, 16, 17, 20, 21, 22, 27, 28
Best Days for Money: 5, 6, 8, 9, 10, 14, 15, 16, 25, 26, 27, 28
Best Days for Career: 1, 8, 16, 26, 27, 28

The financial changes you needed to make last month are really paying off now. On the 20th the Sun will enter your money house and will be there for the remainder of the month. You will be entering a yearly financial peak. But this peak is going to be much greater than usual. For on the 26th Jupiter will enter your money house and will stay there for the rest of the year ahead. Super prosperity is happening. There are many ways that you can earn, and assets you already own will increase in value. You have excellent access to outside capital, especially if you have good business ideas. Money can come from insurance payments or tax refunds. Perhaps you are named in someone's will or appointed to some administrative position in a will. In general, you profit from estates and estate planning. With all this prosperity happening, you need to do some good tax planning.

On the 26th and 27th Jupiter will make fabulous aspects to your love planet Pluto. This can bring interesting and happy romantic opportunities for singles. However, since Pluto goes retrograde on the 2nd there may be delays involved with this.

With your love planet remaining in your 10th house until September 3 love is high on your agenda, and this is good news as it tends to success. But as we've just mentioned, there are delays involved.

Health and energy are excellent this month for the overwhelming majority of Taureans. The Sun is in your own sign until the 20th, and Venus is there too until the 23rd. So you look good. The personal appearance shines.

On the 15th Mercury enters your sign and stays there until the 20th. This brings wonderful financial windfalls to you and is basically a prelude to the prosperity that is happening from the 26th onwards.

June

Best Days Overall: 3, 4, 12, 13, 22, 23, 30
Most Stressful Days Overall: 9, 10, 11, 17, 18, 24, 25
Best Days for Love: 5, 6, 14, 16, 17, 18, 23, 24, 26, 27
Best Days for Money: 5, 6, 14, 15, 16, 17, 24, 26, 27
Best Days for Career: 4, 13, 22, 23, 24, 25

Health and energy are still excellent this month. You can enhance the health further with arm and shoulder massage until the 17th, and after then with right diet and abdominal massage. Massage of the stomach reflex after the 17th will also be helpful. Two important planets in your Horoscope are out of bounds this month. Mercury, your financial planet, is out of bounds from the 11th to the 29th, and Venus, the ruler of your Horoscope and also your health planet, is out of bounds from the 13th to the 29th. Thus, personally and financially, you are outside your normal boundaries. You are not outside the law, but outside your usual sphere. It is like stretching your reach. The same is true in health matters as well.

Finances are still terrific, and you are still in the midst of a yearly financial peak – especially until the 20th. The 3rd and 4th seem like particularly good financial days as your financial planet travels with Jupiter. A nice payday. Mercury is very powerful in his own sign and house and he will be there until the 17th. This is another signal of financial expansion and prosperity.

The new Moon of the 6th is another very strong financial day and you will feel the effect of this until the next new Moon, next month. The Moon will clarify and enlighten your financial consciousness as the days and weeks go by. All the information you need to make good financial judgements will come to you normally and naturally. This is 90 per cent of the battle. Your financial questions will be answered.

Though love and relationships are very important to you, and will ultimately be rewarding, there is a need for patience here; Pluto, your love planet, is still retrograde and will be retrograde for many more months. Singles will certainly date and have romantic opportunity but there is no need to make important love decisions right now. Allow love to play out as it will. No need to rush things. Time and time alone will resolve love issues.

Mars moves into your sign on the 9th and will be there for the rest of the month ahead. Avoid rush and impatience as this can lead to accident or injury. Watch the temper. The good part of this Mars transit is that you have the energy of 10 people. You will excel in sports and exercise regimes. Mars being your spiritual planet will bring a spiritual glow and glamour to your image.

July

Best Days Overall: 1, 9, 10, 11, 19, 20, 27, 28
Most Stressful Days Overall: 7, 8, 14, 15, 16, 21, 22
Best Days for Love: 2, 5, 6, 12, 14, 15, 16, 17, 18, 25, 26, 29
Best Days for Money: 2, 3, 12, 13, 21, 22, 29, 30, 31
Best Days for Career: 1, 10, 20, 21, 22, 28

Health and energy are basically good this month but after the 22nd will need more attention. Enhance the health in the ways mentioned in the yearly report. Until the 11th right diet and emotional harmony seem very important. After the 11th give more attention to the heart. The reflex to the heart should be massaged as well as the chest itself.

Mars is still in your sign until the 20th, so keep in mind our discussion of this last month. Mars travels with your career planet Uranus on the 13th and 14th. This signals some hyperactivity is happening in the career. Also, it indicates that being involved with idealistic enterprises, non-profit organizations or charities helps the career.

On the 20th and 21st Mars makes beautiful aspects to your love planet, Pluto. This can bring an important romantic meeting, perhaps in some type of spiritual venue. But again, as we mentioned in previous months, there can be many delays involved with this. With Pluto still retrograde there is no rush in love. Allow things to happen as they happen.

Mars joins Jupiter in your money house from the 20th onwards. Though this transit makes you a bit more speculative than usual, it is basically a positive for finance. In addition, it indicates a powerful financial intuition. The month ahead should be prosperous. We see prosperity here in other ways as well. The Moon, which normally spends two days in any one house in each month, will be in your money house for five days this month, more than double the usual time.

Your 3rd house of communication and intellectual interests is very strong in the month ahead especially, until the 22nd. This is a good month for students, teachers and intellectual workers. Studying, reading, expanding your stock of knowledge seems a great pleasure this month.

August

Best Days Overall: 5, 6, 7, 15, 16, 23, 24, 25
Most Stressful Days Overall: 3, 4, 11, 12, 17, 18, 30, 31
Best Days for Love: 8, 11, 12, 17, 18, 26, 29
Best Days for Money: 8, 9, 17, 18, 23, 24, 25, 27, 29
Best Days for Career: 11, 12, 15, 16, 19, 20, 28, 29

Continue to watch the health this month, and rest more when tired. Enhance the health with chest massage and massage of the heart reflex until the 5th; from the 5th to the 29th abdominal massage and massage of the small intestine reflex will be helpful.

Your health planet Venus has been in your 4th house of home and family since July 11, and she'll remain there until the 5th of this month. The message here is that good health for you means good emotional health, healthy moods, a healthy domestic life, healthy family relationships. If health problems arise it is probably due to problems in the above areas. Restore harmony in your family life as quickly as possible. From the 5th to the 29th, as your health planet moves to your 5th house, the relationship with your children seems very important. Problems here could impact your own physical health. But there is another message here as well: this is a time when you learn that joy itself, happiness for no reason, is a powerful healing force. If you're feeling under the weather go out and have some fun, watch a funny movie, or go to a concert. You'll start to feel much better.

Overall health and energy will improve dramatically from the 22nd onwards. It seems that you are learning the power of joy as you enter a yearly personal pleasure peak. This would be a very good time to take a vacation and otherwise indulge in leisure activities. Personal creativity is greatly increased. When you emerge from this time of leisure, all kinds of new ideas and insights will come to you.

Your 4th house of home and family is very strong this month, especially until the 22nd. So, this is a month to deal with home and family issues, and – more importantly – with your emotional life. Let career matters go for a while. This is an excellent period for undergoing some type of psychological therapy. If there are health problems a counsellor or therapist can probably help you more than other kinds of health professionals.

Your love planet is still retrograde all this month and receiving stressful aspects. Love and romance could certainly be better, but happily this is a short-term issue.

September

Best Days Overall: 2, 3, 12, 13, 20, 21, 29, 30
Most Stressful Days Overall: 1, 7, 8, 14, 15, 26, 27, 28
Best Days for Love: 3, 4, 5, 7, 8, 13, 14, 15, 21, 23, 24
Best Days for Money: 4, 5, 12, 13, 14, 15, 21, 22, 23
Best Days for Career: 2, 3, 13, 14, 15, 21, 30

A lunar eclipse on the 18th has relatively little effect on you, but it won't hurt to reduce your schedule anyway, and avoid unnecessary driving, or brief journeys. If you must drive, and an eclipse should not prevent us from doing the things that need to be done, drive more carefully. Cars and communication equipment will get tested and will often behave erratically. Sometimes repairs or replacements are necessary.

This eclipse occurs in your 11th house of friends, groups and organizations. There are personal dramas in the lives of friends, and shake-ups and upheavals in trade or professional organizations you are involved with. Siblings, sibling figures and neighbours also experience dramas. There can be strange and perhaps annoying events in your neighbourhood. Mars moves into your 3rd house of communication on the 5th and this amplifies what we have written above. Though the eclipse tends to create drama and excitement, the month ahead is still happy. You're still very much in a yearly personal pleasure peak and this continues until the 22nd. In spite of all the excitement you're still managing to enjoy yourself.

You're also still in a very prosperous time in your life. Jupiter is still in your financial house, expanding earnings, bringing financial opportunity and increasing the value of assets you already own. Furthermore, from the 22nd onwards Jupiter will be receiving very positive aspects. Positive stimulation is happening and thus Jupiter's impact is all the greater.

Health continues to be good this month. You can enhance it further in the ways mentioned in the yearly report and through extra hip massage, kidney massage and, from the 23rd onwards, through detox regimes. Good health after this date is not about adding things to the body but about getting rid of things that shouldn't be there. Sometimes with this kind of aspect surgery is recommended to people. You have a tendency to this kind of thing. However, this doesn't mean that you have to accept it – you would respond equally well to detox regimes.

Pluto, your love planet, moves back into Capricorn on the 3rd and stays there for the rest of the month ahead. You become more conservative in love again, which, right now, is probably a good thing. There is no need to rush romance or hurry things along.

On the 22nd the Sun enters your 6th house of health and work, and so there is more focus here. Generally this focus is a good thing, but with your health basically good the danger is more about hypochondria, the tendency to magnify small things into big things. Your strong 6th house is excellent for those of you who are seeking jobs or for those of you who need to employ others. It is also excellent for doing all those detail-oriented, boring jobs that you keep putting off!

Mars, your spiritual planet, will be out of bounds from the 5th to the 24th. Thus, in your spiritual life you are going outside your usual boundaries. Perhaps you are exploring foreign, esoteric kinds of practices or teachings.

Pluto goes out of bounds on the 25th and will remain out of bounds until November 4. So, you are going out of your normal sphere in your love and romantic life. This will probably not be helpful as Pluto is still retrograde, but you seem to be searching in new places.

October

Best Days Overall: 9, 10, 17, 18, 26, 27, 28
Most Stressful Days Overall: 4, 5, 11, 12, 24, 25, 30
Best Days for Love: 4, 5, 10, 13, 14, 18, 24, 25, 28, 31
Best Days for Money: 1, 2, 11, 12, 13, 19, 20, 21, 22, 29, 30, 31
Best Days for Career: 10, 11, 12, 18, 28

A very strong solar eclipse on the 2nd is the main headline of the month. This is not only a total eclipse, but it also impacts on two important planets in your Horoscope: Mars and Mercury. So, you, parents or parent figures in your life, children and children figures need to take an easy, relaxed schedule while the eclipse is in effect. Things that need to be done, should be done. But anything else, especially if it could be stressful, is better off being rescheduled. An eclipse can be compared to a cosmic storm. When a storm is about to hit your town or neighbourhood, you take normal precautions and ride it out.

This solar eclipse occurs in your 6th house of health and work, signalling a need to make important changes to your health regime – and this will happen over the coming months. The eclipse can also bring job changes, which can either be in your present situation or in another one. You, a parent or parent figure are likely to have financial dramas, which will force important financial changes. The events of the eclipse will show why the financial thinking has not been realistic. Parents or parent figures and children in your life have a need to re-define themselves, their image, their self-concept and how they want to be seen by others. This re-evaluation of the self-concept is basically a healthy thing. We are growing and evolving beings and our concept of ourselves from a year ago or two years ago is probably not valid now. The only difference is that this re-evaluation is rather forced on them and can affect the love relationships of children and parent figures.

The eclipse's impact on Mars causes spiritual changes in your life. These can manifest as changes in your practice, attitudes, teachings or teachers. This sort of eclipse often brings personal dramas to the lives of guru figures in your life. It brings disturbances and upheavals in spiritual or charitable organizations you are involved with. Friends are forced to make important financial changes. Trade and professional organizations, likewise.

November

Best Days Overall: 5, 6, 14, 15, 22, 23, 24
Most Stressful Days Overall: 1, 2, 7, 8, 9, 20, 21, 28, 29
Best Days for Love: 1, 2, 3, 4, 6, 16, 25, 12, 13, 22, 23, 28, 29
Best Days for Money: 3, 8, 9, 12, 13, 16, 17, 20, 21, 26, 27, 29, 30
Best Days for Career: 4, 13, 22, 23, 24, 25

The main headline this month is in your love and social life. It seems very active, and happy. Singles are dating more and attending more parties and gatherings. Furthermore, since October 12 Pluto, your love planet, is now moving forward after many months of retrograde motion. So, the social confidence is strong, as is the social judgement.

You have more clarity in issues of the heart. Singles are likely to meet romantic opportunities. Because Mercury is in your 7th house until the 2nd, this can bring opportunities for love affairs or a business partnership or joint venture.

Health needs more attention this month. As always, make sure to get enough rest. High energy is the first defence against disease and viruses. Until the 11th concentrate on the liver and thighs. Massage the thighs and liver reflex regularly. After the 11th give more attention to the back and knees. They should also be regularly massaged. If you feel under the weather a visit to the chiropractor or osteopath might be a good idea. Your health planet in conservative Capricorn from the 11th onwards shows a tendency to orthodox medicine. Even if you gravitate to alternative treatments you would prefer the therapies that have stood the test of time, the old, traditional kinds of therapies.

Finances are still good this month but are slowing down a bit. Jupiter will be retrograde all month in your money house, and Mercury, your financial planet, will go retrograde on the 26th. This is a time to review your financial goals and see where improvements can be made, rather than splashing out. It is a time for fact-finding and resolving doubts. Later on, when these planets start to move forward again, you can act on your plans. If you must make major purchases or investments this month, especially after the 26th, make sure you do your research.

December

Best Days Overall: 2, 3, 4, 11, 12, 20, 21, 30, 31
Most Stressful Days Overall: 5, 6, 17, 18, 19, 25, 26
Best Days for Love: 2, 3, 4, 5, 13, 14, 22, 23, 24, 25, 26
Best Days for Money: 6, 9, 10, 13, 14, 17, 18, 19, 27, 28, 29
Best Days for Career: 3, 5, 6, 12, 21, 31

Venus, the ruler of your Horoscope and your health planet, is out of bounds until the 8th. So, personally and in health matters you are outside your normal sphere. Perhaps the demands of the workplace also pull you outside your normal boundaries.

Finances are still slow, but they do happen. Your financial planet Mercury is still retrograde until the 15th, and Jupiter remains retrograde in your 2nd house all month. So although finances should improve after the 15th, they will still not be what they should be or will be. If you have to make important purchases or investments, better to wait till after the 15th when Mercury starts to go forward. In the meantime, as we wrote last month, work to attain financial clarity, work to resolve all doubts, and get as much information as you can.

The power of this month is in your 8th house of regeneration until the 21st. So, a good month for detoxifying both the physical body and the mind and emotional life. It's about getting rid of the extraneous and the effete in your life. Possessions that you don't need or use should be sold or given to charity. Needless expenses should be cut (not the necessary expenses). There is a need to create space for the new and better that wants to come to you.

Health is good this month and will get even better from the 21st onwards. You can enhance the health in the ways discussed in the yearly report and, until the 7th, through back and knee massage. After the 7th calf and ankle massage will be beneficial. From the 7th onwards you seem more experimental in health matters and gravitate to new kinds of therapies.

On the 7th and 8th Venus travels with your love planet, Pluto. This brings happy romantic opportunity for singles. This seems to happen with people involved in your career or as you pursue your career goals.

Pluto is now established in your 10th house for the long haul – he will be there for the next 30 or so years. This signals social and romantic success as Pluto is now the most elevated planet in your Horoscope. It is your highest aspiration. This tends to success.

On the 21st the Sun enters your 9th house and will stay there for the rest of the month. This is a happy transit as the 9th house is very beneficent and it can bring foreign travel opportunities. College-level students should hear good news at school. There is a great interest in religion, philosophy and theology. Those involved in these studies will have major breakthroughs.

Mars will spend a month in your 4th house of home and family. If you're planning renovations this would be a great month to do it. With Mars in the 4th house family members, and especially a parent or parent figure, can be short-tempered. Be more patient with them.

Gemini

♊

THE TWINS

Birthdays from
21st May to
20th June

Personality Profile

GEMINI AT A GLANCE

Element – Air

Ruling Planet – Mercury
  Career Planet – Neptune
  Love Planet – Jupiter
  Money Planet – Moon
  Planet of Health and Work – Pluto
  Planet of Home and Family Life – Mercury

Colours – blue, yellow, yellow-orange

Colour that promotes love, romance and social harmony – sky blue

Colours that promote earning power – grey, silver

Gems – agate, aquamarine

Metal – quicksilver

Scents – lavender, lilac, lily of the valley, storax

Quality – mutable (= flexibility)

Quality most needed for balance – thought that is deep rather than superficial

Strongest virtues – great communication skills, quickness and agility of thought, ability to learn quickly

Deepest need – communication

Characteristics to avoid – gossiping, hurting others with harsh speech, superficiality, using words to mislead or misinform

Signs of greatest overall compatibility – Libra, Aquarius

Signs of greatest overall incompatibility – Virgo, Sagittarius, Pisces

Sign most helpful to career – Pisces

Sign most helpful for emotional support – Virgo

Sign most helpful financially – Cancer

Sign best for marriage and/or partnerships – Sagittarius

Sign most helpful for creative projects – Libra

Best Sign to have fun with – Libra

Signs most helpful in spiritual matters – Taurus, Aquarius

Best day of the week – Wednesday

Understanding a Gemini

Gemini is to society what the nervous system is to the body. It does not introduce any new information but is a vital transmitter of impulses from the senses to the brain and vice versa. The nervous system does not judge or weigh these impulses – it only conveys information. And it does so perfectly.

This analogy should give you an indication of a Gemini's role in society. Geminis are the communicators and conveyors of information. To Geminis the truth or falsehood of information is irrelevant, they only transmit what they see, hear or read about. Thus they are capable of spreading the most outrageous rumours as well as conveying truth and light. Geminis sometimes tend to be unscrupulous in their communications and can do both great good and great evil with their power. This is why the sign of Gemini is symbolized by twins: Geminis have a dual nature.

Their ability to convey a message – to communicate with such ease – makes Geminis ideal teachers, writers and media and marketing people. This is helped by the fact that Mercury, the ruling planet of Gemini, also rules these activities.

Geminis have the gift of the gab. And what a gift this is! They can make conversation about anything, anywhere, at any time. There is almost nothing that is more fun to Geminis than a good conversation – especially if they can learn something new as well. They love to learn and they love to teach. To deprive a Gemini of conversation, or of books and magazines, is cruel and unusual punishment.

Geminis are almost always excellent students and take well to education. Their minds are generally stocked with all kinds of information, trivia, anecdotes, stories, news items, rarities, facts and statistics. Thus they can support any intellectual position that they care to take. They are awesome debaters and, if involved in politics, make good orators. Geminis are so verbally smooth that even if they do not know what they are talking about, they can make you think that they do. They will always dazzle you with their brilliance.

Finance

Geminis tend to be more concerned with the wealth of learning and ideas than with actual material wealth. As mentioned, they excel in professions that involve writing, teaching, sales and journalism – and not all of these professions pay very well. But to sacrifice intellectual needs merely for money is unthinkable to a Gemini. Geminis strive to combine the two. Cancer is on Gemini's solar 2nd house of money cusp, which indicates that Geminis can earn extra income (in a harmonious and natural way) from investments in residential property, restaurants and hotels. Given their verbal skills, Geminis love to bargain and negotiate in any situation, and especially when it has to do with money.

The Moon rules Gemini's 2nd solar house. The Moon is not only the fastest-moving planet in the zodiac but actually moves through every sign and house every 28 days. No other heavenly body matches the Moon for swiftness or the ability to change quickly. An analysis of the Moon – and lunar phenomena in general – describes Gemini's financial attitudes very well. Geminis are financially versatile and flexible; they can earn money in many different ways. Their financial attitudes and needs seem to change daily. Their feelings about money change also: sometimes they are very enthusiastic about it, at other times they could not care less.

For a Gemini, financial goals and money are often seen only as means of supporting a family; these things have little meaning otherwise.

The Moon, as Gemini's money planet, has another important message for Gemini financially: in order for Geminis to realize their financial potential they need to develop more of an understanding of the emotional side of life. They need to combine their awesome powers of logic with an understanding of human psychology. Feelings have their own logic; Geminis need to learn this and apply it to financial matters.

Career and Public Image

Geminis know that they have been given the gift of communication for a reason, that it is a power that can achieve great good or cause unthinkable distress. They long to put this power at the service of the highest and most transcendental truths. This is their primary goal, to communicate the eternal verities and prove them logically. They look up to people who can transcend the intellect – to poets, artists, musicians and mystics. They may be awed by stories of religious saints and martyrs. A Gemini's highest achievement is to teach the truth, whether it is scientific, inspirational or historical. Those who can transcend the intellect are Gemini's natural superiors – and a Gemini realizes this.

The sign of Pisces is in Gemini's solar 10th house of career. Neptune, the planet of spirituality and altruism, is Gemini's career planet. If Geminis are to realize their highest career potential they need to develop their transcendental – their spiritual and altruistic – side. They need to understand the larger cosmic picture, the vast flow of human evolution – where it came from and where it is heading. Only then can a Gemini's intellectual powers take their true position and he or she can become the 'messenger of the gods'. Geminis need to cultivate a facility for 'inspiration', which is something that does not originate in the intellect but which comes through the intellect. This will further enrich and empower a Gemini's mind.

Love and Relationships

Geminis bring their natural garrulousness and brilliance into their love life and social life as well. A good talk or a verbal joust is an interesting prelude to romance. Their only problem in love is that their intellect is too cool and passionless to incite ardour in others. Emotions sometimes disturb them, and their partners tend to complain about this. If you are in love with a Gemini you must understand why this is so. Geminis avoid deep passions because these would interfere with their ability to think and communicate. If they are cool towards you, understand that this is their nature.

Nevertheless, Geminis must understand that it is one thing to talk about love and another actually to love – to feel it and radiate it. Talking about love glibly will get them nowhere. They need to feel it and act on it. Love is not of the intellect but of the heart. If you want to know how a Gemini feels about love you should not listen to what he or she says, but rather, observe what he or she does. Geminis can be quite generous to those they love.

Geminis like their partners to be refined, well educated and well travelled. If their partners are more wealthy than they, that is all the better. If you are in love with a Gemini you had better be a good listener as well.

The ideal relationship for the Gemini is a relationship of the mind. They enjoy the physical and emotional aspects, of course, but if the intellectual communion is not there they will suffer.

Home and Domestic Life

At home the Gemini can be uncharacteristically neat and meticulous. They tend to want their children and partner to live up to their idealistic standards. When these standards are not met they moan and criticize. However, Geminis are good family people and like to serve their families in practical and useful ways.

The Gemini home is comfortable and pleasant. They like to invite people over and they make great hosts. Geminis are also good at repairs and improvements around the house – all fuelled by their need to stay active and occupied with something they like to do. Geminis have many hobbies and interests that keep them busy when they are home alone.

Geminis understand and get along well with their children, mainly because they are very youthful people themselves. As great communicators, Geminis know how to explain things to children; in this way they gain their children's love and respect. Geminis also encourage children to be creative and talkative, just like they are.

Horoscope for 2024

Major Trends

Jupiter has been in your 12th house of spirituality since May 2023 and he remains there in the year ahead until May 26. So, you are in a very strong spiritual period in your life. Much spiritual growth has been happening and there have been spiritual breakthroughs. On May 26 this year Jupiter will move into your 1st house, your own sign. This signals a multi-year cycle of prosperity which will continue well into next year. More on this later.

Ever since Saturn moved into your 10th house in March 2023, career has become more challenging. There is now a need to earn your success the hard way, by simply being the best at what you do. So, more work and effort are needed. More on this later.

Pluto's move into your 9th house after more than 30 years in your 8th is a harmonious aspect for you. In the coming years a whole transformation will be happening in your religious, philosophical and metaphysical beliefs. This will be a long-term process, but in the end you will be living your life in a completely different way. Pluto's transition from Capricorn to Aquarius signals changes in the job situation and changes in your health regime, too. It is a good health signal. More on this later on.

Uranus has been in your 12th house of spirituality for many years and will be there in the year ahead as well. So, you have been experimental in these matters. You have been trying out different systems, different practices, different teachings to see what works best for you. This is a normal stage on the spiritual path. More on this later.

From May 26 onwards love is the main headline. The love life is very positive and singles might not remain single for too much longer. More details later.

Your most important areas of interest of this year are spirituality; the body, image and personal appearance from May 26 onwards; career; sex, death, and occult studies from January 1–22 and from September 3 to November 20; and religion, philosophy, theology, higher education and foreign travel from January 22 to September 3 and from November 20 to the end of the year.

Your paths of greatest fulfilment in the year ahead will be friends, groups, group activities and involvement with organizations; spirituality until May 26; and the body, image and personal appearance from May 26 onwards.

Health

(Please note that this is an astrological perspective on health and not a medical one. In days of yore there was no difference, both these perspectives were identical. But these days there could be quite a difference. For a medical perspective, please consult your doctor or health practitioner.)

Ever since Saturn moved into adverse aspect to you in March 2023 the health has needed more watching. Still, I would say that overall health is basically good this year. Sure, as our regular readers know, there will be times during the year when health and energy are less easy than usual and perhaps even stressful. But these are not trends for the year, only temporary blips caused by the transits of short-term planets. When they pass your naturally good health and energy return.

Also, as was mentioned earlier, your health planet is making a major transition this year. It is not yet the full-blown transition, which will happen next year, but is a signal for things to come. Pluto is moving from Capricorn into Aquarius this year and he will spend time in both signs. For many years you have been very conservative in health matters. You gravitated to orthodox medicine. This shift of Pluto is indicating a new attitude; you seem more experimental in health matters and will probably explore alternative types of therapies.

Pluto as your health planet shows a tendency to surgery. You can see them as quick fixes to health problems. But, keep in mind that Pluto also rules detox regimes and you would benefit from these things as well.

Good though your health is, you can make it better. Give more attention to the following – the vulnerable areas of your Horoscope this year (the reflex points are shown in the chart opposite):

- The heart. Do your best to avoid worry and anxiety as this tends to stress out the heart. Regular chest massage would be beneficial.
- The colon, bladder, organs of elimination and sexual organs. Safe sex and sexual moderation also seem very important.

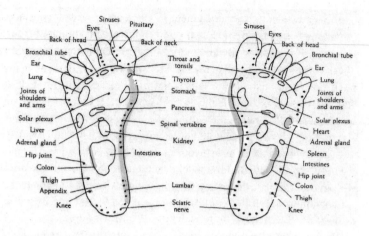

Important foot reflexology points for the year ahead

Try to massage all of the foot on a regular basis – the top of the foot as well as the bottom – but pay extra attention to the points highlighted on the chart. When you massage, be aware of 'sore spots' as these need special attention. It's also a very good idea to massage the ankles and below them.

- The spine, knees, bones, skin and overall skeletal alignment. These areas have been important for many years and remain so from January 1 to the 22nd and from September 3 to November 20. Regular back and knee massage would be wonderful. Regular visits to a chiropractor or osteopath would also be good as the vertebrae in the spine need to be kept in right alignment. Therapies such as Feldenkrais, the Alexander technique and Rolfing, all of which deal with the spine and alignment, would be good. Make sure to get enough calcium for the bones. If you're out in strong sunlight use a good sunscreen. Give the knees more support when you're exercising.
- The ankles and calves. From January 22 to September 3 and from November 20 they should be regularly massaged. A weak ankle can knock the spine and whole skeleton out of alignment, causing all kinds of other problems. Give the ankles more support when exercising.

Saturn as we mentioned is making stressful aspects to you. However, other long-term planets are helping you and so health should be good. However, it is good to understand that Saturn will be revealing your physical limits. Don't be alarmed if you can't jog as far or do as many push-ups as you usually do. This is normal under a Saturn transit. If you are working out and feel pain or discomfort, take a break and go back to it later. Try not to force things. Knowing your physical limits is a good thing. It can prevent all kinds of injuries. When Saturn moves away from his stressful aspect your physical limits will expand.

From May 26 onwards you will be living the good life and the price we pay for this is a tendency to gain weight. So, this needs to be watched more carefully from May 26 onwards and well into next year as well.

Women of childbearing age are much more fertile than usual.

Home and Family

Home and family are always important to you, Gemini, but this year less so than usual. Your 4th house of home and family is not a house of power and is basically empty in the year ahead. Only short-term, fast-moving planets will move through there this year. This tends to the status quo. You seem satisfied with things as they are and have no need to make major changes. Many of you will be travelling more than usual this year but a move is not likely. There is nothing against it, however, but equally there is nothing especially pushing it either.

We mentioned earlier that women of childbearing age are more fertile than usual. This can certainly impact on the home and family life.

Two eclipses in the coming year affect the family's finances. These are the lunar eclipse of March 25 and the solar eclipse of October 2. A parent or parent figure needs to make important financial changes.

A parent or parent figure in your life is having a challenging year and is perhaps overly pessimistic and low in overall energy. He or she could be moving in with you or near you – in close proximity. Parents and parent figures could use some cheering up this year. Siblings' love lives, or current relationships, will be being tested in the coming years. Children and children figures in your life might want to move but it doesn't seem advisable. This could lead to a major renovation of the home instead. They would favour homes that are near water. Grandchildren, if you have them or those who play that role in your life, are likely to move in the year ahead. Perhaps there have been multiple moves for them in the past few years.

This is not an especially strong year for important changes or renovations to the home, but if you choose to do such a thing, August 22 to September 22 would be a good time. If you're merely redecorating, or buying beautiful objects for the home, August 5-29 would be good.

Finance and Career

As we mentioned earlier, from May 26 you begin a multi-year cycle of prosperity. Finances are OK before that date, but they start to really take off after May 26. Jupiter moving through your sign shows someone who is living above their usual standard. There will be more travel, more sensual delights, more indulgence in fine foods and fine wines. You will live as if you were rich, regardless of whether the money is actually there or not. The interesting thing is that the cosmos will tend to support this higher lifestyle. Your balance sheet might not show the extra money, but one way or another it will come to you. Prosperity will be very strong in 2025 too, as Jupiter enters your 2nd money house.

The Moon, the fastest-moving planet in the zodiac, is your financial planet and, as our regular readers know, she moves through all the signs and houses of your Horoscope in any given month. Thus there are many short-term trends in finances that depend on where the Moon is and the kinds of aspects she receives. These are best dealt with in the monthly reports. In general, we can say that the new Moon and full Moon tend to be strong financial days in any given month. Also, earnings should be stronger when the Moon is waxing or growing than when she is waning. When she is waxing is the time to do things that will increase your earnings, make investments or deposit money in your savings account. It is propitious for doing things that you want to see growth in. Conversely, when the Moon is waning and growing smaller is good for paying down debt or paying bills. Good for things that you want to get rid of or reduce. This will vary month-to-month and will be dealt with in the monthly reports. When the Moon moves through your own sign, which varies month-to-month, will also be good financial days.

The Moon as your financial planet indicates the importance of family and family connections in your financial life. It favours residential real estate, the food business, restaurants, hotels and motels and companies and industries that cater to the homeowner. These are always interesting investments for you and you have a good feeling for them. With the Moon as your financial planet, you can be very moody when it comes to finance. In a good mood you feel rich and confident. In a bad mood you can feel very poor. This tends to have nothing to do with the objective reality; it's just your mood. So, try to avoid making important financial decisions based on your mood. Such decisions should be made from a place of peace and emotional tranquillity. Then the inner intuition can flow properly.

Spiritual Neptune has been in your 10th house of career for many years now, and so you have been more idealistic in career matters. Just being successful and making money was not enough for many of you. You wanted to do something meaningful, something that really benefits people on the entire planet. Many of you changed careers to be involved in those things. Others continued in your worldly career but got involved in non-profit organizations and charities on the side. But last year things began to change. Saturn moved into your 10th house in March 2023 and he will be there all of this year. Thus, the idealism is being tempered. There is a need for more practicality in your career goals. Idealism is nice but the bottom line is nicer. So, you are of two minds when it comes to the career this year. One part of you leans towards the worldly side while the other is more idealistic. These two minds argue with each other and create ambivalence. The best career choices satisfy both these sides of you.

With Saturn in your career house there is a need to succeed through sheer merit, through actual performance, through being the best at what you do. This involves work and effort. Your high ideals, good though they are, will not cut it this year. You have to perform. Sometimes with this transit you can come under the dominion of very demanding bosses. They push you to your limit, and sometimes beyond it. This is not punishment, only the cosmos's way of stretching your abilities.

Yes, there is more work involved in your career, but if you put the work in you should be very successful.

Love and Social Life

As we've already said, the love life will be sensational this year. It is really the main headline of the year ahead.

Your love planet Jupiter will move through two signs and houses in the year ahead. This shows different needs and attitudes in love. Until May 26 your love planet will be in your spiritual 12th house. This can be read in a few ways. It indicates a spiritual preparation for love that will manifest after May 26. Until May 26 love is behind the scenes, not overt. Until May 26 spiritual compatibility is ultra-important in love. You need a partner who supports your spiritual goals and who is in harmony with them. If there is spiritual harmony between two people almost any problem, whatever it is, can be corrected. But if this is absent almost nothing can be corrected.

Until May 26 love and social opportunities happen in spiritual types of settings – at a spiritual lecture, prayer meeting, charity event, etc. After May 26 it is a whole different story. Love will pursue you rather than vice versa. There is nothing special that you need to do except just to go about your daily business and love will find you. This looks like serious love. For singles this can lead to marriage or a relationship that is like a marriage. For those of you already in a relationship it enhances the present relationship and makes it more romantic. The spouse, partner or current love is totally on your side and seems completely devoted and dedicated to you. He or she puts your interest above their own. Jupiter in your own sign will also bring all kinds of social opportunities to you, not just romance.

Before May 26 love is spiritual and idealistic. After May 26 love seems more physical and sensual.

Self-improvement

Uranus has been in your 12th house of spirituality for many years now. This has produced constant and serial change in your spiritual life, your spiritual practice and its teachings. Every time you think you have it right you encounter a new idea, a new teaching, and you jump to that. You have been like the wandering mystic of days gone by. He or she would wander the world searching for wisdom, studying with one holy man or another and then moving on. While you haven't done this physically, mentally it's been like that. This wondering and wandering is still in effect this year but is almost over with. In a year or two's time you will have settled on your path and be sticking to it.

Jupiter moving through your 12th house until May 26 has other messages that haven't been mentioned yet. It signals the importance of love in your spiritual life. When you are in love (or in the energy vibrations of love) your connection to spirit is very strong and very reliable. Jupiter's transit also shows a need to delve into the mystical traditions of your native religion. There's no need to travel far and wide; explore the mystical paths of what is close to hand. Every religion has its mystical side. This is what you need to study this year.

We discussed the impact of both Saturn and Neptune being in your 10th house of career earlier. The main challenge is to somehow blend idealism and practicality in the pursuit of career objectives. Your idealism needs to be made more practical and pursued in practical ways, and your practicality needs to become more idealistic. A difficult thing to blend but you can do it. There are no rules about this, everyone finds their own solution in their own way.

For more information on astrology, healing and spiritual topics, please visit my blog at www.spiritual-stories.com.

Month-by-month Forecasts

January

Best Days Overall: 3, 4, 12, 13, 21, 22, 30, 31
Most Stressful Days Overall: 1, 2, 8, 9, 14, 15, 28, 29
Best Days for Love: 1, 2, 8, 9, 10, 11, 18, 19, 27, 28
Best Days for Money: 1, 2, 10, 11, 12, 18, 19, 21, 23, 24, 28, 29
Best Days for Career: 7, 14, 15, 24

Health and energy will steadily improve as the month progresses. Still, with two long-term planets in stressful aspect with you, health still needs watching. With your health planet Pluto moving into Aquarius on the 22nd your health needs and attitudes are undergoing significant change. Right now, it's only the very beginnings of this change but, as time goes on, it will become more pronounced. Until the 22nd enhance the health with back and knee massage. After the 22nd ankle and calf massage will become important. Until the 22nd you seem very conservative in health matters, which has been the case for over 30 years. After the 22nd you seem more open to alternative therapies and to experimental kinds of therapies. In general, you will be more experimental when it comes to health.

Career is prominent this month and seems very demanding. Success comes the old-fashion way, through being the best at what you do. Your 8th house of regeneration is very strong this month, especially until the 20th. This is a good financial signal for the spouse, partner or current love.

Power in the 8th house is good for occult studies and for a deeper understanding of death. Perhaps people you know, or bosses or parents or parent figures, are facing near-death kinds of experiences. Perhaps they are having surgery. These kinds of events force us to think more deeply about what death is all about. It is a good month for getting rid of the extraneous in your life, not the necessary, but the extraneous. A good time for a thorough house clear out, and not just of excess possessions but of mental and emotional patterns that no longer serve you. On the 20th your 9th house becomes very powerful. (It will be even stronger next month but you are experiencing the beginnings of it now.) Thus, it is a good period for foreign travel and religious, philosophical and theological studies. It is a good time for college-level students as well. They should do well in their studies.

Finance doesn't seem a big issue this month; your money house is basically empty and only the Moon will move through there on the 23rd and 24th. In general, finances should be stronger from the 11th to the 25th as the Moon waxes. Until the 11th and after the 25th will be good times to use spare cash to reduce debts or pay bills.

Your love planet Jupiter has been in your spiritual 12th house for many months now and will be there for a few more to come. Singles will find romantic opportunities in spiritual types of settings. It's very important that you and your prospective love be on the same spiritual wavelength. With Mercury, the ruler of your Horoscope, in your 7th house of love until the 14th the social life seems very active and you seem more popular than usual, as you are going out of your way for others. There is happy romantic opportunity from the 14th onwards.

February

Best Days Overall: 8, 9, 17, 18, 26, 27, 28
Most Stressful Days Overall: 4, 5, 10, 11, 24, 25
Best Days for Love: 4, 5, 6, 7, 14, 15, 17, 24, 25, 26, 27
Best Days for Money: 1, 6, 7, 8, 9, 14, 15, 18, 19, 20, 24, 25, 29
Best Days for Career: 2, 3, 10, 11, 20, 29

In spite of the fact that two long-term planets are in stressful aspect to you, health and energy are good this month. Many short-term planets are in harmonious aspect with you, boosting your energy. You can enhance the health even further with ankle and calf massage.

Your 9th house, a beneficent house, became very strong last month and this month is even stronger. Half the planets are either there or moving through there at the start of the month, and with the new Moon of the 9th 60 per cent of the planets will be in your 9th house. When the 9th house is this powerful, a juicy theological discussion or a lecture from a visiting guru is more appealing than a night out on the town. It is an excellent month for college-level students: they should do well in their studies as there is great focus here. The new Moon of the 9th will not only clarify religious and theological issues, but also legal issues if you are involved with these things. The 9th will also be a very strong financial day. Many of you will be travelling to foreign countries this month. It is a good month for taking a trip, and for planning a future trip. A strong 9th house shows a basically happy month ahead. You have the ability to expand beyond your problems, to see what is beyond the bend.

Love also seems happy this month as Mercury, the ruler of your Horoscope, is making beautiful aspects to Jupiter, your love planet.

Romantic opportunities can happen in spiritual-type settings, like last month, or at college, college functions or religious functions.

With your money house still basically empty this month – only the Moon will move through there on the 19th and 20th – finance doesn't seem a major issue. Earnings should be better and stronger from the 9th to the 24th as the Moon waxes. Until the 9th and after the 24th would be good to use spare cash to reduce debt and pay bills.

March

Best Days Overall: 7, 8, 13, 14, 15, 16, 24, 25, 26
Most Stressful Days Overall: 2, 3, 9, 10, 22, 23, 29, 30
Best Days for Love: 2, 3, 4, 5, 7, 8, 13, 14, 17, 18, 22, 23, 27, 28, 29, 30
Best Days for Money: 1, 4, 5, 9, 10, 13, 14, 17, 18, 19, 20, 22, 23, 29, 30
Best Days for Career: 1, 9, 10, 18, 28

On February 19 you began a yearly career peak, which continues until the 20th. This month, however, health needs a lot more attention. Make sure to get enough rest. The demands of the career are strong and probably unavoidable, so focus on essentials and let side issues go. Conserve energy wherever possible. Take short breaks when you work. Enhance the health in the ways mentioned in the yearly report, and also give more attention to the ankles and calves.

The month ahead should be successful, careerwise, but it will be an earned success. Probably you are taking more responsibility in your career, or are being given more responsibility. The 15th to the 17th seems a particularly successful period. Both Mercury and the Sun are travelling with your career planet Neptune.

A lunar eclipse on the 25th occurs in your 5th house and impacts children and children figures in your life. They should be kept out of harm's way while the eclipse is in effect. Things that need to be done should be done but anything else is better off being rescheduled. Children and children figures have a need to re-define themselves, their self-concept, how they think of themselves and how they want others to think of them. This will result in a new presentation, a new look and a new wardrobe over the coming months.

Parents and parent figures are forced to make important financial changes. Most likely their planning and financial strategies were not realistic. Since the eclipsed planet, the Moon, is your financial planet, you too are making important financial changes.

Siblings and sibling figures in your life experience dramatic spiritual changes. They should avoid unnecessary driving, if possible, and drive more carefully over the eclipse period. There can be issues with cars or communication equipment. If siblings are school students there are changes in their educational plans.

April

Best Days Overall: 3, 4, 11, 12, 21, 22, 30
Most Stressful Days Overall: 5, 6, 18, 19, 20
Best Days for Love: 1, 2, 7, 8, 9, 10, 16, 17, 18, 19, 26, 27, 28
Best Days for Money: 1, 2, 7, 8, 9, 10, 13, 14, 15, 17, 18, 19, 28, 29
Best Days for Career: 5, 6, 14, 15, 24, 25

A very strong solar eclipse on the 8th is the main headline of the month ahead. You, family members, siblings and sibling figures, and especially a parent or parent figure, should take it nice and easy while the eclipse is in effect. You will certainly feel the eclipse before it actually happens, and when you do, reduce your schedule. Unnecessary driving or short travel trips are not advisable during this time. If you must drive, do so more carefully.

This eclipse occurs in your 11th house of friends and will bring dramas, often life-changing kinds of dramas, to the lives of friends and turmoil and upheaval in a trade or professional organization that you are involved with. Cars, communication equipment, computers and software will get tested during this eclipse and often repairs or replacements are necessary. Back up important files and avoid opening emails from people you don't know. Be more alert for online scams.

This eclipse also directly impacts two important planets in your chart – Mercury, the ruler of your chart and of your 4th family house, and Venus, the ruler of your 5th house of fun and creativity. The impact on Mercury and Venus shows that you and a parent figure, children and children figures in your life will need to re-define yourselves. Over the coming months you will develop a new self-concept and will present yourself in a different way to others. Often with this kind of eclipse repairs are needed in the home.

May

Best Days Overall: 1, 9, 10, 17, 18, 19, 27, 28
Most Stressful Days Overall: 2, 3, 4, 15, 16, 23, 24, 30, 31
Best Days for Love: 7, 8, 15, 16, 23, 24, 26, 27, 28
Best Days for Money: 1, 7, 8, 11, 12, 15, 16, 18, 19, 26, 27, 28
Best Days for Career: 4, 8, 12, 16, 22, 31

A happy month ahead, Gemini. Enjoy!

You'll begin the month in a very strong spiritual period. This is fitting as spiritual changes and breakthroughs tend to lead to physical ones. Before things happen physically, the spiritual ground needs to be arranged. On the 20th as the Sun enters your sign, you begin a yearly personal pleasure peak. This will be much stronger than usual as Jupiter will move into your sign too on the 26th. This is going to be life-changing, and in a very good way. First off, Jupiter's move will initiate a multi-year cycle of prosperity. This month (and year) it will be more about living at a higher standard than usual. Next year you'll see the actual financial results. But even this year, the cosmos will support your higher living standard.

Jupiter in your sign brings love, serious love, for singles. The beautiful thing about this is that there is nothing much you need to do about it. Love is pursuing you. Just go about your daily business and it will find you. For those of you already in a relationship this transit shows that the spouse, partner or current love is extremely devoted to you, and is putting your interest ahead of his or her own. He or she is very eager to please. Also, this transit shows that social opportunities in general are coming to you. It happens very naturally and with little effort on your part. With the Sun in your sign from the 20th onwards, and Venus also moving in there on the 23rd, the physical appearance shines. There is more personal charisma, grace and glamour to the image. You dress fashionably and probably expensively. The opposite sex certainly takes notice.

Health and energy are also very good this month, in spite of the fact that two long-term planets are in stressful alignment with you. The short-term planets are supporting you. Avoid making important changes to your health regime this month as your health planet goes retrograde on the 2nd. Any changes need a lot more study and this will be the situation for many more months.

Women of childbearing age are extremely fertile this month and in future months.

All of you, male or female, will need to watch the weight more. There is a tendency to pile on the pounds.

Again, finance doesn't seem a major focus this month, with a basically empty money house; only the Moon moves through there on the 11th and 12th. However, as we've said, you are living at a higher standard. You have more enthusiasm for earnings from the 8th to the 23rd, as the Moon is waxing. Spare cash should be put into savings or investment accounts. When the Moon is waning, from the 1st to the 8th and from the 23rd onwards, use spare cash to pay off debt or bills.

June

Best Days Overall: 5, 6, 14, 15, 16, 24, 25
Most Stressful Days Overall: 12, 13, 19, 20, 26, 27
Best Days for Love: 5, 6, 14, 16, 17, 19, 20, 24, 26, 27
Best Days for Money: 5, 6, 7, 8, 14, 15, 24, 26
Best Days for Career: 8, 18, 26, 27

Another happy and prosperous month ahead, Gemini. Enjoy.

Many of the trends discussed last month are still in effect now. You are in one of the most independent times of your year. This is a time to live life on your terms. It is a time to establish your path of personal happiness. If there are changes to be made to improve your personal happiness, by all means make them. Later on, when the planets shift, it will be more difficult.

You are still in a yearly personal pleasure peak until the 20th. So, enjoy all the pleasures of the senses, the good foods, the good wines, etc. A good month to pamper yourself. Also good to get the body and image in the shape that you want.

Health and energy are still wonderful, and you can enhance them further in the ways mentioned in the yearly report and through ankle and calf massage.

The month ahead is prosperous as well. On the 20th as the Sun enters your money house you begin a yearly financial peak. The new Moon of the 5th seems an especially strong financial day. It brings windfalls and also financial opportunities that seek you out rather than vice versa. This new Moon will also clarify your path to personal happiness and issues involving the body and image. This is a process that will go on until the next new Moon next month. All the information you need to make a good decision in these areas will come to you naturally and normally.

Mars's move into your 12th house on the 9th shows a need for spiritual activism. There is a need to express your spiritual ideals and beliefs in physical action. Mere abstract contemplation is certainly not enough for you.

July

Best Days Overall: 2, 3, 12, 13, 21, 22, 29, 30, 31
Most Stressful Days Overall: 9, 10, 11, 17, 18, 23, 24
Best Days for Love: 2, 3, 5, 6, 12, 13, 17, 18, 21, 22, 25, 26, 29, 30
Best Days for Money: 2, 3, 4, 5, 6, 12, 13, 14, 16, 21, 22, 23, 29, 30
Best Days for Career: 6, 16, 23, 24

You're still in the midst of a yearly financial peak. It began last month and will continue until the 22nd: 30 per cent, sometimes 40 per cent of the planets are either in your money house or moving through there. This is a lot of cosmic energy, so earnings are boosted. The new Moon of the 14th is an especially wonderful financial day. Not only will it boost earnings, but as the month goes on, and until the next new

Moon, the financial picture will be clarified. Doubts will get resolved. All the information you need to make good financial decisions will come to you naturally and normally.

With so many planets moving through the money house, earnings can come from many different sources and in many ways.

Health is good this month and you can enhance it even further in the ways mentioned in the yearly report. Continue to give more attention to the ankles and calves. With Pluto, your health planet, still retrograde it is not wise to have medical tests or procedures right now. Sometimes there is no choice about these things, but if there is, reschedule them for another time.

The love life has been super ever since May 26. This month the overall social life, the area of friendships, is also very nice, especially from the 20th onwards. Friends seem more devoted to you and are seeking you out.

Mars travels with Uranus on the 13th and 14th, and friends should be more mindful on the physical plane. There are dramatic changes in trade or professional organizations that you are involved with.

Mars's move into your own sign on the 20th signals that you are more physically active now. From the 20th onwards you excel in sports and exercise regimes, you perform at your personal best. This transit would also indicate that you accessorize in a more high-tech kind of way. Perhaps you are wearing high-tech gadgets as fashion statements. You seem to be more experimental in the way that you dress. There would be a tendency to make political statements in the way that you dress.

Mars in your sign has other meanings as well. There is a need to watch the temper, as you are more aggressive than usual. You need to be careful of rush and impatience as this can lead to accidents or injury. You want things done in a hurry; this is natural with Mars in your sign, but act more mindfully on the physical plane.

On the 22nd the Sun enters your 3rd house of communication and intellectual interests. The cosmos urges you to do what you most love – to read, study and communicate. This is a very happy situation for you. Your normally super communication and intellectual skills become even more super.

Career is basically good, but your career planet Neptune goes retrograde on the 2nd. Many career issues will need time to resolve. In the meantime, avoid making dramatic career moves until you have more information.

August

Best Days Overall: 8, 9, 17, 18, 26, 27
Most Stressful Days Overall: 5, 6, 7, 13, 14, 19, 20
Best Days for Love: 8, 9, 13, 14, 17, 18, 27, 29
Best Days for Money: 1, 2, 3, 4, 8, 9, 13, 14, 17, 18, 23, 27, 28, 29
Best Days for Career: 2, 12, 19, 20, 28, 29

Planetary retrograde activity is nearing its maximum for the year: 40 per cent of the planets will be retrograde from the 4th to the 25th. Only in October will we have more retrogrades than now.

So, the keyword this month is patience. Patience, patience, patience. With Mars still in your sign and wanting everything yesterday, patience will be more difficult to practise. Patience, when understood correctly, is not some verbal platitude, but soul knowledge. It is the understanding that if it takes nine months to make a baby, we allow the nine months. If it takes two hours to bake a cake, we allow the two hours. This is true patience.

Your 3rd house of communication and intellectual interest is still very powerful this month, until the 22nd. While this is basically happy for you, as you get to express your natural gifts, the problem can be too much of a good thing. The mind can easily get overstimulated. It can turn and turn and turn without purpose. This extra intellectual energy that you have needs to be controlled and directed to a good purpose and then turned off when not in use. An out-of-control intellect can lead to insomnia and other nervous problems.

Health is basically good but needs more attention after the 22nd. As always, make sure to get enough rest. High energy is the first defence against disease. Enhance the health in the ways mentioned in the yearly report and continue to give more attention to the ankles and calves. Your health planet is still retrograde so avoid making major changes to the health regime. If changes need to be made, study them more carefully. It is still wise to reschedule medical tests or procedures for a later time, if you can.

On the 22nd the planetary power shifts to your 4th house of home and family. In fact, you'll feel this sooner than the 22nd as other planets energize your 4th house. Career is still very important, but with your career planet Neptune still retrograde, career issues will need time to resolve. It is best to focus on the home and family front. Even more importantly, it is good to focus on your emotional wellness.

September

Best Days Overall: 4, 5, 6, 14, 15, 22, 23
Most Stressful Days Overall: 2, 3, 9, 10, 16, 17, 29, 30
Best Days for Love: 4, 5, 9, 10, 14, 15, 22, 23, 24
Best Days for Money: 2, 3, 4, 5, 12, 13, 14, 15, 21, 22, 23, 24, 25, 30
Best Days for Career: 7, 8, 16, 17, 18, 19, 24, 25

The lunar eclipse of the 18th affects you strongly, so take it nice and easy while the eclipse is in effect. With health and energy more challenging until the 22nd, this advice is good until the 22nd, but especially during the eclipse time. Spend more quiet time at home and reschedule activities if you can, especially if they are stressful. Read a book, watch a movie, or – best of all – meditate.

This solar eclipse occurs in your 10th house of career, bringing important and dramatic career changes to you. Sometimes people actually change the career path, but usually the eclipse manifests as changing the way that you pursue your career goals. There is a change in the way you think and plan it. The events of the eclipse change your career strategy. Since this eclipse is a pretty direct hit on Neptune, your career planet, everything we've said is greatly magnified. With Neptune retrograde all month let the dust settle before you implement your changes.

This eclipse sideswipes Jupiter, your love planet. Happily, it is not a direct hit, but it will still test your current relationship and perhaps bring personal dramas to the current love, spouse or partner. It could also create changes in your social circle. Good relationships survive these things, but flawed ones are in danger.

With the Moon being your financial planet, every lunar eclipse affects your finances and requires course corrections in the financial life. This eclipse is no different. You go through these kinds of dramas twice a year and by now you know how to handle them. Your financial thinking, planning and strategy are not realistic, as the events of the eclipse will show. Thus, changes are necessary.

The good news this month is that health and energy will dramatically improve from the 22nd onwards. Also, you will be having more fun from that time onwards. After a stressful month you deserve some fun.

October

Best Days Overall: 1, 2, 3, 11, 12, 19, 20, 29, 30
Most Stressful Days Overall: 6, 7, 8, 13, 14, 26, 27, 28
Best Days for Love: 2, 4, 5, 6, 7, 8, 11, 12, 13, 14, 19, 20, 24, 25, 29, 30
Best Days for Money: 1, 2, 11, 12, 19, 20, 21, 22, 23, 29, 30
Best Days for Career: 4, 5, 13, 14, 23, 31

A solar eclipse on the 2nd, the second one this year, affects you, siblings and sibling figures, parents and parent figures, children, and the home and family as a whole. They all experience personal dramas. Although this eclipse is not a total eclipse, its impact is strong because it affects other planets.

It occurs in your 5th house of creativity and children and, as we've said, it brings personal dramas to the children and children figures in your life. Those of you involved in the creative arts or entertainment business will make important changes to your creativity.

This eclipse reveals a need for a revision of the self-concept and self-image for yourself, and for children, siblings or sibling figures, and parents and parent figures in your life. It is good every now and then to change our concept of ourselves. After all, we are growing and evolving beings and our image of our self five years ago is not the same as it is now. Our self-concept should evolve as we ourselves evolve. The difference now is that the eclipse forces the issue. This self re-evaluation will lead to wardrobe changes and image changes as the months progress. As with the previous solar eclipse in April, changes in the self-concept seem to affect the marriage or relationship of children figures.

Mars, your planet of friends, is directly impacted by this eclipse. There are dramas in the lives of friends, and often these are life-changing kinds of dramas. Computers and high-tech equipment can behave erratically. Sometimes repairs or replacements are necessary. Keep your antivirus and anti-hacking software up to date. Don't open suspicious emails or attachments. Back up important files.

For students below college level there are changes in educational plans. Sometimes there are disruptions at school and sometimes even a change of schools.

Since Mercury is directly impacted by this eclipse, repairs might be needed in the home. Passions in the family can run high so be more patient with family members.

The two planets that involve driving and short trips, the Sun and Mercury, are both impacted by this eclipse. So, it is probably good to avoid unnecessary driving or unnecessary travel. If you must do these things, drive more carefully. There can be personal dramas in the lives of neighbours and disruptions in your neighbourhood too.

November

Best Days Overall: 7, 8, 9, 16, 17, 25, 26, 27
Most Stressful Days Overall: 3, 4, 10, 11, 22, 23, 24, 29, 30
Best Days for Love: 3, 4, 8, 9, 12, 13, 16, 17, 22, 23, 26, 27, 29, 30
Best Days for Money: 1, 2, 8, 9, 10, 11, 16, 17, 18, 19, 22, 26, 27
Best Days for Career: 2, 10, 11, 19, 29

Health and energy are basically good this month but need some attention from the 21st onwards. As always make sure to get enough rest. Continue to enhance the health in the ways mentioned in the yearly report. Your health planet will be in two signs this month: until the 20th Pluto will be in Capricorn, and after the 20th he will be in Aquarius. So, until the 20th enhance health with back and knee massage and after the 20th with ankle and calf massage.

There is a lot of power in your 6th house this month, especially until the 21st. And your focus on health will stand you in good stead after that date when health becomes more delicate. This is a good month for job-seekers, or for those who employ others. With your health planet now moving forward after many months of retrograde motion it is safer to have medical tests and procedures if you need them.

Mars is in your money house until the 4th. This shows the importance of social connections in the financial life and, more importantly, it favours the technology field and the online world. This would be a good time to upgrade your computers and software as you can earn from these things.

The full Moon of the 15th occurs right on Uranus and will bring enhanced creativity, luck in speculations and sudden, unexpected money. Sometimes this kind of transit brings an unexpected expense as well. But the money to cover it will also come.

Earnings should be better from the 1st to the 15th as the Moon waxes. You have more enthusiasm and energy for finance that period. The new Moon of the 1st is especially good for job-seekers and those who employ others. More importantly, it will clarify health and work issues as the days progress until the next new Moon next month. All the information that you need about these issues will come to you normally and naturally.

The Sun enters your 7th house of love on the 21st, and you begin a yearly love and romantic peak. You have been in a romantic peak since May 26, but now it gets even stronger. The spouse, partner or current love has been very devoted to you since May 26. This month you seem to be devoted to your relationship. You are both devoted to each other. The beloved is having a good month. He or she looks good, there is beauty, grace and charisma to the image. Self-esteem and self-confidence are good. Perhaps he or she is travelling this month, or perhaps planning a foreign trip. If he or she is involved in legal issues they seem to go well.

Mercury, the ruler of your Horoscope, goes retrograde on the 26th. This could weaken your confidence and self-esteem to a degree. But no matter, as this is the kind of month where good comes to you from others and not from personal skills or initiative. It is your social grace that brings your good to you, and you have this. Let others have their way, so long as it isn't destructive, and your good will come to you quite naturally.

December

    Best Days Overall: 5, 6, 13, 14, 22, 23, 24
    Most Stressful Days Overall: 1, 7, 8, 20, 21, 27, 28, 29
    Best Days for Love: 1, 2, 3, 4, 6, 13, 14, 22, 23, 24, 27, 28, 29
    Best Days for Money: 1, 6, 9, 10, 14, 15, 16, 19, 20, 23, 24, 30, 31
    Best Days for Career: 7, 8, 16, 26

Health will improve dramatically from the 21st onwards, although it will still need keeping an eye on. So, as always, make sure to get enough rest and to maintain high energy levels. Both the social demands and career demands are very great these days and you probably can't avoid them. However, you can increase your energy and health by focusing on what is really important to you and letting go of lesser things. Alternate activities. Take short breaks when you work. This will maximize energy.

You are still in a yearly love and social peak until the 21st. Love is happy but complicated. Both you and the current love seem unsure of what you want. You are seeing things from opposite perspectives. If you can bridge the differences the relationship will become stronger than ever. Opposite perspectives, when combined, make for a more powerful whole. The spouse or partner is strong where you are weak, and you are strong where he or she is weak.

The career is improving as Neptune, your career planet, which has been retrograde for many months, starts to move forward on the 7th. Long-stuck career projects become unstuck and start moving forward again. There is more clarity about your career, and this gives more confidence.

Mars is in your 3rd house of communication and intellectual interest all month. This makes you a great debater. However, it can also make you more argumentative. You speak with more passion and perhaps this provokes others to match your passion, and arguments ensue.

Siblings and sibling figures seem more aggressive these days. They need to watch their temper and to avoid rush and haste. If they are college-level students there is good news for them.

On the 21st the Sun moves into your 8th house, initiating a sexually active kind of time. Whatever your age and stage in life the libido is stronger than usual. This will be a good time for detox regimes on all levels – physical, emotional and mental. The spouse, partner or current love begins a very strong period of prosperity.

The full Moon is always a good financial day for you, as the Moon is your financial planet. But this full Moon of the 15th seems especially good as it occurs right on Jupiter, the planet of wealth, bringing a nice payday for you. It is also an excellent love and social day. Romantic feelings are especially strong.

Earning power is good from the 1st to the 15th as the Moon waxes. This is a good time to be saving or investing. From the 15th onwards use spare cash to reduce debts or pay bills. This puts you in harmony with the power of your financial planet.

Cancer

THE CRAB

Birthdays from
21st June to
20th July

Personality Profile

CANCER AT A GLANCE

Element – Water

Ruling Planet – Moon
   Career Planet – Mars
   Love Planet – Saturn
   Money Planet – Sun
   Planet of Fun and Games – Pluto
   Planet of Good Fortune – Neptune
   Planet of Health and Work – Jupiter
   Planet of Home and Family Life – Venus
   Planet of Spirituality – Mercury

Colours – blue, puce, silver

Colours that promote love, romance and social harmony – black, indigo

Colours that promote earning power – gold, orange

Gems – moonstone, pearl

Metal – silver

Scents – jasmine, sandalwood

Quality – cardinal (= activity)

Quality most needed for balance – mood control

Strongest virtues – emotional sensitivity, tenacity, the urge to nurture

Deepest need – a harmonious home and family life

Characteristics to avoid – over-sensitivity, negative moods

Signs of greatest overall compatibility – Scorpio, Pisces

Signs of greatest overall incompatibility – Aries, Libra, Capricorn

Sign most helpful to career – Aries

Sign most helpful for emotional support – Libra

Sign most helpful financially – Leo

Sign best for marriage and/or partnerships – Capricorn

Sign most helpful for creative projects – Scorpio

Best Sign to have fun with – Scorpio

Signs most helpful in spiritual matters – Gemini, Pisces

Best day of the week – Monday

Understanding a Cancer

In the sign of Cancer the heavens are developing the feeling side of things. This is what a true Cancerian is all about – feelings. Where Aries will tend to err on the side of action, Taurus on the side of inaction and Gemini on the side of thought, Cancer will tend to err on the side of feeling.

Cancerians tend to mistrust logic. Perhaps rightfully so. For them it is not enough for an argument or a project to be logical – it must feel right as well. If it does not feel right a Cancerian will reject it or chafe against it. The phrase 'follow your heart' could have been coined by a Cancerian, because it describes exactly the Cancerian attitude to life.

The power to feel is a more direct – more immediate – method of knowing than thinking is. Thinking is indirect. Thinking about a thing never touches the thing itself. Feeling is a faculty that touches directly the thing or issue in question. We actually experience it. Emotional feeling is almost like another sense which humans possess – a psychic sense. Since the realities that we come in contact with during our lifetime are often painful and even destructive, it is not surprising that the Cancerian chooses to erect barriers – a shell – to protect his or her vulnerable, sensitive nature. To a Cancerian this is only common sense.

If Cancerians are in the presence of people they do not know, or find themselves in a hostile environment, up goes the shell and they feel protected. Other people often complain about this, but one must question these people's motives. Why does this shell disturb them? Is it perhaps because they would like to sting, and feel frustrated that they cannot? If your intentions are honourable and you are patient, have no fear. The shell will open up and you will be accepted as part of the Cancerian's circle of family and friends.

Thought processes are generally analytic and dissociating. In order to think clearly we must make distinctions, comparisons and the like. But feeling is unifying and integrative.

To think clearly about something you have to distance yourself from it. To feel something you must get close to it. Once a Cancerian has accepted you as a friend he or she will hang on to you. You have to be really bad to lose the friendship of a Cancerian. If you are related to Cancerians they will never let you go no matter what you do. They will always try to maintain some kind of connection even in the most extreme circumstances.

Finance

The Cancer-born has a deep sense of what other people feel about things and why they feel as they do. This faculty is a great asset in the workplace and in the business world. Of course it is also indispensable in raising a family and building a home, but it has its uses in business. Cancerians often attain great wealth in a family business. Even if the business is not a family operation, they will treat it as one. If the Cancerian works for somebody else, then the boss is the parental figure and the co-workers are brothers and sisters. If a Cancerian is the boss, then all the workers are his or her children. Cancerians like the feeling of being providers for others. They enjoy knowing that others derive their sustenance because of what they do. It is another form of nurturing.

With Leo on their solar 2nd money house cusp, Cancerians are often lucky speculators, especially with residential property or hotels and restaurants. Resort hotels and nightclubs are also profitable for the Cancerian. Waterside properties attract them. Though they are basically conventional people, they sometimes like to earn their livelihood in glamorous ways.

The Sun, Cancer's money planet, represents an important financial message: in financial matters Cancerians need to be less moody, more stable and fixed. They cannot allow their moods – which are here today and gone tomorrow – to get in the way of their business lives. They need to develop their self-esteem and feelings of self-worth if they are to realize their greatest financial potential.

Career and Public Image

Aries rules the 10th solar career house cusp of Cancer, which indicates that Cancerians long to start their own business, to be more active publicly and politically and to be more independent. Family responsibilities and a fear of hurting other people's feelings – or getting hurt themselves – often inhibit them from attaining these goals. However, this is what they want and long to do.

Cancerians like their bosses and leaders to act freely and to be a bit self-willed. They can deal with that in a superior. They expect their leaders to be fierce on their behalf. When the Cancerian is in the position of boss or superior he or she behaves very much like a 'warlord'. Of course the wars they wage are not egocentric but in defence of those under their care. If they lack some of this fighting instinct – independence and pioneering spirit – Cancerians will have extreme difficulty in attaining their highest career goals. They will be hampered in their attempts to lead others.

Since they are so parental, Cancerians like to work with children and make great educators and teachers.

Love and Relationships

Like Taurus, Cancer likes committed relationships. Cancerians function best when the relationship is clearly defined and everyone knows his or her role. When they marry it is usually for life. They are extremely loyal to their beloved. But there is a deep little secret that most Cancerians will never admit to: commitment or partnership is really a chore and a duty to them. They enter into it because they know of no other way to create the family that they desire. Union is just a way – a means to an end – rather than an end in itself. The family is the ultimate end for them.

If you are in love with a Cancerian you must tread lightly on his or her feelings. It will take you a good deal of time to realize how deep and sensitive Cancerians can be. The smallest negativity upsets them. Your tone of voice, your irritation, a look in your eye or an expression on your face can cause great distress for the Cancerian. Your slightest gesture is registered by them and reacted to. This can be hard to get used to, but stick by your love – Cancerians make great partners once you learn how to deal with them. Your Cancerian lover will react not so much to what you say but to the way you are actually feeling at the moment.

Home and Domestic Life

This is where Cancerians really excel. The home environment and the family are their personal works of art. They strive to make things of beauty that will outlast them. Very often they succeed.

Cancerians feel very close to their family, their relatives and especially their mothers. These bonds last throughout their lives and mature as they grow older. They are very fond of those members of their family who become successful, and they are also quite attached to family heirlooms and mementos. Cancerians also love children and like to provide them with all the things they need and want. With their nurturing, feeling nature, Cancerians make very good parents – especially the Cancerian woman, who is the mother *par excellence* of the zodiac.

As a parent the Cancerian's attitude is 'my children right or wrong'. Unconditional devotion is the order of the day. No matter what a family member does, the Cancerian will eventually forgive him or her, because 'you are, after all, family'. The preservation of the institution – the tradition – of the family is one of the Cancerian's main reasons for living. They have many lessons to teach others about this.

Being so family-orientated, the Cancerian's home is always clean, orderly and comfortable. They like old-fashioned furnishings but they also like to have all the modern comforts. Cancerians love to have family and friends over, to organize parties and to entertain at home – they make great hosts.

Horoscope for 2024

Major Trends

Those of you born late in the sign of Cancer (July 20–22) will feel the effects of Pluto's drawn-out move from Capricorn into Aquarius this year. This was going on last year too. Healthwise it can impact on the heart, but also on your finances. It can bring a financial crisis (but nothing you can't handle). For most Cancerians, though, the long-term planets are either in harmonious aspect or leaving you alone. More on this later.

Saturn moved into your 9th house last year and will be there for the rest of the year ahead. College-level students need to knuckle down and be more disciplined in their studies. And if you are involved in legal issues there are many delays and much work and effort involved here. In your religious life Saturn's presence means you seem to favour the traditional teachings.

Jupiter it will be in your 11th house until May 26 and this shows an active and happy social life. You are meeting new and significant people. This transit is also good for your health. On May 26 Jupiter will move into your 12th house of spirituality and will remain there for the rest of the year ahead. This initiates a strong spiritual period for you, a time for expansive spiritual growth and spiritual break-throughs. I see this as preparation for next year when Jupiter moves into your own sign and starts to bring personal happiness and prosperity. It is good to be prepared for these things as they will happen more easily.

Your most important interests in the year ahead are love and romance from January 1–22 and from September 3 to November 20; sex, occult studies and psychology from January 22 to September 3 and from November 20 to the end of the year; religion, philosophy, theology, higher learning and foreign travel; friends, groups, and group activities from January 1 to May 26; and spirituality from May 26 to the end of the year.

Your paths of greatest fulfilment this year will be career; friends, groups and group activities until May 26; and spirituality from May 26 onwards.

Health

(Please note that this is an astrological perspective on health and not a medical one. In days of yore there was no difference, both these perspectives were identical. But these days there could be quite a difference. For a medical perspective, please consult your doctor or health practitioner.)

As we mentioned, for most of you, health should be good in the year ahead with the long-term planets either in harmonious aspect or leaving you alone. Sure, there will be times in the year when health and energy are less easy than usual and perhaps even stressful. But these are not trends for the year, only temporary blips caused by short-term planets. When these stressful transits pass health and energy return.

Good though your health is, you can make it better. Give more attention to the following – the vulnerable areas of your Horoscope this year (the reflex points are shown in the chart opposite):

- The stomach and breasts are always important areas for Cancerians. The reflex to the stomach is shown in the chart above and women should also massage the top of the foot, which is where the reflexes to the breasts are located. Diet is always an issue for you. What you eat is important and should be checked with a professional. But how you eat is just as important. Meals should be taken in a relaxed and calm way. It is helpful to have nice soothing music playing in the background as you eat. Grace, in your own words, should be said before and after meals – food should be blessed. The object here is to elevate the act of eating from mere animal appetite to an act of worship. In other words, to raise the energy vibrations of the act. These practices will ensure that you get the highest and best energy from the food that you eat, and the food will digest better.
- The liver and thighs. Regular thigh massage will not only strengthen the thighs and the liver but the lower back as well. These areas are always important for you, Cancer.
- The neck and throat are important areas until May 26. Regular neck and throat massage will be very beneficial. Be aware of tension in the neck and do your best to release it. Don't let it build up.
- The arms, shoulders, lungs and respiratory system all become important from May 26 onwards. Arms and shoulders should be regularly massaged. Hand reflexology (not shown here) will be especially powerful and effective from that date. Your health planet's position in your 12th house of spirituality shows that you respond well to spiritual-healing techniques. If you feel under the weather, see a spiritual healer. This is a time, from May 26 onwards, to expand your knowledge of spiritual healing. Many of you will.
- The heart (for those of you born between July 20 and July 22). The reflex point is shown above, and chest massage will also

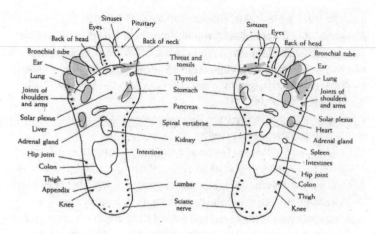

Important foot reflexology points for the year ahead

Try to massage all of the foot on a regular basis – the top of the foot as well as the bottom – but pay extra attention to the points highlighted on the chart. When you massage, be aware of 'sore spots' as these need special attention. It's also a good idea to massage the ankles and below them.

strengthen the heart. The important thing with the heart is to avoid worry and anxiety, the two emotions that stress it out. Replace worry with faith.

Good emotional health is always important for you, Cancer. It is important for all people, of course, but especially for you. Do your best to stay in emotional harmony. Meditation will be a big help.

Home and Family

Home and family are always important to Cancerians. You feel that family is what life is all about. But this year, with your 4th house practically empty (only short-term planets will move through there for short periods), it is not as important as usual. I read this as a good thing. You seem content in this area and have no need to make dramatic changes or overly focus here. It tends to the status quo.

However, two eclipses will occur in your 4th house this year and shake things up in the home and in the lives of family members. The first is a lunar eclipse on March 25, the second is a solar eclipse on October 2. These events can bring personal drama to the lives of family members and perhaps bring a need for repairs in the home. But otherwise, things seem quiet here.

Parents and parent figures need to be more careful about health matters, but moves are unlikely.

Children and children figures are making important transitions in their lives. Their whole focus in life is starting to change. They are becoming less traditional and more experimental in life. They seem more rebellious than usual and more difficult to handle. They are delving deep into psychology and the roots of their emotions. This will be a long-term trend that will last for many years. While they may not move, they are likely to carry out major renovations in their homes. Siblings and sibling figures can have multiple moves in the year ahead. Grandchildren, if you have them, or those who play that role in your life will probably not move this year – nor is it advisable.

This is not a year for making major renovations to your home, but next year might be better. However, if you do decide to do this, September 22 to October 23 would be an OK time. If you're merely redecorating or otherwise beautifying the home, August 29 to September 23 would be a good time.

Finance and Career

Finances are OK this year, but nothing special. Your empty money house signals a quiet, stable kind of year moneywise. Finances will be more or less the same as they were last year. But, as we mentioned earlier, big things are happening behind the scenes and you will see the results in 2025, which will be a super-prosperous year.

The Sun, a fast-moving planet, is your financial planet. Thus, there are many short-term trends in finance that depend on where the Sun is and the kinds of aspects he receives. These are best dealt with in the monthly reports.

Two solar eclipses in the year ahead show important financial changes. The first is on April 8 and the second is on October 2. These kinds of changes are not always comfortable while they are happening, but the end result is beneficial. It is part of the preparation needed for the prosperity to come in 2025.

Job-seekers can find good opportunities online, or through friends and social connections until May 26. After May 26 those looking for employment can find opportunities in spiritual types of venues – at spiritual lectures, prayer meetings, the yoga or tai chi studio or at charity events. Your spiritual practice and meditation will also guide you to the right job.

The Sun as your financial planet signals someone who spends much on the children and children figures in their life but who can also earn from them. When they are young, they inspire you to earn more, and sometimes inadvertently they can come up with profitable ideas. When they are older and more established they can be an actual physical financial support. This aspect also favours investments in electric utilities, power companies and the entertainment industry. It favours industries that cater to the youth market. You have a good feel for these kinds of companies.

Although your 10th house of career is not strong this year, not a house of power, nevertheless pursuing your career objectives brings great fulfilment and personal pleasure. This feeling of fulfilment and joy tends to bring success. The Moon's north node will be in your 10th house all year. This, according to many astrologers, shows fulfilment and happiness. So, it will be good to focus on your career this year and let home and family issues go for a while.

Love and Social Life

Pluto has been in your 7th house of love for over 30 years. So, this has been a tempestuous area of life. Many of you have had divorces and break-ups in the past 30 years. Some of you have lost your partner due to death. Happily, this is about over now as Pluto is leaving your 7th house this year. He will return to the 7th house for brief periods this year, but next year he will leave for the long term. Pluto's purpose in your 7th house was to bring you the love and social life of your dreams. The ideal. After all these years of chaos he's coming to the end of his mission and the love life will be quieter, more serene and happy.

Singles have opportunities for love affairs this year. Marriage is not that prominent in your chart, although serious romance could happen between January 1 and May 27.

Pluto is now going to move through your 8th house of regeneration, completely revamping your sexual life and attitudes. This will be a long-term process.

The social life seems very happy in the year ahead, especially in the area of friendships. This is not really about romance but about friendship. You are meeting people of like mind and like interests. These relationships tend to be Platonic ones. Nevertheless, it seems like a happy area of life.

Saturn, your love planet, made a major move last year from Aquarius, your 8th house, into your 9th house. This signalled a big shift in love attitudes. While Saturn was in your 8th house, sexual magnetism seemed to be the most important thing in love. It is still important, but now you are looking for other things as well. Now you find yourself attracted to people who are well educated, perhaps religious and refined. You are attracted to people you can learn from. You have the aspects of someone who falls in love with their professor, or religious leader. Love and social opportunities happen at religious functions or at your place of worship. Also, at college or university functions.

Self-improvement

Jupiter's move into your spiritual 12th house on May 26 initiates a real spiritual adventure for you. Your path this year seems to revolve around spiritual healing. This will open the door to other spiritual realities. You're going to learn about the relationship between spirit and the physical body. This is a huge, huge subject, but well worth studying. In spiritual healing we see the body as only a side-effect of consciousness. Whatever is going on in the physical body, good or bad, is merely the result of consciousness. Change the consciousness and you change, to that degree, the physical body. This is not something you learn from books but from actual practice. Spiritual healing does not negate orthodox medicine or any other form of medicine. Sometimes these things are needed. But the consciousness of health will lead to a healthy body. Exactly how this happens is not known, nor is it our business. The important thing is that the end result will be good. When this spiritual law is invoked, whatever is needed to keep the body in good health will come, naturally and harmoniously. If a medicine, herb or therapy is needed, it will come. In many cases no external means are necessary. The change in consciousness by itself creates the healing.

For more information on astrology, healing and spiritual topics, please visit my blog at www.spiritual-stories.com.

Month-by-month Forecasts

January

Best Days Overall: 6, 7, 14, 15, 23, 24
Most Stressful Days Overall: 5, 6, 11, 16, 17, 30, 31
Best Days for Love: 6, 8, 9, 10, 11, 14, 20, 23, 27, 28
Best Days for Money: 1, 2, 10, 11, 12, 18, 19, 21, 25, 26, 27, 28, 29
Best Days for Career: 9, 10, 16, 17, 18, 28, 29

Overall, health and energy are basically good, but this month, because of the transits of short-term planets, it's probably a good idea to watch your health more. Make sure to get enough rest. Listen to the messages that your body sends you. Enhance the health with neck and throat massage, and in the ways mentioned in the yearly report. You should see an increase in health and energy from the 20th onwards.

The love and romantic life is the main headline this month. You are in the midst of a yearly love and social peak. It began last month and continues until the 20th. In fact, you will be experiencing an active social life even after the 20th as many planets are either in or moving through your 7th house. The new Moon of the 11th is not only a good romantic day, as it occurs in your 7th house, but it will also clarify love issues as the days go by, until the next new Moon. With so many planets in your 7th house singles have many romantic opportunities. The problem is probably too much of a good thing, and the clarity that the new Moon will bring will be very helpful.

Mars, your career planet, in your 7th house from the 5th onwards indicates that a good part of your socializing is career related. Attending parties and gatherings is not only good for the career but seems to help the bottom line as well: your money planet's presence in the 7th house until the 20th signals that your social grace and likeability are very important in earnings. You seem more open to joint venture and partnership opportunities, and these will come to you. The spouse, partner or current love seems very active in your financial life, in a beneficial way.

Your financial planet in the sign of Capricorn until the 20th is, in my opinion, a positive for earnings. The financial judgement is stable, conservative, down to earth and realistic. There is a distain for gimmicks and short-term fixes. Wealth is attained methodically, over the long term. On the 20th, as your financial planet moves into Aquarius, you become more experimental in financial matters. The Sun travels with Pluto on the 20th and 21st and this can make you more speculative. But it also favours tax efficiency schemes, earnings from insurance payments and from estates. The high-tech and online world also seems very interesting financially.

February

Best Days Overall: 1, 2, 3, 10, 11, 19, 20, 29
Most Stressful Days Overall: 6, 7, 12, 13, 26, 27, 28
Best Days for Love: 6, 7, 17, 26, 27
Best Days for Money: 1, 6, 7, 8, 9, 14, 15, 18, 19, 21, 22, 23, 24, 25, 29
Best Days for Career: 6, 7, 12, 13, 17, 26, 27

Health and energy are improving every day and by the 19th you will be at peak health and energy levels. If you have pre-existing conditions they should be much easier to manage now.

Your financial planet the Sun is still in the sign of Aquarius, your 8th house, until the 19th. This gives many messages. It is a time to get rid of extraneous possessions, investments, or bank and savings accounts – especially the redundant ones. The object of this month is to attain wealth by removing the blockages and obstructions to it. A detox of the financial life will be very helpful to you. Go through your possessions; whatever you don't use or is not needed should either be sold or donated to charity. This will clear the decks for the new wealth that wants to come in. These extraneous possessions are like plaque in the financial arteries. Get rid of the plaque and the financial circulation will flow more strongly.

This is a good month to use spare cash to pay down debt. You will have good access to outside capital this month so getting a loan is also easier. It all depends on your need. You have a knack for creative kinds of financing. The new Moon of the 9th is especially good for these kinds of activities, and it will have other effects as well. It will clarify the finances of the spouse, partner or current love. Tax and estate issues as well. This will go on until the next new Moon, in March. All the information that you need on these issues will come to you normally and naturally.

Your financial planet will travel with Saturn from the 24th to the 26th. This often indicates an extra financial burden, and a need to reorganize the finances. But it can also bring an opportunity for a partnership or joint venture. Your financial planet will be in the spiritual sign of Pisces from the 19th onwards. Thus, your financial intuition is unusually strong. It is also more dependable.

Love is still active, but not as much as last month. Singles have multiple romantic interests. Like last month, much of your socializing is career related.

Mars will travel with Pluto on the 15th and 16th; this can bring a career boost. Children and children figures in your life have career success or opportunity. Surgery could be recommended to a parent or parent figure. Let them get a second opinion about this.

March

Best Days Overall: 1, 9, 10, 17, 18, 27, 28
Most Stressful Days Overall: 4, 5, 6, 11, 12, 24, 25, 26
Best Days for Love: 4, 5, 6, 7, 8, 9, 10, 17, 18, 27, 28, 29
Best Days for Money: 1, 4, 5, 9, 20, 13, 14, 18, 19, 20, 21, 22, 23, 29, 30
Best Days for Career: 7, 8, 11, 12, 15, 16, 27, 28

Health and energy are still good this month but try to get more rest during the lunar eclipse of the 25th, which seems stressful.

The Sun, your financial planet, is still in Pisces until the 20th so it is a time to rely on your financial intuition. This intuition is excellent until the 20th but especially from the 15th to the 17th. The 16th and 17th bring a revelatory and active dream life. Spiritual teaching is being given to you through dreams.

Because the Moon is the ruler of your Horoscope, every lunar eclipse affects Cancerians much more than other signs. This one is no different. It impels you to take stock of yourself, to re-define yourself. Is the way that others see you really how you are? Are the opinions of others about you valid? If not, you need to define yourself for yourself and not let others define you. This will lead over future months to changes in your image and presentation to others. You go through this sort of thing twice every year and by now you should know how to handle it.

Every lunar eclipse also tends to impact on the home, family and the overall emotional life. But this one seems to do so more than usual as it occurs in your 4th house of home and family. There can be dramas – personal dramas – in the lives of family members and perhaps repairs are needed around the home. Siblings and sibling figures will need to make important financial changes. If you haven't been careful in dietary matters, a detox of the body could happen.

The spouse, partner or current love has dramas with friends.

Jupiter, your health planet, travels with Uranus on the 29th and 30th. This can bring a change in your health regime, or a job change. It can also bring a sudden, unexpected sexual encounter.

April

Best Days Overall: 5, 6, 13, 14, 15, 23, 24, 25
Most Stressful Days Overall: 1, 2, 7, 8, 21, 22, 28, 29
Best Days for Love: 1, 2, 5, 6, 7, 8, 16, 17, 23, 24, 27, 28, 29
Best Days for Money: 1, 2, 7, 8, 9, 10, 16, 17, 18, 19, 28, 29
Best Days for Career: 5, 6, 7, 8, 13, 14, 23, 24

The solar eclipse of the 8th, a powerful total eclipse, is the main headline of the month ahead. It has a strong effect on you personally, on parents, parent figures, the home, family and career. So by all means take it nice and easy and reduce your schedule while the eclipse is in effect. Because other planets are directly impacted by this eclipse, its effect will be felt on many areas of your life. A strong eclipse such as this one should be looked at as a cosmic storm or hurricane. We do the things that need to be done and let go of the frivolous. We take normal and natural precautions and stay close to home in a safe area. And we ride it out.

Because the Sun is your financial planet, every solar eclipse forces important changes in your financial thinking, planning and strategy. The events of the eclipse will show you that your financial thinking and strategy have not been realistic. Thus, you will make the changes that need to be made. This is not usually pleasant while it's happening, but the end result should be good. This eclipse occurs in your 10th house of career, which means important career changes are happening. There can be shake-ups and upheavals in your present company. The government can change the rules for your industry. Bosses can experience personal dramas and, in many cases, they are forced to resign or change jobs. Parents and parent figures are also having personal dramas. There can be shake-ups in the powers that be.

Since Mercury is directly impacted by this eclipse, important spiritual changes are happening for you. Generally, these are changes in teachers, teachings, practice and overall attitudes. Guru figures in your life have personal dramas. There are shake-ups and upheavals in spiritual or charitable organizations that you are involved with.

Friends and family are also directly impacted here. There are personal dramas going on in their lives. It would be best to avoid unnecessary driving, as cars and communication equipment are being tested by the eclipse and can behave erratically. If you must drive, be more alert and careful. With such a powerful eclipse such as this, quite frankly it's best to stay close to home, watch a movie, read a book or, best of all, meditate.

May

Best Days Overall: 2, 3, 4, 11, 12, 20, 21, 22, 30, 31
Most Stressful Days Overall: 5, 6, 17, 18, 19, 25, 26
Best Days for Love: 3, 4, 7, 8, 11, 12, 15, 16, 21, 22, 24, 26, 27, 28, 30, 31
Best Days for Money: 1, 7, 8, 13, 15, 16, 18, 19, 26, 27, 28
Best Days for Career: 5, 6, 13, 14, 24

Health and energy are still very good this month. On the 26th your health planet makes a major move from Taurus into Gemini and he will be there for the rest of the year ahead. This shows changes in your health needs. From the 26th onwards the arms, shoulders and respiratory system become more important. In addition, spiritual-healing methods will now be more powerful and effective for you.

Also, Jupiter's move into your 12th house shows a period of spiritual expansion and growth. This will go on for the rest of the year ahead and well into next year as well.

Finances also seem good this month; your financial planet will be in your 11th house, a beneficent house, until the 20th. The Sun will travel with Uranus on the 13th and 14th, which should bring luck in speculations and indicates you are spending money on happy things. From the 18th to the 20th the Sun will travel with benevolent Jupiter and this bring a nice payday. On the 20th the Sun will move into your spiritual 12th house and this transit brings excellent financial intuition. It is said that prayer is making a phone call to the divine, and intuition is the divine making a phone call to you. Intuition can be felt, but it comes from a realm above feeling – a realm of cosmic knowledge. While the Sun is in your 12th house you will be more charitable than usual. You will be, consciously or unconsciously, operating the spiritual laws of affluence.

Love and romance are not big issues this month. Your 7th house is basically empty with only the Moon moving through there on the 25th and 26th. This tends to a status quo. Romance will be more or less the way it was last month.

Your yearly career peak occurred last month, but career still seems strong this month as Mars, your career planet, will be in your 10th house, his own sign and house, all month. Great career progress is happening, and you seem very active and busy there.

June

Best Days Overall: 7, 8, 17, 18, 26, 27
Most Stressful Days Overall: 1, 2, 14, 15, 16, 21, 22, 23, 28, 29
Best Days for Love: 5, 6, 7, 8, 16, 17, 18, 21, 22, 23, 26, 27
Best Days for Money: 5, 6, 9, 10, 11, 14, 15, 24, 26
Best Days for Career: 1, 2, 12, 13, 21, 22, 27, 29, 30

A happy and prosperous month ahead. Enjoy.

You are still in the midst of a very strong spiritual period. Spiritual breakthroughs are happening for those on the path. When these things happen it is the most joyous experience. But even if you are not on a formal spiritual path, the invisible realms will still let you know that they are around. Many of you will experience synchronistic kinds of events, meaningful coincidences that you cannot explain. Many of you will have ESP kinds of experiences. There is more to you than what is beneath your head and above your shoes.

On the 20th the Sun enters your own sign and you begin a yearly personal pleasure peak. This transit is also a fabulous financial transit and brings financial windfalls. Financial opportunity will come to you. In fact, it is as if money is chasing you rather than vice versa. You will dress more expensively and in general project an image of prosperity. Probably you will spend on yourself, and consider yourself to be the best investment there is. The personal appearance will shine. You have more star quality with the Sun in your sign. Venus will also be in your sign from the 17th onwards, giving beauty, grace and glamour to the image. The opposite sex will certainly take notice. The love life seems happy – especially after the 17th. Singles will find love and romantic

opportunities at school and school functions and at religious functions. There can be opportunities for love with people at your place of
worship. Sometimes fellow worshippers like to play Cupid.

Mercury and Venus are both out of bounds this month. Mercury will
be out of bounds from the 11th to the 29th, and Venus will be out of
bounds from the 13th to the 29th. This shows that in your spiritual life
you are exploring paths and teachings outside your normal sphere.
Your taste in reading also seems outside your normal interests.

July

Best Days Overall: 4, 5, 6, 14, 15, 16, 23, 24
Most Stressful Days Overall: 12, 13, 19, 20, 25, 26
Best Days for Love: 2, 3, 5, 6, 15, 16, 17, 18, 19, 20, 23, 25, 26
Best Days for Money: 2, 3, 4, 5, 6, 7, 8, 12, 13, 15, 16, 21, 22, 23,
    29, 30
Best Days for Career: 1, 9, 10, 21, 25, 26, 29, 30

The month ahead is another happy, prosperous and spiritually fulfilling one, Cancer. Enjoy!

You are still in a yearly personal pleasure peak until the 22nd, so you
are continuing to enjoy all the pleasures of the senses. The personal
appearance still shines, and the opposite sex takes notice. This is a
great month to get the body and image into the shape that you want.
Since you are at the maximum point of personal independence in your
chart, it is also a good month to make the changes you need to take to
increase your personal happiness. This is the time to exercise your
personal initiative and create the conditions for your happiness. Later
on, when the planetary power shifts, it will be more difficult to do.
Right now, you have a lot of cosmic support.

The Sun in your sign until the 22nd shows that financial windfalls
and happy money opportunities are coming to you. Like last month,
you are dressing more expensively and projecting an image of wealth
and prosperity. This is a good time to buy clothing or personal acces-
sories – with Venus in your sign until the 11th, your taste is excellent.
Until the 22nd you merely *look* prosperous, but afterwards you will
actually *be* prosperous. Your financial planet moves into your money

house, initiating a yearly financial peak. Earnings should be excellent as the Sun is very strong in his own sign and house.

Love is happy this month, but complicated. You are magnetic and attractive and have many romantic and social opportunities. The problem is that Saturn, your love planet, is now retrograde. So, enjoy love for what it is and don't try to rush things or make important decisions one way or another. Saturn has been in your 9th house since March 2023 and he remains here for the rest of the year ahead. So, as has been the case for some time now, singles find love and romantic opportunities at college, college functions, religious functions, the place of worship and perhaps in foreign lands or with foreigners.

Health and energy are excellent this month. If you have any pre-existing conditions they seem much easier, milder now. You can enhance the health even further in the ways mentioned in the yearly report. If you feel under the weather, try seeing a spiritual healer.

August

Best Days Overall: 1, 2, 11, 12, 19, 20, 28, 29
Most Stressful Days Overall: 8, 9, 15, 16, 21, 22
Best Days for Love: 8, 11, 12, 15, 16, 17, 18, 19, 20, 28, 29
Best Days for Money: 3, 4, 8, 9, 13, 14, 17, 18, 23, 27, 30, 31
Best Days for Career: 8, 9, 17, 18, 21, 22, 26, 27

Retrograde activity increases this month. From the 4th to the 25th 40 per cent of the planets will be retrograde. This is very close to the maximum level for the year. Only in September will we have more retrogrades, but this will only be for a brief time, a few days. So, if things are slowing down in your life or in the world it's not because you're a bad person or that God is punishing you, it is just the astrological, cosmic weather.

Health and energy are still excellent this month, and like last month, if you feel under the weather seek out a spiritual-type healer. You respond very well to spiritual healing techniques.

You are still in a yearly financial peak until the 22nd. So, prosperity is excellent. The new Moon of the 4th occurs in your money house, boosting earnings and making it an exceptional financial day. More importantly, as the days progress towards the next new Moon, your financial picture will clarify. All the information that you need to make good financial decisions, and to resolve doubts, will come to you normally and naturally.

While the Sun is in Leo, you're spending more on the children and children figures in your life and perhaps earning from them as well. This position favours happy money – money that is earned in happy ways and spent on happy things. Financial opportunities can come to you while you're at the theatre, theme park or concert. By the 22nd your short-term financial goals should be achieved, and you are ready to pursue your intellectual interests – to read books, attend lectures and seminars, and otherwise expand your knowledge. The mental faculties are much stronger with the power in the 3rd house.

Mercury will be retrograde from the 4th to the 25th. For students below college level, important educational decisions should not be made during this time. Also, your intuition, and you have experience much of this these days, will need more verification. A real intuition is always right, but our interpretation of it could be amiss.

Your love planet Saturn remains retrograde all month and it is not receiving any especially good aspects. So, love is slowing down. Singles will still go out and date but not as much as usual. This is a time to review your current relationship and your romantic and social goals. See where improvements can be made and, later on, when Saturn moves forward you can take the right actions.

September

Best Days Overall: 7, 8, 16, 17, 24, 25
Most Stressful Days Overall: 4, 5, 6, 12, 13, 18, 19
Best Days for Love: 4, 5, 7, 8, 12, 13, 14, 15, 16, 17, 23, 24, 25
Best Days for Money: 1, 2, 3, 4, 5, 12, 13, 14, 15, 22, 23, 26, 27, 28
Best Days for Career: 7, 8, 16, 17, 18, 19, 24, 25

A lunar eclipse on the 18th is the main headline of the month ahead. With the Moon as your ruling planet, every lunar eclipse impacts you particularly strongly – more than for most people. So, reduce your schedule and relax and take it easy while this eclipse is in effect. It occurs in your 9th house and also impacts very directly on the ruler of the 9th house, Neptune. So, this eclipse will affect college-level students or those who are applying for college. It signals changes in educational plans, disruptions at school and perhaps even a change of schools. In many cases, college applicants wind up in a different institution than they originally planned. While this is sometimes disappointing, over the long term one will see that it is for the best. If you are involved in legal issues, they take a dramatic turn one way or another.

Perhaps the most important thing that will happen is that your religious, theological and philosophical beliefs will get tested by the events of the eclipse. This will lead, over time, to changes, revisions and amendments to your belief system. This is basically a good thing, though it is usually not pleasant while it's happening. Many of the theological and philosophical beliefs that we hold are often no more than superstition. Some are true, but only partially true. Some are correct. But one needs to know what is what. Since we lead our lives according to our religious, theological and philosophical beliefs, these changes will have a profound impact on the way you lead your life. Theology and philosophy are much more powerful forces than psychology. Psychology you understand very well, but your metaphysical beliefs will shape your psychology.

Jupiter is sideswiped by this eclipse – not a direct hit but a glancing blow. This can bring dramas to the workplace, and perhaps even a health scare. Since health is basically good, it is not likely to be more than a scare. However, it will produce changes in your health regime in the coming months.

Every lunar eclipse forces you to take stock of yourself, your image, your appearance and self-concept. As you re-evaluate yourself, this will be reflected in wardrobe changes, changes of the image and presentation, over the next few months.

October

Best Days Overall: 4, 5, 13, 14, 21, 22, 23, 31
Most Stressful Days Overall: 1, 2, 3, 9, 10, 15, 16, 29, 30
Best Days for Love: 4, 5, 9, 10, 13, 14, 21, 22, 23, 24, 25, 31
Best Days for Money: 1, 2, 11, 12, 19, 20, 23, 25, 29, 30
Best Days for Career: 4, 5, 13, 14, 15, 16, 22, 23, 31

The solar eclipse of the 2nd is really the main event of this month. Though it is only a partial eclipse, it has a strong effect on you personally as it is in stressful aspect to your sign *and* because it impacts on two other planets. Thus the eclipse affects many areas of life and many people in your life. So, first off take it nice and easy while the eclipse is in effect. (You should be reducing your schedule anyway, as health and energy are not up to par until the 22nd, but especially during the eclipse time.) It occurs in your 4th house of home and family, thus a parent or parent figure, and family members in general, are experiencing personal dramas. Passions are likely to run high at home, so be more patient with family members. Repairs could be needed in the home. Sometimes this is the result of hidden problems that you knew nothing about; the eclipse reveals them so that you can take proper remedial action.

Since the Sun, the eclipsed planet, is your financial planet, there will be financial dramas. You will need to make course corrections in your financial thinking, planning and strategy. These changes are probably not pleasant while they're happening but the end result will be good. It is preparation for the prosperity that will happen next year. The stage needs to be set. Siblings and sibling figures will also need to make important financial changes.

Mars is one of the planets directly impacted, and so this eclipse springs career changes. That could mean shake-ups and disturbances in your company hierarchy. Bosses and authority figures could experience personal dramas. The government could change the rules for your company or industry and thus you need to pursue your career in a different way. Sometimes there is an actual change of the career, but this is rare.

The impact of the eclipse on Mercury can affect cars and communication equipment. Sometimes repairs or replacements are necessary. It is probably a good idea to avoid unnecessary driving while the eclipse is in effect. Siblings and sibling figures have personal dramas. They have a need to re-define themselves, their self-concept and the image they present to others. This will once again test their current relationship.

Mercury is your spiritual planet so important spiritual changes are happening for you. This would involve teachings, your practice, teachers and general attitudes to spirituality. There are personal dramas in the lives of gurus and guru figures. The dream life is likely to be hyperactive and probably disturbing, but you shouldn't give too much weight to your dreams. They are most likely psychic garbage stirred up by the eclipse. There are disturbances and upheavals in spiritual or charitable organizations that you are involved with.

Enhance the health in the ways mentioned in the yearly report. Regular massage of the arms and shoulders will be helpful. Most of all, make sure to get enough rest.

November

Best Days Overall: 1, 2, 10, 11, 18, 19, 28, 29
Most Stressful Days Overall: 5, 6, 12, 13, 25, 26, 27
Best Days for Love: 1, 2, 3, 4, 5, 6, 10, 11, 12, 13, 18, 19, 22, 23, 28, 29
Best Days for Money: 1, 2, 8, 9, 10, 11, 16, 17, 19, 20, 21, 22, 26, 27
Best Days for Career: 2, 12, 13, 22, 23

Now that the eclipses are behind you, you can enjoy the month ahead. You are in the midst of a yearly personal pleasure peak that will go on until the 21st. Make sure to schedule leisure and fun activities into your busy diary. Having fun and enjoying life is not only healthy but will improve your bottom line. As Andrew Carnegie famously said, 'In leisure there is luck.'

Health and energy are much improved over last month. You can enhance it further in the ways mentioned in the yearly report and with spiritual-healing techniques. Massage of the arms and shoulders is still very beneficial. Deep rhythmic breathing will also help.

Love is improving. Saturn, your love planet, starts moving forward on the 5th – not only that, he receives very wonderful aspects until the 21st. There is clarity in love now, and romantic opportunities are there. Although we don't see a marriage here, we do see a happy love life.

The month ahead also seems prosperous, and this is a happy kind of prosperity. You have the aspects of someone who enjoys the wealth that he or she has. It favours speculations, though you should never indulge in these things except under intuition.

On the 21st as the Sun enters your 6th house, earnings come the old-fashioned way through work and productive service. Still, the financial planet in the sign of Sagittarius shows increased earnings. After the 21st you are in a good period for finding work, if you are unemployed, or for finding good employees if you hire others.

Mars, your career planet, will move into the money house on the 4th and stay there for the rest of the month ahead. This often signals pay rises, official or unofficial, and the financial favour of bosses, parents, parent figures and people in authority over you. Guard your good career reputation as this leads to earnings and opportunities for earnings.

December

Best Days Overall: 7, 8, 15, 16, 25, 26
Most Stressful Days Overall: 2, 3, 4, 9, 10, 22, 23, 24, 30, 31
Best Days for Love: 2, 3, 4, 7, 8, 13, 14, 15, 16, 22, 23, 24, 25, 26, 30, 31
Best Days for Money: 1, 6, 9, 10, 14, 17, 18, 19, 20, 23, 24, 30, 31
Best Days for Career: 9, 10, 17, 18, 19, 27, 28, 29

With your 6th house very strong until the 21st you are in a good period for doing those boring, detail-oriented jobs that you keep putting off. You're in the mood for work and thus these things should go a lot easier.

You seem more focused on health and health issues this month. Generally this is a good thing, especially if the focuses is on a healthy lifestyle. But health and energy are good this month, especially until the 21st, so beware the tendency to magnify small things into big things. Hypochondria is the main danger.

Finances are still good, with your financial planet remaining in the sign of Sagittarius until the 21st. You earn freely and spend just as freely. Overspending is probably the main danger this month.

On the 21st the Sun will move into Capricorn, which will bring sound, conservative financial judgement. You are not likely to over-spend after the 21st. You might buy expensive things, but you will want good value for your money.

Love and romance are the main headlines from the 21st onwards.

Your love planet Saturn is moving forward and your 7th house becomes ultra-powerful. You begin a yearly love and social peak. Love seems happy. With the Sun also in your 7th house a lot of your social-izing seems business related. Singles are attracted to wealthy people. They are attracted to the person who can give them material security. This position can again bring joint venture or partnership opportunities.

If you are already in a relationship you seem to be active in the belov-ed's finances and vice versa. Social connections are playing an impor-tant role in finance, and your social grace and charm are just as important in earnings as your professional skills.

Leo

♌

THE LION

Birthdays from
21st July to
21st August

Personality Profile

LEO AT A GLANCE

Element – Fire

Ruling Planet – Sun
   Career Planet – Venus
   Love Planet – Uranus
   Money Planet – Mercury
   Planet of Health and Work – Saturn
   Planet of Home and Family Life – Pluto

Colours – gold, orange, red

Colours that promote love, romance and social harmony – black, indigo,
   ultramarine blue

Colours that promote earning power – yellow, yellow-orange

Gems – amber, chrysolite, yellow diamond

Metal – gold

Scents – bergamot, frankincense, musk, neroli

Quality – fixed (= stability)

Quality most needed for balance – humility

Strongest virtues – leadership ability, self-esteem and confidence, generosity, creativity, love of joy

Deepest needs – fun, elation, the need to shine

Characteristics to avoid – arrogance, vanity, bossiness

Signs of greatest overall compatibility – Aries, Sagittarius

Signs of greatest overall incompatibility – Taurus, Scorpio, Aquarius

Sign most helpful to career – Taurus

Sign most helpful for emotional support – Scorpio

Sign most helpful financially – Virgo

Sign best for marriage and/or partnerships – Aquarius

Sign most helpful for creative projects – Sagittarius

Best Sign to have fun with – Sagittarius

Signs most helpful in spiritual matters – Aries, Cancer

Best day of the week – Sunday

Understanding a Leo

When you think of Leo, think of royalty – then you'll get the idea of what the Leo character is all about and why Leos are the way they are. It is true that, for various reasons, some Leo-born do not always express this quality – but even if not they should like to do so.

A monarch rules not by example (as does Aries) nor by consensus (as do Capricorn and Aquarius) but by personal will. Will is law. Personal taste becomes the style that is imitated by all subjects. A monarch is somehow larger than life. This is how a Leo desires to be.

When you dispute the personal will of a Leo it is serious business. He or she takes it as a personal affront, an insult. Leos will let you know that their will carries authority and that to disobey is demeaning and disrespectful.

A Leo is king (or queen) of his or her personal domain. Subordinates, friends and family are the loyal and trusted subjects. Leos rule with benevolent grace and in the best interests of others. They have a powerful presence; indeed, they are powerful people. They seem to attract attention in any social gathering. They stand out because they are stars in their domain. Leos feel that, like the Sun, they are made to shine and rule. Leos feel that they were born to special privilege and royal prerogatives – and most of them attain this status, at least to some degree.

The Sun is the ruler of this sign, and when you think of sunshine it is very difficult to feel unhealthy or depressed. Somehow the light of the Sun is the very antithesis of illness and apathy. Leos love life. They also love to have fun; they love drama, music, the theatre and amusements of all sorts. These are the things that give joy to life. If – even in their best interests – you try to deprive Leos of their pleasures, good food, drink and entertainment, you run the serious risk of depriving them of the will to live. To them life without joy is no life at all.

Leos epitomize humanity's will to power. But power in and of itself – regardless of what some people say – is neither good nor evil. Only when power is abused does it become evil. Without power even good things cannot come to pass. Leos realize this and are uniquely qualified to wield power. Of all the signs, they do it most naturally. Capricorn, the other power sign of the zodiac, is a better manager and administrator than Leo – much better. But Leo outshines Capricorn in personal grace and presence. Leo loves power, whereas Capricorn assumes power out of a sense of duty.

Finance

Leos are great leaders but not necessarily good managers. They are better at handling the overall picture than the nitty-gritty details of business. If they have good managers working for them they can become exceptional executives. They have vision and a lot of creativity.

Leos love wealth for the pleasures it can bring. They love an opulent lifestyle, pomp and glamour. Even when they are not wealthy they live as if they are. This is why many fall into debt, from which it is sometimes difficult to emerge.

Leos, like Pisceans, are generous to a fault. Very often they want to acquire wealth solely so that they can help others economically. Wealth to Leo buys services and managerial ability. It creates jobs for others and improves the general well-being of those around them. Therefore – to a Leo – wealth is good. Wealth is to be enjoyed to the fullest. Money is not to be left to gather dust in a mouldy bank vault but to be enjoyed, spread around, used. So Leos can be quite reckless in their spending.

With the sign of Virgo on Leo's 2nd money house cusp, Leo needs to develop some of Virgo's traits of analysis, discrimination and purity when it comes to money matters. They must learn to be more careful with the details of finance (or to hire people to do this for them). They have to be more cost-conscious in their spending habits. Generally, they need to manage their money better. Leos tend to chafe under financial constraints, yet these constraints can help Leos to reach their highest financial potential.

Leos like it when their friends and family know that they can depend on them for financial support. They do not mind – and even enjoy – lending money, but they are careful that they are not taken advantage of. From their 'regal throne' Leos like to bestow gifts upon their family and friends and then enjoy the good feelings these gifts bring to everybody. Leos love financial speculations and – when the celestial influences are right – are often lucky.

Career and Public Image

Leos like to be perceived as wealthy, for in today's world wealth often equals power. When they attain wealth they love having a large house with lots of land and animals.

At their jobs Leos excel in positions of authority and power. They are good at making decisions – on a grand level – but they prefer to leave the details to others. Leos are well respected by their colleagues and subordinates, mainly because they have a knack for understanding and relating to those around them. Leos usually strive for the top positions even if they have to start at the bottom and work hard to get there. As might be expected of such a charismatic sign, Leos are always trying to improve their work situation. They do so in order to have a better chance of advancing to the top.

On the other hand, Leos do not like to be bossed around or told what to do. Perhaps this is why they aspire so for the top – where they can be the decision-makers and need not take orders from others.

Leos never doubt their success and focus all their attention and efforts on achieving it. Another great Leo characteristic is that – just like good monarchs – they do not attempt to abuse the power or success they achieve. If they do so this is not wilful or intentional. Usually they like to share their wealth and try to make everyone around them join in their success.

Leos are – and like to be perceived as – hard-working, well-established individuals. It is definitely true that they are capable of hard work and often manage great things. But do not forget that, deep down inside, Leos really are fun-lovers.

Love and Relationships

Generally, Leos are not the marrying kind. To them relationships are good while they are pleasurable. When the relationship ceases to be pleasurable a true Leo will want out. They always want to have the freedom to leave. That is why Leos excel at love affairs rather than commitment. Once married, however, Leo is faithful – even if some Leos have a tendency to marry more than once in their lifetime. If you are in love with a Leo, just show him or her a good time – travel, go to casinos and clubs, the theatre and discos. Wine and dine your Leo love – it is expensive but worth it and you will have fun.

Leos generally have an active love life and are demonstrative in their affections. They love to be with other optimistic and fun-loving types like themselves, but wind up settling with someone more serious, intellectual and unconventional. The partner of a Leo tends to be more political and socially conscious than he or she is, and more libertarian. When you marry a Leo, mastering the freedom-loving tendencies of your partner will definitely become a life-long challenge – and be careful that Leo does not master you.

Aquarius sits on Leo's 7th house of love cusp. Thus if Leos want to realize their highest love and social potential they need to develop a more egalitarian, Aquarian perspective on others. This is not easy for Leo, for 'the king' finds his equals only among other 'kings'. But perhaps this is the solution to Leo's social challenge – to be 'a king among kings'. It is all right to be regal, but recognize the nobility in others.

Home and Domestic Life

Although Leos are great entertainers and love having people over, sometimes this is all show. Only very few close friends will get to see the real side of a Leo's day-to-day life. To a Leo the home is a place of comfort, recreation and transformation; a secret, private retreat – a castle. Leos like to spend money, show off a bit, entertain and have fun. They enjoy the latest furnishings, clothes and gadgets – all things fit for kings.

Leos are fiercely loyal to their family and, of course, expect the same from them. They love their children almost to a fault; they have to be careful not to spoil them too much. They also must try to avoid attempting to make individual family members over in their own image. Leos should keep in mind that others also have the need to be their own people. That is why Leos have to be extra careful about being over-bossy or over-domineering in the home.

Horoscope for 2024

Major Trends

Now that Saturn has moved away from his stressful aspect to you, most of you will be feeling better and more energetic this year. Health and energy are definitely improved. And, since Saturn moved out of your 7th house last year, the love and social life should also be much improved in the year ahead.

Those of you born early in the sign of Leo, July 22 and 23, are feeling the effects of Pluto's move into Aquarius – a stressful aspect to you. This signals a need to take better care of the heart and to avoid dangerous situations. Most of you, however, will not be feeling these effects much this year, though you will in later years.

Last year, with Jupiter's move into your 10th house of career, you were very successful careerwise. Promotions at work or with businesses that you are involved with should have happened. And this is still the case in the year ahead, especially until May 26.

This is more of a career year than a financial year, Leo. Status and prestige seem more important than the bottom line. However, career success generally brings financial benefits, but finance doesn't seem a major focus. More on this later.

Pluto is right at the very beginning of a long-term 30-year transit through your 7th house of love. This is very significant. Over the coming years a cosmic alchemical process will be happening in your love and social life. You will be giving birth to the love life of your dreams. New births tend to be a messy business and there is usually a lot of blood and gore. The same is likely to happen in your love life. But the end result will be good.

Your most important areas of interest in the year ahead will be sex, personal transformation, occult studies and psychology; career until May 26; friends, groups and group activities from May 26 onwards; health and work from January 1–22 and from September 3 to November 20; and love and romance from January 22 to September 3 and from November 20 onwards.

Your paths of greatest fulfilment will be higher education, religious, philosophical and theological studies; career until May 26; and friends, groups and group activities from May 26 onwards.

Health

(Please note that this is an astrological perspective on health and not a medical one. In days of yore there was no difference, both these perspectives were identical. But these days there could be quite a difference. For a medical perspective, please consult your doctor or health practitioner.)

For most of you, the overwhelming majority, health is much improved this year and should be basically good. Those Leos born early in your sign, July 22–23, will need to be a little bit more watchful healthwise. But most of the planets, especially the long-term ones, are either making nice aspects to you or leaving you alone. So, health should be good. Sure, there will be periods where health and energy are less easy than usual. But these times are only temporary blips caused by short-term planetary transits. When they pass your normally good health and energy return.

Good though your health is, you can make it better. Give more attention to the following – the vulnerable areas of your Horoscope this year (the reflex points are shown in the chart opposite):

- The heart is always important for Leo and this year it is especially important for those of you born on July 22 and 23. Chest massage is also good for the heart. Try to avoid worry and anxiety, the two emotions that stress the heart. The good news here is that Leos are usually not worriers.
- The back, spine, knees, bones and overall skeletal alignment. These areas too are always important for Leo, and back and knee massage should be part of your regular health regime. Regular visits to a chiropractor or osteopath are also beneficial; it's very important to keep the vertebrae in right alignment. Therapies such as Feldenkrais, Alexander Technique, yoga or Rolfing are excellent for the spine. Make sure to get enough calcium for the bones, and if you are out in the sun make sure to use a good sunscreen.
- The feet became more vulnerable last year in March as your health planet Saturn moved into Pisces, and this is still the case this year.

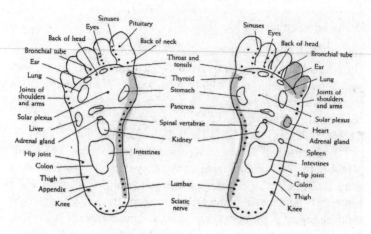

Important foot reflexology points for the year ahead

Try to massage all of the foot on a regular basis this year – the top of the foot as well as the bottom – but pay extra attention to the points highlighted on the chart. When you massage, be aware of 'sore spots' as these need special attention. It's also a good idea to massage the ankles and below them.

Regular foot massage (as indicated on the chart above) will not only strengthen your feet but the entire body as well. Regular foot massage should be part of your regular health regime. There are machines, not expensive, that massage the feet, which you might want to invest in. They also sell machines that give foot whirlpool baths. This too would be very good for you.

With your health planet in a Water sign this year you benefit from the healing powers of the water element, which are considerable. It will be very beneficial to be around water – oceans, rivers, lakes, natural bodies of water. Good to swim or soak in natural waters. If you feel under the weather, a nice leisurely soak in the tub will make you feel much better.

Home and Family

Your 4th house of home and family is not prominent this year so it is not a major focus. Normally this would tend to the status quo. But with your home and family planet Pluto in the process of a major transition from Capricorn to Aquarius, this is not a status quo kind of year. Many changes are happening in the family and with children and children figures. This year you see only the beginning of this, but as time goes on the changes will become more and more pronounced. The family planet in the sign of Aquarius signals many things. It would show a need for building up a team spirit in the family. It would show a tendency to upgrade the home's technology, to install all kinds of high-tech equipment in the home – the latest and most modern. And, since Pluto is starting to move through your 7th house you will be doing more entertaining from home. There would be a tendency to beautify the home: the home itself becomes a work of art. All this will not happen overnight but is a process that goes on for many years.

A parent or parent figure will embark on in-depth psychology studies. These studies will go on for many years. He or she seems bent on completely transforming the psyche. He or she will probably be exploring past incarnations as well. This parent or parent figure needs to pay more attention to the stomach and digestive system. Surgery could be recommended here, but a detox regime could do the job as well.

The other parent, or parent figure, is prospering this year and travelling more. A move is not likely, however, though there is nothing against it. Siblings and sibling figures should probably not move in the year ahead. Instead, they should make good use of the space that they have. The same is true for children and children figures in your life. Use the space you have more creatively and a move becomes unnecessary.

Major renovations in the home are better done next year than this. However, if you plan on doing such things, October 23 to November 22 would be a reasonable time. If you're redecorating in a cosmetic kind of way, or otherwise beautifying the home, September 23 to October 18 would be a good time.

Finance and Career

Your 2nd house of finance is basically empty this year, with only short-term planets moving through there for short periods. Thus, it tends to the status quo. Earnings will more or less be in line with last year. You seem content with finances as they are and have no pressing need to make major changes. If financial problems occur, it is probably due to a lack of attention, so you need to give some focus to this area.

You are, however, in a great career year, although you seem to be more interested in status and prestige than in the bottom line. This is OK; some years are like that. If you had a choice between two jobs, one that paid more and the other that had more prestige, you would most likely choose the latter.

Fast-moving Mercury is your financial planet. In any given year he will move through all the signs and houses of your Horoscope. Thus, there are many short-term financial trends that depend on where Mercury is at any given time and the kinds of aspects he receives. These trends are best dealt with in the monthly reports.

Mercury does double duty in your Horoscope. He is your financial planet and also the ruler of your 11th house of friends. Thus, your social connections are very important in your financial life. Also, it is good for you to be involved with trade and professional organizations as these benefit the bottom line. Good use of technology and online activities are also important financially.

Generally, Mercury goes retrograde four times a year, although this year he will be properly retrograde only three times (his retrograde on January 1 will last only one day). This is a good financial signal. Overall, there will be greater financial confidence and clarity than usual. Mercury will be retrograde from April 2–24; August 5–26; and from November 26 to December 14. These are times to avoid making major purchases or investments. These things need to be researched and studied more carefully. These are times to attend to financial clarity rather than overt actions.

Mercury as the financial planet favours buying, selling, retailing and trading. It also favours good use of the media, sales, marketing, advertising and PR.

Career, as we mentioned above, is fabulous this year. (It was good last year as well.) Those of you who work for others are probably being promoted in the year ahead. (This could have happened last year too.) You seem to be enjoying your career path these days. It seems like fun. And you have a light-hearted attitude towards it. Jupiter in your 10th career house favours a creative kind of career. This feeds into your natural strengths as you are a very creative kind of person. Uranus has been in your 10th house for many years now, and so there have been many career changes in recent years. This year the changes seem very positive. You know all the right people who can help you. By May 26 your career goals will have been attained – the short-term ones at least – and your focus will shift to the social life – friends, groups and group activities.

Love and Social Life

With Uranus as your love planet you tend to have an exciting and dramatic love life. Love and romantic opportunity can happen for you at any time, in any place and at times when you least expect it. But love tends to be unstable. Instability is the price we pay for excitement.

This year Jupiter is travelling with your love planet, so romance is in the air. This could be serious committed love, or a serious kind of love affair.

Uranus has been in your 10th house of career for many years and is still there in the year ahead. This gives many messages. People of power and prestige, people above you in status, are very attractive to you. Henry Kissinger's famous remark that 'power is the ultimate aphrodisiac' certainly applies to you these days. It would also show that there are love opportunities with people involved in your career. An office romance, especially with the boss, is very likely. The problem with this is that you could be prone to relationships of convenience rather than of true love. However, another way to read this is that, as you focus on your career, love will find you. Get your career straight and love will fall into place.

Your love planet in the 10th house is very favourable for love. It shows focus. Love is high on your priorities and this tends to success. Focus, in my opinion, is more important than easy aspects. This year you have both, focus *and* easy aspects. So, love is happy and successful.

However, Pluto's move into your 7th house this year is going to bring long-term change and transformation in your love and social life. This is a process that will go on for the next 30 or so years. It can bring break-ups and shake-ups in existing relationships. Your whole social sphere will be transformed in the coming years. Many of your assumptions about love and relationships will also get transformed. This is usually not pleasant, but the end result is good. You're not being punished, only giving birth to the love life of your dreams, the ideal marriage and the ideal love life.

In the meantime, enjoy your happiness in love. You have plenty of time to deal with the coming challenges. And, when they come, you'll know how to deal with them.

Self-improvement

Neptune, the most spiritual of the planets, has been moving through your 8th house of regeneration for many years now. He will be there for the year ahead but is getting ready to leave. This transit shows, as we have mentioned in reports in earlier years, that the sexual act is becoming spiritualized. The object of this transit has been to lift the sexual act from mere animal lust to an act of worship. Thus, you have been, and still are, a good candidate for the spiritual teachings on sex. Kundalini and Tantra yoga as well as the hermetic sciences would be good studies for you. In addition, Saturn has been in your 8th house since last year and will remain there for the rest of the year ahead. This also signals a need to elevate the quality of the sexual act. You seem to be more choosy about it. Less but higher-quality sex is to be preferred over lots of sex. This will also improve the health.

We discussed Pluto's move into your 7th house earlier. But there is a spiritual component to this transit. An alchemical process is happening in your love and social life over the next 30 years. Good though your love life might be, it might not be good enough for you. All the dramas that will happen with this transit are only there to make the love life more perfect – to bring it closer to your ideal. You are meant to have the best and all these dramas are happening to make sure that you get the best. Sometimes an old building needs to be torn down and rebuilt in a new and better way. This is the process that will happen in your love and social life over the coming years.

For more information on astrology, healing and spiritual topics, please visit my blog at www.spiritual-stories.com.

Month-by-month Forecasts

January

Best Days Overall: 8, 9, 16, 17, 25, 26, 27
Most Stressful Days Overall: 6, 7, 12, 13, 18, 19
Best Days for Love: 2, 8, 9, 11, 12, 13, 19, 27, 28, 29
Best Days for Money: 1, 2, 9, 10, 11, 18, 19, 28, 29, 30, 31
Best Days for Career: 8, 9, 18, 19, 27, 28

Health needs a lot of watching this month, especially from the 20th onwards. The good news is that you are paying attention to health as your 6th house is very strong. This focus will prevent many problems from happening. The new Moon of the 11th, which occurs in your 6th house, is another positive for health as it will clarify health issues as the days go by, right up to the next new Moon next month. The important thing is to rest when tired. Avoid pushing yourself too hard. Listen to the messages that your body gives you. Enhance your health in the ways mentioned in the yearly report. You respond very well to spiritual-healing techniques, and if you feel under the weather a visit to a spiritual type of healer might be the answer.

Leos tend to be independent types of people, but this month less so than normal. Most of the planets are in the Western, social sector of your Horoscope so the focus now is on others and their needs. This is especially so from the 20th onwards as the Sun moves through your 7th house. Your way is probably not the best way right now. Let others have their way, so long as it isn't destructive. Your good will come to you through the grace of others and not so much from personal initiative. The good news is that you seem very popular this month, especially from the 20th onwards. You go out of your way for others. You put them first. People pick up on this and appreciate it.

With your financial planet moving forward again on the 2nd, finances seem much improved. Job-seekers have many job opportunities. Even those of you who are already employed will have opportunities for side jobs and extra assignments.

Mercury in Sagittarius, your 9th house, until the 14th indicates expanded earnings. Foreign investments, foreign companies and foreigners in general seem important in your financial life. You tend to be a risk-taker, a speculator when it comes to finance, Leo, and this is especially so until the 14th. Afterwards, as Mercury moves into Capricorn, these urges become more restrained. Financial judgement improves. You are taking a more long-term perspective on wealth. You are more restrained in your spending, and like value for your money. I consider this a positive for wealth.

On the 20th and 21st the Sun travels with Pluto. You seem closer to family and family members, and especially to a parent or parent figure. This is a good time for detox regimes or weight-loss regimes.

From the 20th you enter a yearly love and social peak. This will go on well into February and will be even stronger next month.

February

Best Days Overall: 4, 5, 12, 13, 21, 22, 23
Most Stressful Days Overall: 1, 2, 3, 8, 9, 14, 15, 29
Best Days for Love: 6, 7, 8, 9, 14, 15, 16, 17, 24, 25, 26, 27
Best Days for Money: 6, 7, 8, 9, 14, 15, 18, 24, 25, 29
Best Days for Career: 6, 7, 14, 15, 17, 26, 27

The love and social life, your 7th house, is the main headline this month, with 60 per cent of the planets either residing there or moving through there this month. This is an enormous amount of cosmic power and the love life is happy and very active. Singles have many romantic opportunities, perhaps too many. The problem this month is too much of a good thing. Still, it is a nice problem to have. Happily, the new Moon of the 9th, which occurs in your 7th house, will clarify your social confusion as the days go by, and well into next month. All the information you need to make a good social or romantic decision will come to you very naturally and normally.

With so many planets moving through your 7th house you get along and are attracted to all kinds of people, all kinds of personality types.

The Sun, the ruler of your Horoscope, is not very comfortable in this sign of Aquarius. He is considered weakened in that sign. So, self-esteem and self-confidence are not as strong as usual. However, with so many planets in your 7th house and with the Western sector of your chart so powerful, this doesn't really matter. Too much self-confidence and self-esteem might actually be a handicap this month. This is a time to let others have their way and allow your good to come through others.

The Sun's move into your 8th house on the 19th shows the prosperity of the spouse, partner or current love. It shows too that you are very involved in the finances of others. It is a more erotic kind of period – the natural consequence of an active love life. Saturn's position in your 8th house, however, cautions you not to overdo it. Focus on quality rather than quantity.

March

Best Days Overall: 2, 3, 11, 12, 19, 20, 21, 29, 30
Most Stressful Days Overall: 1, 7, 8, 13, 14, 27, 28
Best Days for Love: 4, 5, 7, 8, 13, 14, 17, 18, 22, 23, 27, 28
Best Days for Money: 1, 4, 5, 9, 11, 13, 14, 19, 20, 22, 23, 29, 30
Best Days for Career: 7, 8, 13, 14, 17, 18, 27, 28

Health and energy are much better than last month but still need watching. As always, make sure not to get overtired and to rest when necessary. Enhance the health in the ways mentioned in the yearly report. Although the love and social life has calmed down a bit it still seems happy. Jupiter will travel with your love planet Uranus on the 29th and 30th and this should bring happy romantic experiences for singles. It also brings happy social experiences for those already in relationships.

A lunar eclipse on the 25th is relatively mild in its effects on you but it won't hurt to reduce your schedule a bit. This eclipse occurs in your 3rd house and impacts siblings, sibling figures, neighbours and the neighbourhood in general. There are personal dramas with siblings, sibling figures and neighbours. There are probably weird kind of events happening in the neighbourhood too. Siblings and sibling figures need to re-define themselves, to take stock of themselves, their image and personality and the kinds of impressions they make on others. This re-evaluation will manifest in wardrobe and image changes over the coming months.

Since the Moon is your spiritual planet, important spiritual changes are happening for you – and for parents, parent figures and family members. You could change teachings, teachers and your spiritual practice. Your attitudes to spirituality will also change. Often such an eclipse brings personal dramas to the lives of guru figures. There are disruptions and upheavals in spiritual or charitable organizations that you are involved with.

Since this eclipse occurs in your 3rd house, cars and communication equipment can behave erratically and often repairs or replacements are necessary. It would be a good idea to avoid unnecessary driving while the eclipse is in effect. If you must drive, be more careful and mindful as you do so. Students below college level will experience disruptions at school, and perhaps even changes of school. Educational plans will change.

April

Best Days Overall: 7, 8, 16, 17, 26, 27
Most Stressful Days Overall: 3, 4, 9, 10, 23, 24, 25, 30
Best Days for Love: 2, 3, 4, 7, 8, 10, 16, 17, 27, 28, 29, 30
Best Days for Money: 1, 2, 7, 8, 9, 10, 16, 17, 18, 19, 20, 26, 27
Best Days for Career: 7, 8, 9, 10, 16, 17, 27, 28

There is another eclipse this month too – a solar eclipse. Every solar eclipse affects you strongly, Leo, but this one on the 8th seems especially strong. Not only is it a total eclipse but it also impacts other important planets in your Horoscope – Mercury and Venus, your money and career planets. So many areas of life and many people in your life are affected by this eclipse. So, take the same approach to this eclipse as you would to a storm or hurricane that was about to hit your neighbourhood. Take normal and sane precautions. If you don't need to drive, don't. Stay close to home, read a book, watch a movie, or – best of all – meditate. If you must drive, do so in a more careful manner. Things that need to be done should be done, but anything else, especially if it's stressful, is best rescheduled for another time.

If you haven't been careful in dietary matters this eclipse can bring a detox of the body. Often this is confused with disease, but it's not disease. It's just the body getting rid of things that don't need to be there. The eclipse forces you to take stock of yourself, your image, self-concept and the way you present yourself to others. Perhaps people are slandering or bad-mouthing you. So, there is a need for you to define yourself for yourself, or others will define you as they see fit. This is not pleasant. This redefinition of yourself will lead to wardrobe changes and changes in your image and presentation to others as the months go by.

This eclipse also brings dramatic and important financial changes, as it directly affects your financial planet. Your financial thinking, planning and strategizing have not been realistic, as the events of the eclipse will show. A course correction is necessary and will happen.

Since Mercury is also your planet of friends, there are dramas, life-changing kinds of events, in the lives of friends. There are shake-ups and upheavals in trade or professional organizations that you're involved with. Cars and communication equipment, computers and technology can behave erratically and often repairs or replacements are necessary. Be on the alert for computer and online scams. Avoid opening emails from people you don't know and don't open suspicious attachments.

The impact of this eclipse on Venus shows career changes happening. Often it indicates changes in the corporate hierarchy or dramas in the lives of bosses and authority figures in your company. In many cases the government changes the regulations in your industry or company and so now you have to play by different rules. You haven't changed your career but must pursue it in a different way.

Parents, parent figures, siblings and sibling figures, as well as friends, should all take it nice and easy while the eclipse is in effect.

May

Health needs more attention this month, especially until the 20th. After the 26th, however, you will see a dramatic improvement. In the meantime be sure to get enough rest, as always, and enhance the health in the ways mentioned in the yearly report.

You are in the midst of a yearly career peak and it looks very success-ful. The 18th to the 20th, as the Sun travels with Jupiter, seems espe-cially successful. With your family planet Pluto going retrograde on the 2nd, home and family issues will need time to resolve themselves and so you may as well focus on your career and external, outer objectives now. The Sun, the ruler of your Horoscope, is at the top of your chart this month. So, there is personal elevation, perhaps honour and recognition as well. This is not just because of your professional abilities, but for who you are as a person. People look up to you and aspire to be like you.

Career has been successful all year but this month even more so. On the 26th Jupiter makes a major move out of your 10th house into your 11th, where he will stay for the rest of the year ahead. On the 20th the Sun will join him in the 11th house and on the 23rd Venus will also join the party. So the month ahead is a strong social month. It is not necessarily romantic, more about friendships and Platonic kinds of relationships. Yet, romance is happening for singles as well: on the 13th and 14th the Sun travels with your love planet Uranus. And Jupiter has been travelling with your love planet since the end of last month. Both these transits show serious romance happening.

Finances seem good this month. Mercury, your financial planet, crosses your Mid-heaven and enters your 10th house on the 15th. This puts him at the top of your chart and indicates great focus. Finance is high on your list of priorities from the 15th onwards and this tends to success. Also, it shows that bosses, parents, parent figures and author-ity figures in your life are kindly disposed to your financial goals. Often such transits show a pay rise, official or unofficial. It also shows that your good career reputation leads to earnings and opportunities for earnings.

Drive more carefully on the 18th and 19th.

June

Best Days Overall: 1, 2, 9, 10, 11, 19, 20, 28, 29
Most Stressful Days Overall: 3, 4, 17, 18, 24, 25, 30
Best Days for Love: 4, 5, 6, 13, 16, 17, 22, 23, 24, 25, 26, 27
Best Days for Money: 5, 6, 12, 13, 14, 15, 16, 17, 24, 26, 27
Best Days for Career: 3, 4, 5, 6, 16, 17, 26, 27, 30

Health is much better than last month. Now that Jupiter has moved away from his stressful aspect, health looks good. Enhance the health with back and knee massage, foot massage and spiritual-healing techniques. Your health planet Saturn will go retrograde on the 29th so if you need to make important changes to the health regime do so before the 29th. Spiritual-healing techniques work especially well during the full Moon of the 22nd.

The month ahead looks happy. The planetary power is mostly in the beneficent 11th house. This is the house where fondest dreams and wishes come true. It is the house of friendships and Platonic kinds of relationships. These seem happy and fulfilling. You are meeting new friends and they seem significant kinds of friendships. They seem important.

Mercury, your financial planet, travels with Jupiter on the 3rd and 4th. This signals a nice payday or financial windfall. There is luck in speculations at this time as well. Keep in mind that the cosmos has many ways to enrich you, however – it doesn't have to be by speculation. Your financial planet has been travelling with Uranus from the end of May and does so until the 2nd of this month. This transit can bring sudden and unexpected money to you. It shows money that comes out of the blue. On the 17th Mercury enters your spiritual 12th house and stays there for the rest of the month. This indicates strong financial intuition. You're a generous person by nature but especially from the 17th onwards.

On the 20th the Sun enters your 12th house of spirituality and will be there for the rest of the month ahead. It is a good time to study the holy books, to meditate and to pursue your spiritual practice. This is a time for spiritual breakthroughs for those who want them. Even the career can be boosted by spiritual and charitable kinds of activities. Being involved in spiritual activities is likely to bring connections that will boost the career.

July

Best Days Overall: 7, 8, 17, 18, 25, 26
Most Stressful Days Overall: 1, 14, 15, 16, 21, 22, 27, 28
Best Days for Love: 1, 10, 17, 18, 20, 21, 22, 25, 26, 28
Best Days for Money: 2, 3, 7, 8, 9, 10, 11, 12, 13, 17, 18, 21, 22, 27, 28, 29, 30
Best Days for Career: 1, 5, 6, 17, 18, 25, 26, 27, 28

Basically a happy month ahead, Leo, especially from the 22nd onwards.

Health is good this month and will get even better after the 20th. You can improve it even further in the ways mentioned in the yearly report. With your health planet retrograde all month it is probably not a good idea to make drastic changes to your health regime. Nor very advisable to have medical tests or procedures done if you have the choice. If you can, reschedule such things for another time.

Mars is moving through your 10th house until the 20th, indicating a lot of career activity. It would also indicate that you see your children or children figures in your life as your mission during this time. You're working hard on the career but it does seem to be enjoyable. This turns to success.

Your 12th house of spirituality remains very powerful until the 22nd. You are in a strong spiritual period and this is an excellent time to study holy scripture, meditate, and pursue your spiritual practice. In general, you experience a more active dream life and supernatural kinds of experiences, experiences that can't be explained logically.

Be more patient with a parent or parent figure and with family in general from the 21st to the 22nd. You seem to be at odds. You and they see things from opposite perspectives. Both of you have a point.

Your own house becomes very strong this month. Mercury moves in on the 2nd, Venus moves in on the 11th and the Sun on the 22nd. You begin a yearly personal pleasure peak and are in a period of maximum personal independence. Personal initiative matters now. Your way is the best way these days. No one knows better than you where your path of happiness lies. Make the changes that need to be made to enlarge your happiness. Your happiness is really up to you.

The month ahead is also a prosperous one. Mercury is in your own sign from the 2nd to the 25th, bringing financial windfalls. Happy financial opportunities are pursuing you rather than vice versa. The money people in your life seem devoted to you and are on your side. You spend on yourself and project an image of prosperity.

Venus in your sign from the 11th onwards shows happy career opportunities coming to you. You are seen as a successful person. You are dressing the part.

On the 13th and 14th as Mars travels with your love planet there is a happy romantic opportunity. It seems more like fun and games than something very serious.

August

Best Days Overall: 3, 4, 13, 14, 21, 22, 30, 31
Most Stressful Days Overall: 11, 12, 17, 18, 23, 24, 25
Best Days for Love: 6, 7, 8, 15, 16, 17, 18, 24, 25, 29
Best Days for Money: 5, 6, 7, 8, 9, 17, 18, 21, 22, 27, 30, 31
Best Days for Career: 8, 17, 18, 23, 24, 25, 29

The month ahead continues to be happy and prosperous.

Health is still good, and the personal appearance shines. Your natural Leo charisma is unusually strong with the Sun in your sign until the 22nd. Venus has been in your sign since July 11 and is still there until the 5th, giving beauty, grace and charm to the image. You are still in an excellent period for creating your own happiness and making the changes that will foster this.

You remain very much in a yearly personal pleasure peak. This will go on until the 22nd. So, continue to enjoy all the pleasures of the body and the five senses. The body can use some extra pampering this month. The new Moon of the 4th occurs in your own sign and is an especially happy day. It also brings spiritual understanding and illumination to you. Issues involving the body and personal appearance will clarify themselves as the days go by – until the next new Moon next month. Romance seems stable this month. Singles should focus on their career and romantic opportunities will come to them.

Personal independence is a wonderful thing, but not so good for love. Love doesn't seem that important to you right now – you are in a 'me'-oriented kind of month. And with your love planet Uranus retrograde the social judgement and thinking are not up to scratch and could be a lot better.

With Jupiter now established in your 11th house, the month ahead is more about friendship and Platonic kinds of relationships. These seem happy and fortunate.

Your financial planet Mercury will be retrograde from the 4th to the 25th. Yet, with your money house very powerful from the 22nd onwards, the month ahead is still prosperous. Mercury's retrograde could slow things down a bit but it won't stop earnings from happening. Also, when Mercury starts to go forward on the 25th you will be entering a yearly financial peak. You should end the month more prosperous than when it began. As always, avoid making important purchases or investments while your financial planet is retrograde. Do these things either before the 4th or after the 25th.

September

Best Days Overall: 1, 9, 10, 18, 19, 26, 27, 28
Most Stressful Days Overall: 7, 8, 14, 15, 20, 21, 26
Best Days for Love: 2, 3, 4, 5, 13, 14, 15, 21, 23, 24, 30
Best Days for Money: 1, 2, 3, 4, 5, 12, 13, 14, 15, 21, 22, 23, 29, 30
Best Days for Career: 4, 5, 14, 15, 20, 21, 23, 24

Now that Mercury is moving forward, and with your money house still very powerful until the 22nd, prosperity is very strong this month. There is good financial clarity and your decisions should be good.

The main headline of the month is the lunar eclipse on the 18th, which occurs in your 8th house of regeneration and impacts on the ruler of the 8th house.

This shows various things. The spouse, partner or current love is forced to make very important financial changes. The events of the eclipse will reveal where the financial thinking, planning and strategy have been amiss. It can also bring dramas involving taxes or insurance payments. There can be psychological encounters with death. Generally, this is not a literal death but psychological kinds of encounters. Perhaps you have dreams of death. Perhaps people you know have near-death kinds of experiences. Perhaps surgery is recommended for you. Perhaps you yourself have a close call or brush with death. Perhaps you hear of a literal death of someone you know. The cosmos has its way of bringing your attention to the matter. This is not any sort of punishment. Instead, the cosmos is showing there is a need for a deeper understanding of death. In many cases this is merely a love letter from the divine telling you to get more serious about life and to be about the business that you were born to do. Life is short and can end at any time. No more postponing of your life mission and purpose.

The eclipsed planet, the Moon, is your spiritual planet. This reinforces the spiritual agenda behind all these phenomena.

The dream life is likely to be active and probably not pleasant over the period of the eclipse, but it shouldn't be taken too seriously. Much of what you see is merely astral garbage stirred up by the eclipse.

This eclipse will cause important spiritual changes. (Every lunar eclipse has this effect.) There are important changes in your spiritual practice, teachings and perhaps even teachers. There are personal dramas in the lives of guru figures in your life. There are disturbances and changes in spiritual or charitable organizations that you are involved with.

October

Best Days Overall: 6, 7, 8, 15, 16, 24, 25
Most Stressful Days Overall: 4, 5, 11, 12, 17, 18, 30
Best Days for Love: 4, 5, 10, 11, 12, 13, 14, 18, 24, 25, 28
Best Days for Money: 1, 2, 11, 12, 13, 19, 20, 21, 22, 25, 27, 28, 29, 30, 31
Best Days for Career: 4, 5, 13, 14, 16, 18, 24, 25

The main event this month is the solar eclipse of the 2nd. With the Sun as your ruling planet, every solar eclipse affects you more than most people, but the good news is that this eclipse is nowhere near as powerful as the one we had in April. Still, it would be wise to reduce your schedule while the eclipse is in effect. Children and children figures in your life should also take it easier. Things that need to be done should be done, but other activities, especially if they are stressful, are better off being rescheduled.

This eclipse occurs in your 3rd house of communication and intellectual interests. Students below college level have dramas at school and perhaps even change schools. There are important changes in educational plans. Siblings and sibling figures are also impacted by this eclipse. They experience personal dramas and will need to redefine themselves, their self-concept, their opinion of themselves and the presentation and impression they make on others. This will lead to wardrobe and image changes in the coming months. The same holds true for you and for children and children figures in your life. Leos go through this re-evaluation twice a year, and by now you know how to handle it. It is probably more dramatic on children figures and siblings who may not be used to this.

The solar eclipse forces you to make important financial changes. Your thinking, planning and strategizing have not been realistic, as the events of the eclipse will show. A course correction is necessary now.

Try to avoid unnecessary driving while the eclipse is in effect. If you must drive, be more mindful and careful. Cars, computer and communication equipment and high-tech gadgets generally will probably be tested by the eclipse. They can behave erratically and sometimes repairs or replacements are necessary. Technology is wonderful when it's working properly, but it is hell on earth when it doesn't. Take the normal precautions with your online activities: back up important files and don't open emails or attachments from people you don't know. Even if you know the people, avoid opening suspicious attachments.

November

  Best Days Overall: 3, 4, 12, 13, 20, 21, 29, 30
  Most Stressful Days Overall: 1, 2, 7, 8, 9, 14, 15, 28, 29
  Best Days for Love: 3, 4, 6, 7, 8, 9, 12, 13, 15, 22, 23, 24
  Best Days for Money: 3, 8, 9, 12, 13, 16, 17, 20, 21, 22, 23, 24,
      26, 27, 29, 30
  Best Days for Career: 3, 4, 12, 13, 15, 22, 23

Health needs some attention until the 21st. There is nothing serious afoot, only temporary stresses caused by the short-term planets. You should see major improvement from the 21st onwards. In the meantime, make sure to get enough rest and enhance the health in the ways mentioned in the yearly report.

The planetary power this month is in your 4th house of home and family, and this has been the case since October 22. So, though career is still important, give more attention to the home and family and, most importantly, to your emotional wellness. You are in a nostalgic kind of mood these days. There is a great interest in the past, both your personal past and history in general. This nostalgia is not something random, but part of the cosmic therapeutic process. It is bringing up old memories from the past, good and bad, so that you can look at them from your present state of consciousness. This will not erase the past but will redefine it in a new way. Much of the sting and hurt of past events will dissolve as you look at them from your present state of consciousness. This brings emotional understanding and healing. This emotional healing will set the stage for future career success later on. The new Moon of the 1st occurs in your 4th house, making it an especially good day for emotional healing. And, as the days go by, the new Moon will clarify many emotional and family issues.

On the 21st the Sun enters your 5th house of fun, children and creativity. So, it is party time in your life. Take a vacation from your cares and worries and just have some fun. This is a good month to be more involved with your children or children figures in your life. They seem very devoted to you. Mars, your planet of children, enters your own sign on the 4th and will be there for the rest of the month ahead. Leos are very creative kinds of people and this month even more so than usual. Mars in your own sign gives more energy, enthusiasm and courage. You get things done in a fraction of the normal time. You will excel in sports and exercise regimes. You could be taking more risks with your body, so be careful about this. But Mars has a downside too. He can make you short-tempered, prone to arguments, too much in a hurry, and this could lead to accidents or injury. So, make haste by all means, but in a mindful kind of way.

Finances look good this month as Mercury will be in beneficent Sagittarius from the 2nd onwards. This will expand earnings. You earn big but you spend big as well. Always a speculator, this month even more so than usual. Your financial planet will go retrograde at the end of the month, from the 26th onwards. Thus, make any important purchases or investments before then. Mercury will also be out of bounds from the 7th to December 2, signalling that in your financial affairs you are outside your normal sphere – in unknown territory. With Venus also out of bounds all month you are outside your normal sphere in career matters as well.

December

Best Days Overall: 1, 9, 10, 17, 18, 19, 27, 28, 29
Most Stressful Days Overall: 7, 8, 13, 14, 20, 21
Best Days for Love: 2, 3, 4, 5, 6, 12, 13, 14, 21, 22, 23, 24, 31
Best Days for Money: 1, 6, 9, 10, 14, 17, 18, 19, 20, 21, 23, 24
Best Days for Career: 2, 3, 4, 11, 12, 13, 14, 22, 23, 24

You're still very much in a party period this month, especially until the 21st. So continue to enjoy your life and engage in leisure kinds of activities. With Mars going retrograde on the 6th the party slows down a bit but it is still happening. Be more careful about speculations from the 6th onwards. Children and children figures seem to lack direction this month. They seem confused. The new Moon of the 1st should ease the situation for them and will clarify their confusion. As the days go on, they will receive all the information they need to make the right choices and decisions.

Health and energy are excellent this month. Dynamic Mars is in your sign all month so you have the energy of 10 people. But keep in mind our discussion of this last month. Avoid rush and impatience and watch the temper.

Your financial planet Mercury starts to move forward on the 15th and he spends the month in benevolent Sagittarius. Thus, finances will be good. Earnings should increase. You're a big earner and a big spender. Money comes easily and is spent just as easily. With Mars, the ruler of your 5th house, retrograde from the 6th onwards, you should curb the temptation for speculation, as we've said – although you will be sorely tempted.

Personal creativity was very strong last month and is still very strong in the month ahead. Venus, your career planet, will be out of bounds from the 1st to the 8th, showing that in career matters and the way you pursue your career you are outside your normal sphere. Siblings and sibling figures also seem outside their normal sphere this period. Your taste in reading also seems more experimental.

Love will go better after the 21st than before. But the real action, as has been the case for many months now, is in the area of friendships and group activities. The month ahead favours Platonic relationships rather than romantic ones.

The full Moon of the 15th, which occurs right on Jupiter, is especially happy and creative. For those on the spiritual path it brings spiritual illumination and breakthroughs.

On the 21st the Sun moves into your 6th house of health and work and stays there for the rest of the month. You've had enough partying and you're ready for some serious work. This is a wonderful period for job-seekers, or for those who employ others. Even if you are already employed there are opportunities for overtime and second jobs.

Virgo

♍

THE VIRGIN

Birthdays from
22nd August to
22nd September

Personality Profile

VIRGO AT A GLANCE

Element – Earth

Ruling Planet – Mercury
  Career Planet – Mercury
  Love Planet – Neptune
  Money Planet – Venus
  Planet of Home and Family Life – Jupiter
  Planet of Health and Work – Uranus
  Planet of Pleasure – Saturn
  Planet of Sexuality – Mars

Colours – earth tones, ochre, orange, yellow

Colour that promotes love, romance and social harmony – aqua blue

Colour that promotes earning power – jade green

Gems – agate, hyacinth

Metal – quicksilver

Scents – lavender, lilac, lily of the valley, storax

Quality – mutable (= flexibility)

Quality most needed for balance – a broader perspective

Strongest virtues – mental agility, analytical skills, ability to pay attention to detail, healing powers

Deepest needs – to be useful and productive

Characteristic to avoid – destructive criticism

Signs of greatest overall compatibility – Taurus, Capricorn

Signs of greatest overall incompatibility – Gemini, Sagittarius, Pisces

Sign most helpful to career – Gemini

Sign most helpful for emotional support – Sagittarius

Sign most helpful financially – Libra

Sign best for marriage and/or partnerships – Pisces

Sign most helpful for creative projects – Capricorn

Best Sign to have fun with – Capricorn

Signs most helpful in spiritual matters – Taurus, Leo

Best day of the week – Wednesday

Understanding a Virgo

The virgin is a particularly fitting symbol for those born under the sign of Virgo. If you meditate on the image of the virgin you will get a good understanding of the essence of the Virgo type. The virgin is, of course, a symbol of purity and innocence – not naïve, but pure. A virginal object has not been touched. A virgin field is land that is true to itself, the way it has always been. The same is true of virgin forest: it is pristine, unaltered.

Apply the idea of purity to the thought processes, emotional life, physical body and activities and projects of the everyday world, and you can see how Virgos approach life. Virgos desire the pure expression of the ideal in their mind, body and affairs. If they find impurities they will attempt to clear them away.

Impurities are the beginning of disorder, unhappiness and uneasiness. The job of the Virgo is to eject all impurities and keep only that which the body and mind can use and assimilate.

The secrets of good health are here revealed: 90 per cent of the art of staying well is maintaining a pure mind, a pure body and pure emotions. When you introduce more impurities than your mind and body can deal with, you will have what is known as 'dis-ease'. It is no wonder that Virgos make great doctors, nurses, healers and dieticians. They have an innate understanding of good health and they realize that good health is more than just physical. In all aspects of life, if you want a project to be successful it must be kept as pure as possible. It must be protected against the adverse elements that will try to undermine it. This is the secret behind Virgo's awesome technical proficiency.

One could talk about Virgo's analytical powers – which are formidable. One could talk about their perfectionism and their almost superhuman attention to detail. But this would be to miss the point. All of these virtues are manifestations of a Virgo's desire for purity and perfection – a world without Virgos would have ruined itself long ago.

A vice is nothing more than a virtue turned inside out, misapplied or used in the wrong context. Virgos' apparent vices come from their inherent virtue. Their analytical powers, which should be used for healing, helping or perfecting a project in the world, sometimes get misapplied and turned against people. Their critical faculties, which should be used constructively to perfect a strategy or proposal, can sometimes be used destructively to harm or wound. Their urge to perfection can turn into worry and lack of confidence; their natural humility can become self-denial and self-abasement. When Virgos turn negative they are apt to turn their devastating criticism on themselves, sowing the seeds of self-destruction.

Finance

Virgos have all the attitudes that create wealth. They are hard-working, industrious, efficient, organized, thrifty, productive and eager to serve. A developed Virgo is every employer's dream. But until Virgos master some of the social graces of Libra they will not even come close to fulfilling their financial potential. Purity and perfectionism, if not handled correctly or gracefully, can be very trying to others. Friction in human relationships can be devastating not only to your pet projects but – indirectly – to your wallet as well.

Virgos are quite interested in their financial security. Being hard-working, they know the true value of money. They do not like to take risks with their money, preferring to save for their retirement or for a rainy day. Virgos usually make prudent, calculated investments that involve a minimum of risk. These investments and savings usually work out well, helping Virgos to achieve the financial security they seek. The rich or even not-so-rich Virgo also likes to help his or her friends in need.

Career and Public Image

Virgos reach their full potential when they can communicate their knowledge in such a way that others can understand it. In order to get their ideas across better, Virgos need to develop greater verbal skills and fewer judgemental ways of expressing themselves. Virgos look up to teachers and communicators; they like their bosses to be good communicators. Virgos will probably not respect a superior who is not their intellectual equal – no matter how much money or power that superior has. Virgos themselves like to be perceived by others as being educated and intellectual.

The natural humility of Virgos often inhibits them from fulfilling their great ambitions, from acquiring name and fame. Virgos should indulge in a little more self-promotion if they are going to reach their career goals. They need to push themselves with the same ardour that they would use to foster others.

At work Virgos like to stay active. They are willing to learn any type of job as long as it serves their ultimate goal of financial security. Virgos may change occupations several times during their professional lives, until they find the one they really enjoy. Virgos work well with other people, are not afraid to work hard and always fulfil their responsibilities.

Love and Relationships

If you are an analyst or a critic you must, out of necessity, narrow your scope. You have to focus on a part and not the whole; this can create a temporary narrow-mindedness. Virgos do not like this kind of person. They like their partners to be broad-minded, with depth and vision. Virgos seek to get this broad-minded quality from their partners, since they sometimes lack it themselves.

Virgos are perfectionists in love just as they are in other areas of life. They need partners who are tolerant, open-minded and easy-going. If you are in love with a Virgo do not waste time on impractical romantic gestures. Do practical and useful things for him or her – this is what will be appreciated and what will be done for you.

Virgos express their love through pragmatic and useful gestures, so do not be put off because your Virgo partner does not say 'I love you' day-in and day-out. Virgos are not that type. If they love you, they will demonstrate it in practical ways. They will always be there for you; they will show an interest in your health and finances; they will fix your sink or repair your video recorder. Virgos deem these actions to be superior to sending flowers, chocolates or Valentine cards.

In love affairs Virgos are not particularly passionate or spontaneous. If you are in love with a Virgo, do not take this personally. It does not mean that you are not alluring enough or that your Virgo partner does not love or like you. It is just the way Virgos are. What they lack in passion they make up for in dedication and loyalty.

Home and Domestic Life

It goes without saying that the home of a Virgo will be spotless, sanitized and orderly. Everything will be in its proper place – and don't you dare move anything about! For Virgos to find domestic bliss they need to ease up a bit in the home, to allow their partner and children more freedom and to be more generous and open-minded. Family members are not to be analysed under a microscope, they are individuals with their own virtues to express.

With these small difficulties resolved, Virgos like to stay in and entertain at home. They make good hosts and they like to keep their friends and families happy and entertained at family and social gatherings. Virgos love children, but they are strict with them – at times – since they want to make sure their children are brought up with the correct sense of family and values.

Horoscope for 2024

Major Trends

Saturn's move into Pisces last year not only tested your current relationship but also your overall health and energy. This situation continues in the year ahead. More on this later.

Uranus has been in your 9th house for many years now and will remain there in the year ahead. Thus, your religious, philosophical and theological beliefs are undergoing a dramatic change. Most likely you are dealing with scientific conflicts with these beliefs. At the same time Jupiter is also moving through your 9th house, greatly increasing your interest in religion and philosophy. You will be merging, marrying your religious beliefs with science.

Love has been idealistic for many years now, but with Saturn in your 7th house practical issues become very important as well. More details later.

When Jupiter enters your 10th house of career on May 26 you begin a cycle of career success and advancement. Many of you will receive promotion in your current job, and if you are in business your business will be elevated in status. There will be increased honour and recognition for your professional skills in the year ahead. More on this later.

Pluto's move into Aquarius brings changes to the health regime and health attitudes. For many of you it brings a tendency for surgery; for others a tendency to detox regimes. More on this later.

Your most important interests in the year ahead are fun, creativity and children until January 22 and from September 3 to November 20; health and work from January 22 to September 3 and from November 20 onwards; love, romance and social activities; religion, philosophy, theology, higher education and foreign travel until May 26; and career from May 26 onwards.

Your paths of greatest fulfilment in the year ahead will be sex, psychology and occult studies; religion, philosophy, theology, foreign travel and higher education until May 26; and career from May 26 onwards.

Health

(Please note that this is an astrological perspective on health and not a medical one. In days of yore there was no difference, both these perspectives were identical. But these days there could be quite a difference. For a medical perspective, please consult your doctor or health practitioner.)

Since the body is basically a dynamic energy system, the movement of the planets, especially the long-term ones, affects the energy of the world and thus the energy of the body. Pluto has been in harmonious aspect to you for more than 30 years but is now leaving his harmonious aspect. Last year Saturn moved into adverse aspect with you. Neptune has been in adverse aspect for many years now and this is the case in the year ahead. So, health needs more watching.

This is especially so from May 26 onwards when Jupiter starts to make an adverse aspect with you.

The good news is that health is always a major focus for Virgo and this year will become an even greater focus. This is a positive for health. It would be much more dangerous if you were ignoring things.

Also, there is much you can do to enhance your health and prevent problems from developing. And, even if you can't totally prevent problems, you can soften them when they do happen. They need not be devastating. Things that ordinarily would be knockout blows become mere taps.

So, pay more attention to the following – the vulnerable areas of your Horoscope this year (the reflex points are shown in the chart opposite):

- The small intestine. This area is always important for Virgo, and the reflex is shown above.
- The heart. This only became important since March 2023 and it remains important in the year ahead. The reflex point is shown above, and chest massage is also good for the heart as it sends energy and stimulation there. Do your best to avoid worry and anxiety, the two emotions that stress the heart. Virgos tend to be worriers so this is especially important for you. Replace worry with faith. Regular meditation will help you achieve this.
- The ankles and calves should be regularly massaged. A weak ankle can knock the spine and skeleton out of alignment and can cause all kinds of other problems. If you're exercising give the ankles more support.
- The neck and throat. These areas have been important for some years now and are still important in the year ahead. Regular neck and throat massage will help release tension in the neck.
- The colon, bladder, organs of elimination and sexual organs. These are starting to become very important health areas for you this year and will be important for decades to come. Safe sex and sexual moderation are becoming more important now.

Uranus, your health planet, rules your health from an Earth sign. You have a special connection to the healing powers of the Earth element, and these are considerable. Crystal therapy, an Earth-based therapy, would be very effective this year. If you feel under the weather go off to the mountains or caves, or old forests, the older the better, and just hang out. These are places where the Earth energy is very strong. You should feel better. If there is a particular part of the body that bothers you, a mudpack applied to the area should be helpful.

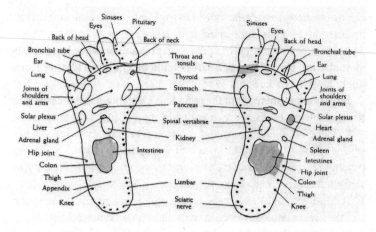

Important foot reflexology points for the year ahead
*Try to massage all of the foot on a regular basis – the top of the foot as well as
the bottom – but pay extra attention to the points highlighted on the chart.
When you massage, be aware of 'sore spots' as these need special attention.
It's also a good idea to massage the ankles, especially, and below them.*

Home and Family

Although your 4th house of home and family is not prominent this
year, your family planet Jupiter is receiving much stimulation. So, big
and dramatic changes are happening in the home and with the family.
For the first half of the year, until May 26, Jupiter is travelling with
Uranus, the planet of sudden change and in your case your health and
work planet. This signals many things. You're working more from
home. You're installing equipment to boost your health in the home.
There is a tendency to emotional instability both in yourself and in
family members. There can be sudden and swift mood changes.
Maintaining emotional equilibrium is a challenge both for you and for
family members. The good news is that this will ease up after May 26.
Until May 26 you could be living in different places for long periods of
time. You might not actually move, but just spend time in different
places. The health of a parent or parent figure seems a concern. There

can be multiple, serial renovations of the home. The home is a work in progress and is constantly being updated.

A parent or parent figure is prospering in the year ahead, especially after May 26. He or she needs to watch the weight more. A move is not likely for him or her this year. The other parent figure might feel cramped in the present home, but a move is not advisable. Better to make creative use of the space available.

A sibling or sibling figure seems about to embark on a major renovation of the home, but also on a deep psychological journey. Deep psychology and reincarnations seem an important interest for this sibling. A move is not likely this year.

Children and children figures in your life could have moved last year, and they seem content where they are right now. Grandchildren, if you have them, or those who play that role in your life, are likely to move in the year ahead. They could have moved in previous years as well. The home situation is far from settled.

If you're planning major renovations or repairs to the home, January 1–5 would be a good time. If you're redecorating or otherwise beautifying the home, January 1–23 and October 18 to December 7 would be excellent times.

Finance and Career

Your money house is basically empty this year; no long-term planets move through that house. Only short-term planets will temporarily energize your 2nd house. So, finance is not a big deal this year. You seem satisfied with things as they are and have no need to make major changes or to unduly focus here. However, two eclipses in the coming year occur in the money house. The first is a lunar eclipse on March 25 and the second is a solar eclipse on October 2. These events will temporarily shake up the financial life and force important changes and course corrections.

You are, however, in a very strong career year – especially from May 26 onwards. I read this as status, prestige and recognition are more important to you than the bottom line. The good news is that career success tends to translate into financial success over time. But this doesn't seem the main motivation this year.

Our regular readers will know that with Venus as your financial planet, a fast-moving planet, there are many short-term trends in finance that depend on where Venus is and the kinds of aspects she receives. These short-term trends are best dealt with in the monthly reports.

Venus as your financial planet indicates the importance of social connections in your financial life. With you, real wealth cannot be determined by looking at a financial statement or profit-and-loss account. Who you know is more important than how much you have. Also, it signals a good feeling for the beauty industry as a whole – fashion, cosmetics, art, jewellery, companies that beautify people or the world. Venus does double duty in your chart; she is your financial planet and the ruler of the beneficent 9th house. This in general is a positive financial signal. Your financial goals tend to be larger than life. Just earning your living is not interesting to you. You are interested in big wealth. Higher goals tend to manifest as higher earnings. But this also shows a good intuition for airlines, travel agencies and institutions of higher learning. You also have a good feeling for foreign companies and foreign investments. Foreigners in general seem important in your financial life.

Careerwise you are more ambitious than usual this year. Most of the long-term planets are above the horizon in your Horoscope, in the day side of your chart. Not only that but your 10th house of career becomes very powerful from May 26 onwards. This is not only a successful period for you but for the family as a whole. The family is elevated in status in the year ahead. Perhaps more importantly, family is supporting your career goals. This year we don't see the usual tension between family and career. The family is on board. Perhaps they see your success as a family project.

Your family planet Jupiter in your career house shows that the distinctions between home and career are blurred this year. Perhaps you pursue career goals from the comfort of your home. Others might make the office more homely.

Your family planet moving through your 10th house favours careers that involve residential real estate, psychology, restaurants, the food business, hotels and motels. Family connections also seem very helpful in your career goals. In some cases, this transit could be read as that being there for the family *is* the actual career this year.

Love and Social Life

Saturn's move into your 7th house of love last year started to complicate the love life, as we mentioned earlier. Existing relationships are getting tested. Though this is not usually comfortable, it is a good thing. It is through these kinds of testings that we know whether love is real or not. Many of you got involved in serious relationships in recent years, especially in 2022, and you have been in a kind of honeymoon period. Now you'll see how deep the love goes.

For singles, we see another love complication. We see two love interests with radically different types of people. One interest is very idealistic and with someone who is not especially materialistic, but more artistic and spiritual. The other love interest is someone more corporate, more materialistic, more down to earth. You are not sure whom to choose. Both have their strong points. The spiritual person is probably more fun to be with, but the corporate person is a better provider. The ideal would be to find someone who is poetic, musical and spiritual but who is also an entrepreneur! Not so easy to find in one person.

Saturn moving through your 7th house also has other meanings. You won't socialize as much as usual. You will be more choosy as to the parties and events that you attend. You would prefer less frequent but higher quality socializing than merely attending every single event.

Singles are not likely to marry this year, nor should they. However, there are many opportunities for love affairs.

Self-improvement

Spiritual Neptune has been in your 7th house of love for many years now. Your intuition is being trained in love and social matters. Also, as we have mentioned in previous years, Neptune is leading you to the spiritual dimensions of love. The perfect love that you seek is already there in your spirit. The reality is that you are loved perfectly every second of every day, but you have to open up to the vibration of that energy.

Neptune is leading you to the understanding that we don't get love from the world but are channels for bringing it into the world. By the cosmic law, as you project love into the world love will come back to you, one way or another. Perhaps you won't see it immediately, but you'll see it eventually.

Neptune in your 7th house has an obvious meaning that when you are in love, or in a state of love, you are close to the divine and able to receive its messages.

The Sun is your spiritual planet. He is a fast-moving planet and during the year he will move through every sign and house in your Horoscope. Thus, there are many short-term trends in spirituality, depending on where the Sun is and the kinds of aspects he is receiving, that are best dealt with in the monthly reports. The Sun as the spiritual planet favours the solar religions: Christianity, Krishna, Surya and Kriya yoga. Those of you who study Kabbalah would benefit from meditations on the sixth sefira, the sefira of Tifareth.

For more information on astrology, healing and spiritual topics, please visit my blog at www.spiritual-stories.com.

Month-by-month Forecasts

January

Best Days Overall: 1, 2, 10, 11, 18, 19, 28, 29
Most Stressful Days Overall: 8, 9, 14, 15, 21, 22
Best Days for Love: 7, 8, 9, 14, 15, 24, 27, 28
Best Days for Money: 1, 2, 3, 4, 8, 9, 10, 11, 18, 19, 27, 28, 29, 30, 31
Best Days for Career: 1, 2, 9, 18, 19, 21, 22, 30, 31

Although Saturn is still making a stressful aspect to you, health and energy should be good this month as the short-term planets are relieving distress and giving you energy. You can enhance the health even further in the ways mentioned in the yearly report.

The month ahead is basically happy. You are in the midst of a yearly personal pleasure peak. This one should be even stronger than usual as your 5th house is very powerful: 60 per cent of the planets are either there or moving through there this month, a big percentage. This is very much a party month. Even the love life seems less serious than usual. Your chart favours love affairs rather than serious committed love this month. It favours fun kinds of relationships. The new Moon of the 11th occurs in the 5th house and is an especially fun kind of day. And, as the days go by, issues involving children or children figures in your life will be clarified. This is also true for issues involving your personal creativity.

Virgos are always interested in health but after the 20th even more so. The Sun's move into your 6th house on the 20th favours spiritual-healing techniques. Pluto will move into your 6th house of health shortly afterwards, on the 22nd. This favours detox regimes. Good health is not about adding things to the body but about getting rid of things that don't belong there.

Although finance does not seem a big issue this month, nevertheless it seems good that Venus, your financial planet, will be in your 4th house until the 23rd, signalling good family support and someone who spends more on the home and family. The financial planet in the sign of Sagittarius shows someone who earns freely and spends freely. The danger comes from a tendency to overspend and impulse buy. This will change after the 23rd as Venus moves into conservative Capricorn. Although you are still a speculator, it will be a more conservative kind of speculation. Your speculations will tend to be well thought out and well hedged. Not casino-type gambles. You will spend but you will want value for your money. The financial judgement is sound. Further, from the 23rd onwards Venus will start making nice aspects to Jupiter, which would show financial expansion, and also good family support.

Love is mixed this month. There is no clear pattern here. Saturn in your 7th house is testing a current relationship, and this will go on for the rest of the year ahead. If your relationship can survive this Saturn transit it can pretty much survive anything. For singles and the young attached this transit would show a tendency to love affairs rather than serious committed love, as we have mentioned.

February

Best Days Overall: 6, 7, 14, 15, 24, 25
Most Stressful Days Overall: 4, 5, 10, 11, 17, 18
Best Days for Love: 2, 3, 6, 7, 10, 11, 17, 20, 26, 27, 29
Best Days for Money: 6, 7, 14, 15, 17, 18, 24, 25, 26, 27, 28
Best Days for Career: 8, 9, 17, 18, 29

A busy month ahead, Virgo, but productive. The main headline this month is the power in your 6th house of health and work. You are always focused on health but this month even more so. Over half of the planets are either in your 6th house or moving through there. Since health is reasonably good this month (though not as good as last month), this excess focus on health can show a tendency to hypochondria – a tendency to magnify small things into big things. You need to be careful about this. Most Virgos are employed. But if you are one of those rare ones that are unemployed, this month will change the situation. You have many, many job opportunities. But, even if you are already employed, there will be opportunities for overtime and side jobs.

The new Moon of the 9th also occurs in your 6th house, enhancing your already strong productivity. Issues involving health and work will clarify day by day until the next new Moon next month. All the information that you need to make good decisions in these areas will come to you very naturally and normally as the days go by.

Children and children figures in your life are having a robust and prosperous financial life. Financial issues involving the children will also clarify as the days go by.

Your financial planet Venus is still in your 5th house and the sign of Capricorn until the 17th. This is a positive for finance as it shows good financial judgement, and happy money. You earn in happy ways and spend on happy things. You are enjoying the wealth that you have. On the 17th Venus moves into Aquarius and your 6th house. This shows earning in the old-fashioned way, through your work and productive service. As we've mentioned, there are many opportunities for extra earnings this month.

On the 19th the Sun will enter your 7th house of love and romance and you'll begin a yearly love and social peak. Singles have many romantic opportunities. Marriage is not seen this month, and probably not this year either, but singles will date more and attend more parties and gatherings. The Sun's move into your 7th house signals an attraction for spiritual-type people. This just emphasizes a tendency that has been there for many years with Neptune's presence in your 7th house.

Mercury, the ruler of your Horoscope, enters your 7th house on the 23rd and will be there for the rest of the month ahead. This also indicates an active love and social life. It shows more personal popularity as well. You are there for your friends and current relationship and you put their interests ahead of your own. Mercury is far from his home in the 7th house and this could weaken your self-esteem and self-confidence. You could feel like a stranger in a strange land, as if you were in exile. But no matter, with the Western sector of your Horoscope very strong at the moment, this is a time to let others have their way, so long as it isn't destructive. Strong self-esteem and self-confidence aren't necessary these days. Your good comes to you from others and not so much from your personal skills, initiative or confidence.

March

Best Days Overall: 6, 7, 14, 15, 24, 25
Most Stressful Days Overall: 2, 3, 9, 10, 15, 16, 29, 30
Best Days for Love: 1, 7, 8, 9, 10, 17, 18, 27, 28
Best Days for Money: 4, 5, 7, 8, 13, 14, 17, 18, 22, 23, 24, 25, 26, 27, 28
Best Days for Career: 1, 9, 11, 15, 16, 19, 20, 29, 30

Health needs a lot more attention this month. You have two long-term planets in stressful aspect to you and the short-term planets are also joining in. So, make sure to get enough rest. You like to work, and this is good, but make sure to rest when tired, and try not to overwork. Your body will give you the message.

You are still in the midst of a yearly love and social peak, and love seems relatively happy. Mercury travels with your love planet Neptune on the 16th and 17th and these are excellent romantic days. The Sun will also be travelling with Neptune on the 15th and the 16th. This is good for romance but is especially good for your spiritual life as it will bring spiritual insights and growth to you.

A lunar eclipse on the 25th is relatively mild in its effect on you, as far as eclipses go; however, it won't hurt to reduce your schedule during that time. This eclipse occurs in your money house and will force important and dramatic financial changes. Probably your financial thinking and planning have not been realistic and the events of the eclipse will reveal that. Changes are necessary.

Every lunar eclipse affects friends and brings personal dramas to their lives. This one is no different. Also, it will tend to test your computers and high-tech gadgetry. They can behave erratically. Sometimes repairs or replacements are necessary. Make sure your antivirus and anti-hacking software is up to date. Back up important files. Avoid opening emails from people you don't know or suspicious attachments.

This eclipse will bring important financial changes to parents and parent figures as well.

April

Best Days Overall: 1, 2, 9, 10, 18, 19, 20, 28, 29
Most Stressful Days Overall: 5, 6, 11, 12
Best Days for Love: 5, 6, 7, 8, 14, 15, 16, 24, 25, 17, 27, 28
Best Days for Money: 1, 2, 7, 8, 9, 10, 16, 17, 18, 19, 21, 22, 27, 28
Best Days for Career: 7, 8, 11, 12, 16, 17, 26, 27

A very strong solar eclipse on the 8th is the main headline this month. This eclipse is strong for many reasons. First, it is a total eclipse. Secondly, it impacts other planets, important ones, and thus it affects many other areas of life and also important people in your life. There will be two more eclipses this year but none as strong as this one, and you should take the same precautions this month as you would if you heard that there was a hurricane or bad storm coming to your neighbourhood. There is no need to panic, of course, that never helps, but common-sense precautions should be taken. Stay close to home, avoid unnecessary driving or trips, reschedule any events you can for another time, read a book, watch a movie, meditate.

The eclipse occurs in your 8th house of regeneration and this gives many meanings. The spouse, partner or current love experiences financial dramas and needs to make important financial changes. It looks to me that the changes will be good ones as he or she is in a prosperous time right now. This eclipse can bring dramas that involve taxes or insurance payments. It can bring psychological encounters with death, and these can take many forms. Perhaps you experience a close call or a near-death kind of experience. Perhaps you have dreams of death, or perhaps you hear of the death of someone that you know or of some celebrity that you like. The cosmos is forcing you to look deeper into this matter. Sometimes it is just a love message from above showing you that life is short and can end at any time and you need to be more serious about life. You need to be focused on the reason that you were born.

Mercury, the ruler of your Horoscope, is directly impacted by this eclipse. Thus, you need to review your self, your self-concept, your opinion of yourself and the way that you want others to think of you. This is a healthy thing to do periodically, but this month the events of the eclipse force the issue. You don't have much of a choice in the matter. This re-evaluation will manifest as changes in your image and wardrobe changes over the coming months. You will be presenting a whole new look to others. Sometimes this kind of eclipse forces a detox of the physical body. This is not to be confused with disease, although sometimes the symptoms are similar. This is just the body getting rid of things that don't belong there. (What we've said above also applies to parents and parent figures.)

Career changes are likely now. Usually, one doesn't completely change the career, but there are changes in the way that it is pursued. Sometimes these changes happen because of shake-ups in the hierarchy of your company. Sometimes these changes happen because the government changes the rules for your company or industry.

Since Venus, your financial planet, is directly impacted by this eclipse, important financial changes are happening for you. A course correction in finance is necessary. It's usually not comfortable while it's happening, but the end result is usually good. Venus is also the ruler of your 9th house. Thus, your religious, theological and philosophical beliefs will get tested by the events of the eclipse. Again, while this is not comfortable the end result will be good. Some of your beliefs will be discarded entirely, as they are little more than superstition. Some will get amended. The eclipse will force you to think more deeply on these issues. In coming months you could live your life in a whole different way.

Every solar eclipse affects your spiritual life, because the Sun is your spiritual planet. Important spiritual changes are happening now, and could involve your practice, teachings and teachers. Your overall attitudes to spirituality will change. Guru figures in your life will have personal dramas – it can be disconcerting to see them affected by mundane events. There are probably spectacular shake-ups and upheavals in spiritual or charitable organizations that you are involved with.

May

Best Days Overall: 7, 8, 15, 16, 25, 26
Most Stressful Days Overall: 2, 3, 4, 9, 10, 23, 24, 30, 31
Best Days for Love: 2, 3, 4, 7, 8, 12, 15, 16, 22, 27, 28, 30, 31
Best Days for Money: 7, 8, 15, 16, 17, 18, 19, 26, 27, 28
Best Days for Career: 5, 6, 9, 10, 14, 25, 26

The career changes brought on by last month's eclipse seem to be very good ones, and Jupiter's move into your 10th house of career on the 26th initiates tremendous career success for the rest of the year ahead. From the 20th onwards, as the Sun also moves into your 10th house, you begin a yearly career peak. You have career peaks every year, of course, but this one will be much stronger than previous ones and will last longer. We don't see the usual conflict between home and career in this year's chart. Both areas of life are cooperating with each other. Family, and especially a parent or parent figure, is very supportive of your career. Perhaps it is seen as a family project and not something personal. The lines between home and career are blurred these days. Perhaps you will be working on your career from the comforts of home, or you will make your office more like home.

Finances should be good this month as your financial planet will be in your beneficent 9th house until the 23rd. Venus travels with Uranus on the 18th and 19th, which often brings sudden and unexpected money. This can come from work or from a job opportunity. On the 23rd Venus crosses your Mid-heaven and enters your 10th house. This too is good for finance as Venus will be very elevated in the Horoscope and is in your chart's most powerful position. It shows the financial favour of bosses, parents or parent figures. It shows that your good career reputation brings earning opportunities to you. Often it shows pay rises, official or unofficial.

Your 9th house is very strong until the 20th, and there is a great focus on religion, theology and philosophy. A good juicy theological discussion or the visit of a guru is more enticing than a night out on the town. This is an excellent month for college students as they seem successful in their studies.

The new Moon of the 8th occurs in your 9th house. It brings happy social experiences, but, more importantly, it will clarify issues involving higher education, religion, theology and philosophy. This seems important as last month's eclipse probably created confusion in these areas. Day by day until the next new Moon next month, your philosophical and theological thinking will start to clarify.

Health needs more watching from the 20th onwards. As always, make sure to get enough rest. Enhance the health in the ways mentioned in the yearly report.

June

Best Days Overall: 3, 4, 12, 13, 22, 23, 30
Most Stressful Days Overall: 5, 6, 19, 20, 26, 27
Best Days for Love: 5, 6, 8, 16, 17, 18, 26, 27
Best Days for Money: 5, 6, 14, 15, 16, 17, 24, 26, 27
Best Days for Career: 5, 6, 15, 16, 17, 26, 27

You are still very much in a yearly career peak this month and much outer success is happening. Family and family connections are boosting the career or playing important roles in the career. You are there for your family, and family is supporting the career.

Health needs watching until the 20th, but it won't hurt to keep an eye on the health after the 20th as well. Don't allow yourself to get overtired or low in energy. It might be wise to book a massage, reflexology session or acupuncture treatment this month. These therapies tend to boost the energy, which is what is needed. You can further enhance your health in the ways mentioned in the yearly report.

Be more mindful on the physical plane on the 1st and 2nd. A happy job opportunity can come to you those days as well.

Mercury travels with Jupiter on the 3rd and 4th and this should bring increased earnings and good family support. Mercury will be in your 10th house until the 17th. This is another indication of success which we discussed earlier. Mercury elevated in your Horoscope shows your elevation in the world. On the 17th Mercury moves into your 11th house, as does Venus. On the 20th the Sun moves into your 11th house as well, and you should see a dramatic improvement in health and energy after the 20th. You are less career focused and more socially focused from the 20th onwards. This social life is more about Platonic kinds of friendships rather than necessarily romantic ones. It is a very good time to be more involved with friends, groups, group activities, and trade and professional organizations. Such activities are not only fun in their own right but boost both career and the bottom line. Your financial planet in the 11th house shows the fulfilment of fondest hopes and wishes on the financial level. And, when this happens you will most likely create a new set of fondest hopes and wishes.

When the 11th house is this strong people often have their Horoscopes cast. There is great interest not only in astrology but in astronomy, science and technology in general over this period. Your financial planet in the 11th house shows that you probably spend on these things, but you can also earn from them.

Though marriage is still not on the cards, the love life is much improved this month, especially from the 17th onwards. Singles will go out more, date more and attend more parties and gatherings. There can be romantic opportunities but there is no need to rush into anything.

July

Best Days Overall: 1, 9, 10, 11, 19, 20, 27, 28
Most Stressful Days Overall: 2, 3, 17, 18, 23, 24, 29, 30, 31
Best Days for Love: 5, 6, 16, 17, 18, 23, 24, 25, 26
Best Days for Money: 2, 3, 5, 6, 12, 13, 14, 15, 16, 17, 18, 21, 22, 25, 26, 29, 30
Best Days for Career: 2, 3, 7, 8, 17, 18, 27, 28, 29, 30, 31

Three long-term planets are in stressful alignment with you early on this month, and on the 20th Mars will join the party and make stressful aspects to you. So, health needs more attention from the 20th onwards. Career is successful and is likely taking up much energy. You probably can't avoid the demands of the career. However, you can work in a steadier way and take breaks when you are tired. Keep your focus on the important things in your life and let go of the trivia. This will save a lot of energy. Listen to the messages your body gives you, and rest when you are tired. Enhance the health in the ways mentioned in the yearly report. This month I would give more attention to the heart.

Mars will be in your 10th house of career from the 20th onwards. This shows not only more career activity, but also a lot of turmoil involved with the career. Perhaps bosses or authority figures involved with your career undergo surgery or have other personal dramas. Surgery could be recommended to a parent or parent figure as well.

Though your love planet Neptune goes retrograde on the 2nd, complicating the love life, love still seems happy until the 22nd. Neptune is receiving wonderful aspects until then. However, the social life is slowing down a bit. It is not stopping but is slowing down. Now and for the next few months, this is a time for gaining clarity in love and social matters. Review your love life and see where things can be improved. Later on, when Neptune starts to move forward again, you can implement your improvements.

Your financial planet will be in the sign of Cancer until the 11th and then moves into Leo, your 12th house. Finances should be good this month. While Venus is in Cancer you can be too moody about finance and about spending. Make sure to sleep on things before making a decision. After the 11th and Venus's move into Leo, you become more speculative and risk-taking. When the financial intuition is good, which it seems to be, these things work out. You seem more charitable and generous from the 11th onwards. Friends prosper from the 11th onwards.

On the 22nd your spiritual planet the Sun moves into your 12th house where he is very strong. It is his own sign and house. You are in a time of spiritual growth. Your focus on spirituality is not only good in its own right but it will boost the bottom line and improve your personal appearance.

The planetary power is now mostly in the Eastern sector of self. So, you are in a good point in the planetary cycle for pursuing your path of personal happiness. Personal independence is stronger now than it has been all year. Your happiness is up to you. Make the changes that need to be made to enhance your happiness.

With your love planet retrograde, it is good to focus on other kinds of social relationships, friendships and Platonic kinds of relationships. These seem active and happy.

August

Best Days Overall: 5, 6, 7, 15, 16, 23, 24, 25
Most Stressful Days Overall: 13, 14, 19, 20, 26, 27
Best Days for Love: 2, 8, 12, 17, 18, 19, 20, 28, 29
Best Days for Money: 8, 9, 17, 18, 27, 29
Best Days for Career: 5, 6, 7, 12, 21, 22, 26, 27, 30, 31

A happy and prosperous month ahead, Virgo. Enjoy. You are entering a time of maximum personal independence and the cosmos supports your efforts at personal happiness. The problem is that with Mercury retrograde from the 4th to the 25th, you are not sure of what personal happiness is. However, once this is clarified in your mind, it is the perfect time to make the changes that need to be made after the 25th, when Mercury moves forward again.

The power in your own sign from the 22nd onwards is great for health, personal appearance and finance. Not so great for love and romance, though. With Mercury, the ruler of your Horoscope, and Neptune your love planet both retrograde, neither you nor the beloved are sure of what you want. This really complicates the love life. Both of you have serious doubts. On top of this, you and the beloved don't seem in agreement on things. You have diametrically opposite views of things. This often creates conflict. However, if you can bridge your differences, respect the other's point of view as being valid from their perspective, the relationship can become stronger than ever. Both of your perspectives are true.

Career is still wonderful, but with Mercury retrograde most of the month, important career decisions should not be made. Things might not be as they seem. Study things more, resolve your doubts. By the 25th there should be more clarity in the career and a proper decision can be made.

Though Mars is still in stressful aspect to you, health is much improved over the last month; the short-term planets are in harmonious aspect and nullifying the effect of the long-term planets. Still, health needs watching. As always, make sure to get enough rest and to maintain high energy levels. Enhance the health in the ways mentioned in the yearly report and continue to give attention to the heart.

Finances seem excellent this month, especially from the 5th to the 29th. Your financial planet Venus will be in your own sign, bringing windfalls and happy financial opportunities. Money pursues you rather than vice versa. The personal appearance shines and you dress more expensively and beautifully. You have the image of a prosperous person.

With the Sun in your sign from the 22nd onwards you are entering a yearly personal pleasure peak. But the pleasure seems more physical – these are the pleasures of the body. A good time for getting the body and image in the shape that you want. A time to pamper the body now.

September

Best Days Overall: 7, 8, 16, 17, 24, 25
Most Stressful Days Overall: 9, 10, 16, 17, 22, 23
Best Days for Love: 4, 5, 8, 14, 15, 16, 17, 23, 24, 25
Best Days for Money: 4, 5, 6, 14, 15, 23, 24
Best Days for Career: 1, 12, 13, 21, 22, 23

You remain in a yearly personal pleasure peak this month until the 22nd. But a lunar eclipse on the 18th complicates things. This eclipse affects you strongly, so, as always, take a more relaxed, easy schedule. Stressful activities that can be put off are better rescheduled for another time.

The short-term planets are basically kind to you this month and Mars moves away from his stressful aspect on the 5th. So, health and energy should be better than last month.

Love has been complicated for some time now, and the eclipse of the 18th complicates it even further. It occurs in your 7th house of love and will test your current relationship. Sometimes the problems are not with the relationship itself but are because of personal dramas in the life of the spouse, partner or current love. Generally, repressed grievances and resentments, dirty laundry in the relationship, surface so that they can be dealt with. Often you are not even aware of these grievances, but now you find out. A basically sound relationship will survive this kind of eclipse but one that is fundamentally flawed is in trouble.

Every lunar eclipse brings dramas in the lives of friends and this one is no different. Often these personal dramas are life-changing in nature. Computer equipment, high-tech gadgetry, software, etc., can behave erratically while the eclipse is in effect. Sometimes repairs or replacements are necessary. Technology is a wonderful thing when things are working but hell when they're not. Take the normal precautions with your computer. Back up important files, make sure your antivirus and anti-hacking software is up to date. Avoid opening suspicious attachments, even if they are from people that you know. Avoid suspicious websites.

Jupiter, your home and family planet, is sideswiped by this eclipse. Happily, it is not a direct hit, but it can bring minor home repairs, and minor dramas in the lives of family members.

October

Best Days Overall: 9, 10, 17, 18, 26, 27, 28
Most Stressful Days Overall: 6, 7, 8, 13, 14, 19, 20
Best Days for Love: 4, 5, 13, 14, 23, 24, 25, 31
Best Days for Money: 1, 2, 4, 5, 11, 12, 13, 14, 19, 20, 24, 25, 29, 30
Best Days for Career: 1, 12, 13, 19, 20, 21, 22, 31

A solar eclipse on the 2nd, though not as strong as the one in April, is still pretty powerful as it impacts other planets in your Horoscope. It not only affects you but other important people in your life. So, as always, take a more relaxed, easy schedule while the eclipse is in effect. Do what needs to be done and reschedule anything else for another time.

This eclipse occurs in your money house and will bring important and dramatic financial changes – not only to you personally but also for the spouse, partner or current love. The events of the eclipse will show you where your financial thinking and planning have been amiss.

Mercury, the ruler of your Horoscope and your career planet, is directly impacted by this eclipse. There is a need to take stock of yourself, your self-image, your self-concept, your opinion of yourself. This will lead to a new wardrobe and new presentation to others in the coming months. And this not only applies to you but to the parents and parent figures in your life as well. A detox of the body would not be a surprise. But this shouldn't be confused with illness, though the symptoms are often similar. It is just the body getting rid of what should not be there. This is so for parents and parent figures as well.

Career changes are also in order these days. These changes are likely to be good ones as your career seems very successful. Most likely blockages and obstructions to your progress will be blasted away, one way or another. There can be shake-ups, reshuffles, perhaps resignations in the hierarchy of your company. The government can change the rules governing your industry or company. So, there is a need to pursue the career in a different way.

The impact of this eclipse on Mars, the ruler of your 8th house of regeneration, is more serious. It can bring psychological encounters with death and perhaps near-death kinds of experiences. Close calls. The dark angel is letting you know that he is around. The good part of this is that your understanding of death should deepen. When we understand death, we understand life.

Although the eclipse shakes up your financial life, the month ahead still seems prosperous as you are in the midst of a yearly financial peak.

Planetary retrograde activity hits its maximum extent of the year briefly, from the 9th to the 11th. Half the planets will be retrograde over this period. You probably won't be able to avoid delays, but you can minimize them by being perfect in all that you do.

November

Best Days Overall: 5, 6, 14, 15, 22, 23, 24
Most Stressful Days Overall: 3, 4, 10, 11, 16, 17, 29, 30
Best Days for Love: 2, 3, 4, 10, 11, 12, 13, 19, 22, 23, 29
Best Days for Money: 3, 4, 8, 9, 12, 13, 16, 17, 22, 23, 25, 26, 27
Best Days for Career: 3, 12, 13, 16, 17, 20, 21, 29, 30

Your 3rd house of communication is very strong until the 21st. This is a great month for attending lectures, seminars and generally expanding your knowledge base. It is a wonderful aspect for students below college level; they seem successful in their studies. The mental faculties are much enhanced this month. Learning is easier.

Your love planet is still retrograde, but love seems much happier than usual this month as Neptune is receiving very positive aspects. Romantic opportunities are happening, though there is still a need to go slow in love. No need to rush into anything just yet.

Your financial planet is in Sagittarius, your 4th house, until the 11th. You earn freely and spend freely. You have a happy-go-lucky attitude to money. Excessive risk-taking and perhaps overspending are the main dangers here. Until the 11th you are an impulse kind of spender. On the 11th, as your financial planet moves into Capricorn, the financial judgement becomes more sound and reliable. Now, you don't rely on luck but on steady, slow, secure step-by-step methods to attain wealth. This is a good time to set up disciplined investment and savings plans. You will spend but you will be more cautious about it and want value for money. If you speculate it will be in a well-hedged kind of way.

Your financial planet in your 5th house from the 11th shows happy money. You earn in happy ways and you spend on happy things. It is a time to enjoy the wealth that you have.

Mars moves through your 12th house of spirituality from the 4th onwards. This shows various things. First, it indicates a need to express your spiritual ideals and knowledge in physical actions. It is a time for acting on your ideals. Also, it shows that spiritual progress will happen by ridding the mind of the things that block it. It's not about adding things to the mind but getting rid of things that don't belong there.

December

Best Days Overall: 2, 3, 4, 11, 12, 20, 21, 30, 31
Most Stressful Days Overall: 1, 7, 8, 13, 14, 27, 28, 29
Best Days for Love: 2, 3, 4, 7, 8, 13, 14, 16, 22, 23, 24, 26
Best Days for Money: 2, 3, 4, 6, 13, 14, 22, 23, 24
Best Days for Career: 3, 12, 13, 14, 20, 21, 29, 30

The power this month is in your 4th house of home and family. So, though career is still very successful, this month is a home and family month. The pleasures of home and hearth appeal to you. This is a good month for those of you who are exploring psychological-type therapies, as much progress will be made. Many deep psychological insights are coming to you. When the 4th house is strong people tend to be more nostalgic. They remember the past and perhaps yearn for it. Your spiritual practice is also bringing up old memories. Those of you who are deep into the spiritual path are remembering past lives as well. Even those starting out on the path are remembering past incarnations, but probably not in a conscious way. They would experience it as irrational fears, longings, attractions or repulsions.

Mars is still in your 12th house of spirituality all month, so keep in mind our discussion of this last month.

Love is very much improved this month. You love planet Neptune, who has been retrograde for many months, starts to move forward on the 7th and there is a new-found clarity about love, and about a current relationship. The social judgement is much improved. Love decisions will likely be good ones. Love will go better after the 21st than before.

Health needs watching until the 21st so, as always, make sure to get enough rest. Enhance the health in the ways mentioned in the yearly report. Health will dramatically improve from the 21st onwards as the short-term planets start to make harmonious aspects to you.

Venus, your money planet, is still in your 5th house until the 7th. This shows, as we saw last month, happy money. Money that is spent in happy ways and earned in happy ways. Money is spent on children and children figures and can also come from that source. On the 7th Venus moves into Aquarius and your 6th house of health and work. On the 7th and 8th money can come from trading, buying and selling. But the main message here is that from the 7th onwards you earn in the old-fashioned ways, through hard work and productive service.

Libra

THE SCALES

Birthdays from
23rd September to
22nd October

Personality Profile

LIBRA AT A GLANCE

Element – Air

Ruling Planet – Venus
  Career Planet – Moon
  Love Planet – Mars
  Money Planet – Pluto
  Planet of Communications – Jupiter
  Planet of Health and Work – Neptune
  Planet of Home and Family Life – Saturn
  Planet of Spirituality and Good Fortune – Mercury

Colours – blue, jade green

Colours that promote love, romance and social harmony – carmine, red, scarlet

Colours that promote earning power – burgundy, red-violet, violet

Gems – carnelian, chrysolite, coral, emerald, jade, opal, quartz, white marble

Metal – copper

Scents – almond, rose, vanilla, violet

Quality – cardinal (= activity)

Qualities most needed for balance – a sense of self, self-reliance, independence

Strongest virtues – social grace, charm, tact, diplomacy

Deepest needs – love, romance, social harmony

Characteristic to avoid – violating what is right in order to be socially accepted

Signs of greatest overall compatibility – Gemini, Aquarius

Signs of greatest overall incompatibility – Aries, Cancer, Capricorn

Sign most helpful to career – Cancer

Sign most helpful for emotional support – Capricorn

Sign most helpful financially – Scorpio

Sign best for marriage and/or partnerships – Aries

Sign most helpful for creative projects – Aquarius

Best Sign to have fun with – Aquarius

Signs most helpful in spiritual matters – Gemini, Virgo

Best day of the week – Friday

Understanding a Libra

In the sign of Libra the universal mind – the soul – expresses its genius for relationships, that is, its power to harmonize diverse elements in a unified, organic way. Libra is the soul's power to express beauty in all of its forms. And where is beauty if not within relationships? Beauty does not exist in isolation. Beauty arises out of comparison – out of the just relationship between different parts. Without a fair and harmonious relationship there is no beauty, whether in art, manners, ideas or the social or political forum.

There are two faculties humans have that exalt them above the animal kingdom: their rational faculty (expressed in the signs of Gemini and Aquarius) and their aesthetic faculty, exemplified by Libra. Without an aesthetic sense we would be little more than intelligent barbarians. Libra is the civilizing instinct or urge of the soul.

Beauty is the essence of what Librans are all about. They are here to beautify the world. One could discuss Librans' social grace, their sense of balance and fair play, their ability to see and love another person's point of view – but this would be to miss their central asset: their desire for beauty.

No one – no matter how alone he or she seems to be – exists in isolation. The universe is one vast collaboration of beings. Librans, more than most, understand this and understand the spiritual laws that make relationships bearable and enjoyable.

A Libra is always the unconscious (and in some cases conscious) civilizer, harmonizer and artist. This is a Libra's deepest urge and greatest genius. Librans love instinctively to bring people together, and they are uniquely qualified to do so. They have a knack for seeing what unites people – the things that attract and bind rather than separate individuals.

Finance

In financial matters Librans can seem frivolous and illogical to others. This is because Librans appear to be more concerned with earning money for others than for themselves. But there is a logic to this financial attitude. Librans know that everything and everyone is connected and that it is impossible to help another to prosper without also prospering yourself. Since enhancing their partner's income and position tends to strengthen their relationship, Librans choose to do so. What could be more fun than building a relationship? You will rarely find a Libra enriching him- or herself at someone else's expense.

Scorpio is the ruler of Libra's solar 2nd house of money, giving Libra unusual insight into financial matters – and the power to focus on these matters in a way that disguises a seeming indifference. In fact, many other signs come to Librans for financial advice and guidance.

Given their social grace, Librans often spend great sums of money on entertaining and organizing social events. They also like to help others when they are in need. Librans would go out of their way to help a friend in dire straits, even if they have to borrow from others to do so. However, Librans are also very careful to pay back any debts they owe, and like to make sure they never have to be reminded to do so.

Career and Public Image

Publicly, Librans like to appear as nurturers. Their friends and acquaintances are their family and they wield political power in parental ways. They also like bosses who are paternal or maternal.

The sign of Cancer is on Libra's 10th career house cusp; the Moon is Libra's career planet. The Moon is by far the speediest, most changeable planet in the horoscope. It alone among all the planets travels through the entire zodiac – all twelve signs and houses – every month. This is an important key to the way in which Librans approach their careers, and also to what they need to do to maximize their career potential. The Moon is the planet of moods and feelings – Librans need a career in which their emotions can have free expression. This is why so many Librans are involved in the creative arts. Libra's ambitions wax and wane with the Moon. They tend to wield power according to their mood.

The Moon 'rules' the masses – and that is why Libra's highest goal is to achieve a mass kind of acclaim and popularity. Librans who achieve fame cultivate the public as other people cultivate a lover or friend. Librans can be very flexible – and often fickle – in their career and ambitions. On the other hand, they can achieve their ends in a great variety of ways. They are not stuck in one attitude or with one way of doing things.

Love and Relationships

Librans express their true genius in love. In love you could not find a partner more romantic, more seductive or more fair. If there is one thing that is sure to destroy a relationship – sure to block your love from flowing – it is injustice or imbalance between lover and beloved. If one party is giving too much or taking too much, resentment is sure to surface at some time or other. Librans are careful about this. If anything, Librans might err on the side of giving more, but never giving less.

If you are in love with a Libra, make sure you keep the aura of romance alive. Do all the little things – candle-lit dinners, travel to exotic locales, flowers and small gifts. Give things that are beautiful, not necessarily expensive. Send cards. Ring regularly even if you have nothing in particular to say. The niceties are very important to a Libra. Your relationship is a work of art: make it beautiful and your Libran lover will appreciate it. If you are creative about it, he or she will appreciate it even more; for this is how your Libra will behave towards you.

Librans like their partners to be aggressive and even a bit self-willed. They know that these are qualities they sometimes lack and so they like their partners to have them. In relationships, however, Librans can be very aggressive – but always in a subtle and charming way! Librans are determined in their efforts to charm the object of their desire – and this determination can be very pleasant if you are on the receiving end.

Home and Domestic Life

Since Librans are such social creatures, they do not particularly like mundane domestic duties. They like a well-organized home – clean and neat with everything needful present – but housework is a chore and a burden, one of the unpleasant tasks in life that must be done, the quicker the better. If a Libra has enough money – and sometimes even if not – he or she will prefer to pay someone else to take care of the daily household chores. However, Librans like gardening; they love to have flowers and plants in the home.

A Libra's home is modern, and furnished in excellent taste. You will find many paintings and sculptures there. Since Librans like to be with friends and family, they enjoy entertaining at home and they make great hosts.

Capricorn is on the cusp of Libra's 4th solar house of home and family. Saturn, the planet of law, order, limits and discipline, rules Libra's domestic affairs. If Librans want their home life to be supportive and happy they need to develop some of the virtues of Saturn – order, organization and discipline. Librans, being so creative and so intensely in need of harmony, can tend to be too lax in the home and too permissive with their children. Too much of this is not always good; children need freedom but they also need limits.

Horoscope for 2024

Major Trends

Pluto's major transition out of Capricorn and into Aquarius this year is a positive for your health, Libra. Overall health and energy should improve dramatically in the year ahead. More on this later.

Jupiter has been in your 8th house of regeneration since last year and remains there until May 26 of the current year. Thus, you are in a more erotic time in your life. It is also a very nice financial transit for the spouse, partner or current love. Jupiter moves into Gemini, your 9th house, on May 26 and stays there well into 2025. This is a wonderful transit for college-level students or for those applying to college. It shows good fortune and success in your studies. If you are involved in legal actions, there is good fortune in that too. This transit will also bring more foreign travel.

Pluto's gradual move into Aquarius, only beginning this year, signals important changes in the financial life and financial attitudes. More details later.

Two eclipses will occur in your own sign in the year ahead. The first is a lunar eclipse on March 25 and the second is a solar eclipse on October 2. These will bring personal shake-ups and can also bring changes to your paths of personal happiness. The events of the eclipses could reveal that your thinking has been unrealistic. More importantly they will bring a need to re-define yourself, your image and self-concept. This will produce changes in your image and presentation and the way that you want others to think of you.

Your most important areas of interest this year are home and family until January 22 and from September 3 to November 20; children, fun and creativity from January 22 to September 3 and from November 20 to the end of the year; health and work; sex, psychology and occult studies until May 26; and religion, philosophy, theology, higher studies and foreign travel from May 26 onwards.

Your paths of greatest fulfilment this year will be love and romance; sex, psychology and occult studies until May 26; and religion, philosophy, theology, higher learning and foreign travel from May 26 to the end of the year.

Health

(Please note that this is an astrological perspective on health and not a medical one. In days of yore there was no difference, both these perspectives were identical. But these days there could be quite a difference. For a medical perspective, please consult your doctor or health practitioner.)

As we mentioned above, health and energy should improve this year. Pluto is moving away from a stressful aspect to you into a harmonious one. This is a major positive shift. The other long-term planets are either in harmonious aspect with you or leaving you alone. Health should be good. If you have any pre-existing conditions they seem better controlled these days. Sure, there will be times in the year where health and energy are less easy than usual, but these are not trends for the year but temporary blips caused by the transit of short-term planets. When the planets pass on your normally good health and energy return.

Your 6th house of health is a house of power this year, indicating a strong focus on health. Basically this is a good thing, but in your case it could lead to overkill. There could be a tendency to hypochondria, a tendency to magnify little things into big things. You need to be careful about that.

Good though your health is, you can make it better. Give more attention to the following – the vulnerable areas of your Horoscope this year (the reflex points are shown in the chart opposite):

- The kidneys and hips are always important for Libra and the reflexes are shown above. Regular hip massage should be part of your usual health regime. This will not only strengthen the kidneys and hips but also the lower back as well. The back is important this year.

- The feet. Regular foot massage will not only strengthen the feet but the entire body as well. There are gadgets that automatically massage the feet and this could be a good investment for you. There are also gadgets that give foot whirlpool treatments and these too seem like good investments.

- The spine, knees, skin and overall skeletal alignment. These areas became important for you last year and remain important in the year ahead. The reflexes are shown above. Regular back and knee massage would be wonderful. Therapies such as yoga, Feldenkrais, Alexander Technique and Rolfing, all of which deal with the spine and skeletal alignment, are good. If you're out in the sun make sure to use a good sunscreen, and to get enough calcium to strengthen the bones. Regular visits to a chiropractor or osteopath also seem advisable.

Saturn, your home and family planet, has been in your 6th house since last year – signalling a need for good emotional health. Good health for you means a healthy domestic life and healthy family relationships. If health problems arise, restore harmony with family members as quickly as possible. Saturn in your health house could also show that you are more concerned with the health of family members than with your own.

Spiritual Neptune, your health planet, has been in your 6th house, his own house and sign, for many years now. Thus, you have been delving deeper into spiritual healing. You always respond well to this but lately even more so. So, if you feel under the weather see a spiritual healer. With Saturn also in your 6th house I like a combination of spiritual and hands-on healing for you.

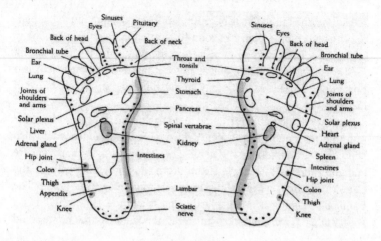

Important foot reflexology points for the year ahead

Try to massage all of the foot on a regular basis – the top of the foot as well as the bottom – but pay extra attention to the points highlighted on the chart. When you massage, be aware of 'sore spots' as these need special attention. It's also a good idea to massage the ankles and below them.

Your health planet has been in Pisces, a Water sign, for many years. Thus, you have a good connection with the healing powers of the Water element. You benefit from being around water, especially large bodies of water such as oceans, rivers, lakes and natural springs. Swimming is a healthy exercise, as are all water sports. If you don't feel right, try a soak in a lake or natural spring and let the water work its magic on you. If this is impractical, a nice long, leisurely soak in the tub will also rejuvenate you. If there is a part of the body that bothers you, hold it under the tap or shower – under running water.

Home and Family

With Pluto in your 4th house for the past 30 or so years, this has been a major focus for a long time. The family situation has been very turbulent. Probably there have been deaths in the family or near-death experiences in the lives of family members, and important renovations made in the home. Happily, the *Sturm und Drang* is mostly over with.

The home and family life is becoming more stable, and much happier.

With your money planet in your 4th house for so many years, many of you have been earning money from the home and perhaps setting up home offices. The home is as much a place of business as it is a home, and the family and family connections an important source of income.

Your family planet Saturn now in a Water sign indicates an attraction to homes on or near water. Saturn in your 6th house would also show that you're making the home a healthier place. Perhaps you are spending money to remove toxins from the paint, the walls or the pipes. You could be installing health equipment in the home. The home is becoming as much a health spa as a home.

Though a move is not likely this year, renovation of the home could happen.

Although the health of a parent or parent figure seems a concern, generally parents or parent figures are having a stable home and family year. They seem satisfied with the status quo.

Children or children figures in your life could have moved last year, but if not can move this year as well. Their home situation has been unstable for many years. Probably they have had multiple moves over the years.

Siblings and sibling figures feel cramped in the present home, but a move is not wise this year. Let them make better use of the space that they have. They need to be careful of tendencies to depression.

Grandchildren, if you have them, or those who play that role in your life, seem prosperous in the year ahead and are travelling more this year. If they are of childbearing age, they are much more fertile than usual.

If you are planning on renovating the home – and this seems likely – January 5 to February 13 would be a good time.

If you're redecorating the home, in a cosmetic kind of way, January 23 to February 16 and December 7 to the end of the year would be good times. These are also good times for buying objects of beauty for the home.

Finance and Career

Pluto's move out of Capricorn this year signals very important changes in your financial life and financial moves. Your financial planet has been in Capricorn for over 30 years, which means that you have been very conservative in financial matters. I consider this a good thing. You took a long-term view of wealth and learned to achieve wealth step by step, by methodical means. You gravitated to conservative types of investments, blue-chip companies listed on major stock exchanges. You still have this tendency this year, but you will be more speculative too. Your financial planet is moving into the sign of Aquarius. This favours the high-tech sector of the stock market and the online world. Perhaps in coming years you will start your own website and engage in e-commerce. You have a good feeling for the tech world. Probably you will spend more and invest more in technology. Being up-to-date technologically seems important in your financial life. The financial planet in Aquarius favours investments in start-ups, especially high-tech start-ups.

The financial planet in your 5th house indicates someone who spends more on children and children figures in your life. And you can earn from them as well. When they are young they can inspire you to earn more and, as often happens, they can come up with ideas that are profitable. Many a successful business arose from simply observing what the founder's children gravitated to. If the children are older and more established, they can become financially supportive in a material way. Sometimes the children lead to connections to other parents that lead to business and financial opportunities.

The financial planet in the 5th house also favours investments in electric utilities – power companies – and the entertainment industry. Companies and industries that cater to the youth market are interesting and probably lucrative. You have a good natural intuition for these kinds of companies.

Although Pluto is moving into your 5th house, he still spends part of the year in your 4th. So, family and family connections remain important in the year ahead.

For the past 30 years you've basically followed the rules of finance. You went by the book. Now you are becoming more experimental in finance. The rule books will get thrown out and you will learn what works for you through trial, error and experiment. Not every experiment succeeds but they all bring new and true knowledge. And many of your experiments will succeed.

Jupiter is travelling with Uranus early in the year – a transit that is favourable for speculations. There should be good fortune in these things. Of course, never speculate blindly but only under intuition.

Career seems stable and quiet this year. Things will go more or less the way they went last year. Next year, however, will be a banner career year and you should be very successful. This year seems more of a year of preparation for the future success that is going to happen.

With the Moon as your career planet, the two lunar eclipses, on March 25 and September 18, will force you to make the changes that need to be made for future success.

Love and Social Life

Love and social activities are always a focus for Libra. This is where your genius lies. And, although your 7th house is basically empty this year, the north node of the Moon will be in your 7th house all year. This shows that this house is a path to happiness and fulfilment. So, your naturally good love and social interests are likely to be happy and fulfilling – more so than usual.

The year ahead seems to be a sexually active kind of year, and while sex and love are two different things, this does point to increased social activity.

Mars is your love planet. While not as fast-moving as the Sun, Moon, Mercury or Venus, he is relatively fast-moving compared to the long-term planets. This year, he will move through eight signs and houses of your Horoscope. Thus, there will be many short-term trends in love that depend on where Mars is and the kinds of aspects he receives. These are best dealt with in the monthly reports.

Mars makes one of his rare retrogrades in 2024, from December 6 to the end of the year. This will be a time to review your love and social goals but not to take any overt actions or decisions about them. The retrograde might slow down the social life but it won't stop it.

Mars as your love planet shows that you tend to be aggressive and proactive when it comes to love. You're not someone who sits around waiting for the phone to ring. You like to make social events or romantic events happen. If you like someone, they will know it.

I don't see a marriage for singles this year. On the other hand, there is nothing against it either.

Your 11th house of friends is not prominent this year and this will tend to the status quo. Friendships will be more or less like last year and you seem content about this.

Siblings and sibling figures have had a tumultuous love and social life in recent years, and this continues in the year ahead. There is romance for them, perhaps even serious romance, but the stability of it is in question. Parents and parent figures have a stable love and social year. Children and children figures have love affairs this year but they don't seem too serious. Grandchildren of an appropriate age, if you have them, or those who play that role in your life have serious romantic opportunities. Love seems to pursue them rather than vice versa.

Self-improvement

Neptune, your health planet, has been in your 6th house for many years now, and he will still be there for the year ahead. So, as we have written in past years, this is a time in your life to go deeper into spiritual healing. By now you already understand much about it, but there is always more to learn. Spiritual healing is not just about healing the physical body, it involves healing any aspect of life that troubles you or is problematic. Seen from the spiritual perspective, if there is an area of life that is troubling or less than perfect, we are not completely well. Applying the spiritual laws of healing doesn't negate orthodox medicine or other forms of medicine – sometimes these methods are necessary. But applying the laws of spiritual healing will lead you to whatever the body needs to be in perfect health. This can manifest as a pill, a herb, a drug, sometimes even surgery in certain cases. Whatever is needed will come to you very naturally. Often, problems clear up without any outside intervention. This year, though, it seems that it will lead to hands-on kinds of therapies.

Pluto's move into Aquarius has other implications aside from financial ones. Over the coming years there will be a whole transformation of your creative life and creative abilities. Also, children and children figures in your life will completely transform their images and physical bodies. Little by little they will grow into the body and image of their dreams. Their ideal body and image. It can get messy at times, but the end result will be good.

For more information on astrology and spiritual healing, please visit my blog at www.spiritual-stories.com.

Month-by-month Forecasts

January

Best Days Overall: 3, 4, 12, 13, 21, 22, 30, 31
Most Stressful Days Overall: 11, 16, 17, 23, 24
Best Days for Love: 8, 9, 10, 16, 17, 18, 27, 28, 29
Best Days for Money: 1, 2, 3, 6, 7, 10, 11, 12, 18, 19, 20, 28, 29, 31
Best Days for Career: 11, 12, 28, 29, 21, 23, 24

Health needs some attention until the 20th. This doesn't seem anything serious, merely short-term stress caused by the short-term planets. By the 20th you should see a remarkable improvement. In the meantime, as always, make sure to get enough rest and enhance the health in the ways mentioned in the yearly report.

The planetary power this month is mostly in your 4th house of home and family: 60 per cent of the planets are either there or moving through there this month. By contrast, your 10th house of career is basically empty. Only the Moon will move through there, briefly, between the 25th and 27th. You can safely let career matters go and focus on the home front. More importantly, this is a month for making psychological progress, for finding and functioning from your personal point of emotional harmony. Once this is attained you can succeed in your career from that point.

If you are involved in any formal type of psychological therapy, much progress and insight will come. But even if you're not in formal therapy, you will make psychological progress. The cosmos has its own way of doing this. Your feelings of nostalgia are the cosmos's way of bringing up old memories so that you can look at them from your present state of consciousness. You can't change the facts of your past but you can change your interpretation. And this will make all the difference.

Pluto, your financial planet, is still in your 4th house until the 22nd. Thus, there is good family support; family and family connections are playing a very big role in your finances. There is a tendency to earn money from home, from a home office and the like. This has been the case for over 30 years. On the 22nd Pluto will move into Aquarius, your 5th house, and stay there until September 3. The whole financial attitude will start to change. You will be less conservative and more speculative. With this transit you'll earn your money in happy ways and spend it on happy things. You will enjoy the wealth that you have. The 20th and 21st seem like excellent financial days.

The power in your 6th house this year is a positive indicator for health. Health, as we mentioned, needs more watching and more focus this month and you seem to be on the case. Children and children figures in your life have an excellent social month, especially from the 20th onwards. If they are of an appropriate age there is romance in their lives.

Your love planet Mars is in your 3rd house until the 5th. Thus, love and romantic opportunity can be found in your neighbourhood, close to home. Romantic opportunities happen at school, school functions, lectures, seminars, the bookshop or the library. After the 5th Mars moves into your 4th house of home and family and this gives many messages. You're socializing more from home and with the family. Family members are playing a role in your love life, perhaps by playing Cupid. An old flame can come back into the picture. (Sometimes it is the person him- or herself, sometimes it is someone who reminds you of the old flame.) This might not lead to anything serious, but it does help to resolve old issues. After the 5th you gravitate to people with whom you can share emotional intimacy. You like people with strong family values. A romantic evening at home is probably preferable to a night out on the town.

February

Best Days Overall: 8, 9, 17, 18, 26, 27, 28
Most Stressful Days Overall: 6, 7, 12, 13, 19, 20
Best Days for Love: 6, 7, 12, 13, 17, 26, 27
Best Days for Money: 1, 2, 3, 6, 7, 8, 14, 15, 17, 24, 25, 26, 29
Best Days for Career: 8, 9, 18, 19, 20, 29

The main headline this month is the unusual degree of power in your 5th house of fun and creativity. Well over half the planets are either there or moving through there. You began your yearly personal pleasure peak last month on January 20, but this month the peak is even stronger. Librans have a great sense of beauty and are very creative people. This month the creativity is unusually strong. If you are in the creative arts, and many of you are, this is where your focus should be.

Health and energy are excellent this month, much better than last month. With your 6th house of health very strong let's hope that your focus is more on unhealthy lifestyles than temporary symptoms. There is a danger of hypochondria – a tendency to magnify small things into big things, a tendency to invent pathology where there is none. Be careful about this.

Children and children figures had a tremendous social month last month, but this month even more so.

Your love planet moves into your 5th house on the 13th and stays there for the rest of the month ahead. This favours love affairs rather than serious romance and you are attracted to people who can show you a good time; to people you can have fun with. Love, from the 13th onwards, seems little more than another form of entertainment, like going to the movies or the theatre. Still, there is something to be said for fun.

You've had excellent job prospects for over a year now, and especially this month after the 19th. Most of you are probably employed. Even so, you will have many opportunities for overtime or side jobs.

Finances are good, as Pluto is receiving much stimulation from the other planets. The spouse, partner or current love is also prospering greatly this year and this month.

All the planets are moving forward this month, so the events of life are fast-paced and you tend to make fast progress towards your goals.

The Sun travels with Saturn between the 24th and 26th. So be more patient with friends. They seem troubled and pessimistic.

March

Best Days Overall: 7, 8, 13, 14, 15, 16, 24, 25, 26
Most Stressful Days Overall: 4, 5, 6, 11, 12, 17, 18
Best Days for Love: 7, 8, 11, 12, 15, 16, 17, 18, 27, 28
Best Days for Money: 1, 4, 5, 7, 13, 14, 15, 22, 23, 24, 27, 28
Best Days for Career: 1, 9, 10, 17, 18, 19, 20, 29, 30

Mars, your love planet, is travelling near Venus, the ruler of your Horoscope. He is near her but has not quite caught up. So, someone is pursuing you romantically, but you have not yet allowed yourself to be caught. This person seems eager and ardent. Perhaps it is someone you work with. Perhaps it is someone who is involved with your health.

Health is still good and you are still very focused on it. With Venus in your 6th house from the 11th onwards, good health also means looking good. There is a vanity component to health after the 11th. The cosmic message is stay healthy and your appearance will shine. Plain good health will do more for your looks than hosts of lotions and potions.

On the 23rd Mars moves into your 6th house. Thus, good health for you also means a happy, harmonious love and social life. If problems occur, restore harmony in your love life as quickly as possible. You always respond well to spiritual-healing techniques but this month even more so. The 15th to the 17th are especially good for spiritual healing. The 16th and 17th bring spiritual insights and enhanced ESP abilities. Make a note of your dreams on those days, as they seem revelatory and important.

A lunar eclipse on the 25th is relatively mild in its effects on you. (However, if it hits something sensitive in your personal Horoscope, the Horoscope cast especially for you, it can be strong indeed.) It occurs in your own sign but doesn't have much impact on other planets or the rest of your Horoscope. The eclipse will force you to re-evaluate yourself, your opinion of yourself, your self-concept and the way that you want others to see you. Thus, over the coming months you will change your wardrobe, appearance and overall presentation to the world. These changes are the normal side-effects of a change in your opinion about yourself. If you haven't been careful in dietary matters the eclipse can bring a detox of the physical body – a mild one for most of you. All of you will feel this eclipse to some degree, but those of you born early in the sign of Libra, from September 26–29, will feel it most strongly. If you fall into this category, definitely reduce your schedule while the eclipse is in effect.

Since the Moon is your career planet, every lunar eclipse brings career changes and shake-ups. This one is no different. Often there are shake-ups and reshuffles in your corporate hierarchy. Often bosses and authority figures experience personal dramas. The government can change the rules of your industry or company and this requires you to change how you pursue your career. Parents and parent figures can have personal dramas as well.

April

Best Days Overall: 3, 4, 11, 12, 21, 22, 30
Most Stressful Days Overall: 1, 2, 7, 8, 13, 14, 15, 28, 29
Best Days for Love: 5, 6, 7, 8, 13, 14, 16, 17, 23, 24, 27, 28
Best Days for Money: 1, 2, 3, 9, 10, 11, 18, 19, 21, 23, 24, 25
Best Days for Career: 7, 8, 13, 14, 15, 17, 28, 29

We have a very strong solar eclipse on the 8th of this month. Of all the eclipses this year this one is the strongest. So, take a nice, easy, relaxed schedule while the eclipse is in effect. There is no need to panic – this never helps anyway – but it would be good to take normal common-sense precautions. Stay close to home, do what is absolutely necessary to do, but reschedule anything else. Take a short break. Stay close to home, read a book, watch a movie, or, best of all, meditate.

This eclipse occurs in your 7th house of love and will test your current relationship. Perhaps the spouse, partner or current love is having his or her own personal dramas. Perhaps he or she is short-tempered and touchy. Perhaps old long-buried grievances surface and need to be dealt with. The eclipse forces them into the open and you can deal with them. Before the events of the eclipse you might not have been aware of these grievances and they would continue to fester. Now at least you know what they are and can mitigate them. Venus, the ruler of your Horoscope, is directly impacted by this eclipse. This is another good reason to stay close to home and take it easy.

Like last month there is a need to re-define yourself, your self-concept, your image and presentation to others. You tend to believe that presentation is everything, Libra. So, in the coming months the wardrobe, hairstyle, perhaps hair colouring and general presentation will change. This will reflect the inner changes that you have made. A detox of the body could also happen, and it seems much more powerful than last month.

Venus is the ruler of both your Horoscope and your 8th house of regeneration. Thus, this eclipse can bring psychological encounters with death and even near-death experiences. The thousand-eyed angel is letting you know that he's around. Those of you on the spiritual path can even have a conversation with this angel and he will explain to you what death is all about. Some people encounter death in their dreams or through hearing of the death of someone they know. None of this is any sort of punishment, but is designed to get you to be more serious about life and your mission in life.

The impact of the eclipse on Mercury will bring spiritual, religious, theological and philosophical changes. Your theological and spiritual beliefs will get tested by the events of the eclipse. Some beliefs will get discarded, some will get amended. There are shake-ups and upheavals in your place of worship and in spiritual or charitable organizations that you are involved with. Worship leaders and guru figures have personal dramas.

Friends will tend to experience life-changing dramas. Computers, high-tech gadgetry and software will behave erratically. Back up important files, avoid opening emails from people you don't know and avoid suspicious websites and suspicious attachments. Sometimes your high-tech equipment needs repair or replacement.

May

Best Days Overall: 1, 9, 10, 17, 18, 19, 27, 28
Most Stressful Days Overall: 5, 6, 11, 12, 25, 26
Best Days for Love: 5, 6, 7, 8, 13, 14, 15, 16, 24, 27, 28
Best Days for Money: 8, 15, 16, 26, 27, 28
Best Days for Career: 1, 7, 8, 11, 12, 18, 19, 27

Your financial planet Pluto goes retrograde on the 2nd and will remain so for many months. This will not stop earnings but will slow things down a bit. It can introduce unnecessary financial delays. You can minimize these delays by being more perfect in your financial dealings. Make sure every detail is correct. If possible, avoid making major investments or purchases while Pluto is retrograde, although, since it goes on for many months, this might not be practical. However, you can study things more carefully before you plunge in.

Jupiter has been in your 8th house for the past year or so, but now, on the 26th, he makes a major move into your 9th house. This is excellent for college-level students or for those who are applying to college. There is good news here. Students are successful in their studies and applicants have good fortune. If you are involved in legal issues, there is good fortune there too.

Until the 20th, the planetary power is in your 8th house. Thus, the spouse, partner or current love is having a prosperous month. It also seems like a more sexually active kind of month. Whatever your age or stage in life, the libido is stronger than usual. A strong 8th house shows a great interest in personal transformation and projects involving such things. It favours detox regimes of all kinds, physical, emotional and mental. This is a time for getting rid of the extraneous in your life. Things that are no longer serving you.

Health looks good this month and will get even better from the 20th. You can improve it even further in the ways mentioned in the yearly report.

Mars, your love planet, will be in his own sign and house from the beginning of the month. He is strong in this position and this indicates an active kind of social life. However, the people you are meeting seem very self-centred and full of themselves. You will need a double dose of your Libran social genius to deal with this.

Though Pluto is still retrograde, the 20th and 26th bring financial increase and opportunity. However, there can be delays involved with this.

June

Best Days Overall: 5, 6, 14, 15, 16, 24, 25
Most Stressful Days Overall: 1, 2, 7, 8, 21, 22, 23, 28, 29
Best Days for Love: 1, 2, 5, 6, 12, 13, 16, 17, 21, 22, 26, 27, 28, 29, 30
Best Days for Money: 5, 14, 17, 18, 23, 24
Best Days for Career: 5, 6, 7, 8, 14, 15, 26

Basically, a happy and healthy month ahead, Libra. Enjoy. Health is generally good but after the 20th will need more watching. There is nothing serious afoot; it is merely short-term stress caused by short-term planets. This will pass next month. Make sure to get enough rest and enhance the health in the ways mentioned in the yearly report.

With Mars as your love planet, you are attracted to physical types of people. The physical attraction seems the primary thing. With Mars in your 7th house since May 1 – and remaining there until the 9th of this month – this tendency has become even stronger. On the 9th, as Mars moves into your 8th house, it is the sexual magnetism that seems most important in love. Physical attraction is not the same as sexual magnetism. Someone can be physically attractive but sexually not up to par, and the reverse is also true – someone can have strong sexual magnetism and not be that physically attractive. Good sex covers many sins; however, it is not enough to build a long-term relationship.

The month ahead seems very successful for you, Libra. On the 17th Venus, the ruler of your Horoscope, crosses the Mid-heaven and enters your 10th house of career. This shows personal success. You seem empowered, you are honoured and appreciated not so much for your professional abilities but for who you are as a person. On the 20th the Sun moves into your 10th house and you begin a yearly career peak.

You can let go of home and family issues for a while and focus on your career. This is where the power and the action are from the 20th onwards. Keep in mind, too, that your home and family planet, Saturn, starts to retrograde on the 29th, signalling that family issues need time to resolve. You may as well focus on the career.

July

Best Days Overall: 2, 3, 12, 13, 21, 22, 29, 30, 31
Most Stressful Days Overall: 4, 5, 6, 19, 20, 25, 26
Best Days for Love: 1, 5, 6, 9, 10, 17, 18, 20, 25, 26, 28
Best Days for Money: 2, 3, 12, 13, 14, 15, 16, 21, 22, 29, 30
Best Days for Career: 4, 5, 6, 15, 16, 23

Continue to be more mindful about your health until the 22nd. High energy levels are the first defence against disease. Low energy tends to weaken the immune system and make one more vulnerable to all kinds of problems. If you feel under the weather, see a spiritual-type healer. Continue to enhance the health in the ways mentioned in the yearly report. Health improves dramatically from the 22nd onwards.

You're still in a yearly career peak until the 22nd. Much progress and success are happening. The new Moon of the 5th occurs in your 10th house, which makes it an especially good career day. Friends and social connections are also successful these days and they are boosting your career. Very important to be up-to-date technologically, as this seems to play an important role in success. The new Moon of the 5th not only boosts the career directly but will have indirect effects as the days go on. The new Moon will clarify and illuminate career issues and you will receive all the information necessary to make good career moves. This will go on until the next new Moon next month.

Love is still very sexual and hands on. Keep in mind our discussion of this last month. On the 20th Mars, your love planet, enters your 9th house and your love attitudes, and needs, change. After the 20th love becomes more cerebral and intellectual. You are attracted by the person's mind and intelligence as much as by their physical body. A good body with a good mind would be the ideal. You are attracted to people who are easy to communicate with, with whom you can share ideas, and people you can learn from. Romantic opportunities can happen at college or school functions, religious functions, your place of worship, at lectures, seminars, the library and even the bookstore. Foreigners are also very appealing. Mars makes very nice aspects to your financial planet Pluto on the 20th and 21st. This boosts the finances, but there can be delays involved. Keep in mind that your financial planet is still retrograde.

Your health planet, Neptune, goes retrograde on the 2nd and will be retrograde for many more months. Avoid making major changes to your health regime during this retrograde. If you do, these things need more study. Also, it is not a good idea to have medical tests or procedures while Neptune is retrograde. If you can, if the tests and procedures are not urgent, reschedule them for a later time.

On the 22nd the Sun enters your 11th house of friends and the social life becomes more active, and happy. This socializing is more Platonic in nature, it is more about friendship and group activities, and not necessarily romantic. Still, it seems happy.

The 22nd and 23rd are stressful financial days, but happily this is a short-term issue. The problems will resolve rather quickly.

August

Best Days Overall: 8, 9, 17, 18, 26, 27
Most Stressful Days Overall: 1, 2, 15, 16, 21, 22, 28, 29
Best Days for Love: 8, 9, 17, 18, 21, 22, 26, 27, 29
Best Days for Money: 8, 9, 11, 12, 17, 18, 26, 27
Best Days for Career: 1, 2, 3, 4, 13, 14, 23, 28, 29

The social life, both Platonic and romantic, is the main headline this month.

Your love planet travels with Jupiter from the 11th to the 14th. This shows a very serious romantic meeting or opportunity for singles. Perhaps a foreign trip happens with the beloved. Love can happen in foreign lands at this time. Your love planet is also receiving harmonious aspects from other short-term planets, so your social grace is unusually strong. Like last month there is great involvement with friends, group activities, trade and professional organizations. Platonic kinds of relationships are also very important this month. So, you will have both friendship and romance.

If you are already in a relationship, the beloved seems more romantic and amorous than usual.

Power in your 11th house of friends tends to bring happiness as the 11th house is a beneficent one. It is the house where fondest dreams and wishes come true. When the 11th house is very powerful many people have their Horoscopes done. Their knowledge of science, astronomy and technology tends to expand. Most likely you will be spending more time than usual online.

This month 40 per cent of the planets are retrograde, close to the maximum for the year. (In October for a few days half of the planets will be retrograde.) There can be many delays and slowdowns both in the world and in your life now. It is not your fault. It's just the cosmic weather.

On the 22nd the Sun enters your 12th house. Venus, the ruler of your Horoscope, enters there on the 5th. You are in a very strong spiritual cycle. This is the time to meditate, engage in your spiritual practice, and to read and study the holy books. The spiritual understanding you receive will help you deal with all the delays that are happening. Spirit, of course, is never delayed. But its manifestation can appear that way here on the material plane.

Health and energy are good, much better than last month.

September

Best Days Overall: 4, 5, 6, 14, 15, 22, 23
Most Stressful Days Overall: 12, 13, 18, 19, 24, 25
Best Days for Love: 4, 5, 7, 8, 14, 15, 16, 17, 18, 19, 23, 24, 25
Best Days for Money: 3, 4, 5, 7, 8, 13, 14, 15, 21, 22, 23
Best Days for Career: 2, 3, 12, 13, 24, 25

A lunar eclipse on the 18th is relatively mild in its impact on you, but it won't hurt to take it more easily over this period. (If this eclipse hits a sensitive point in your personal Horoscope, the one cast especially for you, it can be powerful indeed.)

The eclipse occurs in your 6th house, and impacts on Neptune, your health and work planet and ruler of that house. So, the eclipse is announcing job changes or changes in the conditions of work. Perhaps there are dramas and upheavals in your place of work. Perhaps you change jobs, either in your present situation or in a new situation. There can be health scares as well, but as your health is good, these are likely to be no more than scares. However, there will be important and dramatic changes in the health regime in the coming months. Keep in mind that your health planet is still retrograde and will be for a while, so don't be too quick to make these changes – study them thoroughly.

Jupiter is sideswiped by this eclipse. It is not a direct hit. This can bring minor dramas in the lives of siblings and sibling figures. Students can have dramas at school and make changes to educational plans.

Cars and communication equipment can behave erratically. It's probably a good idea to avoid unnecessary driving while the eclipse is in effect.

With the Moon as your career planet, every lunar eclipse affects the career – and this one is no different. Career changes are afoot. Sometimes this comes from changes in the hierarchy of your company. Perhaps you get a new boss, or the company board changes its policies. Sometimes the government changes the rules that regulate your company or industry and you must pursue your career in a different way. There are personal dramas in the lives of parents, parent figures and bosses. It is rare that there is an actual career change, but it does happen sometimes.

October

Best Days Overall: 1, 2, 3, 11, 12, 19, 20, 29, 30
Most Stressful Days Overall: 9, 10, 15, 16, 21, 22, 23
Best Days for Love: 4, 5, 13, 14, 15, 16, 22, 23, 24, 25, 31
Best Days for Money: 2, 10, 11, 12, 18, 19, 20, 28, 29, 30, 31
Best Days for Career: 1, 11, 12, 20, 21, 22, 23

The solar eclipse on the 2nd is the main headline this month. Though it is not as strong as the one in April, it is still pretty powerful in its effect on you. So, as always, reduce your schedule and avoid stressful activities where possible. The eclipse occurs in your own sign and forces you again to take stock of yourself and your opinion of yourself, your self-concept, and to upgrade it. You don't have much of a choice in this – either you define yourself for yourself, or others will define you their way. The latter will not be very pleasant. Over the coming months this self-reflection will manifest as a new wardrobe, a new look, and a new presentation to the world. This eclipse will also bring changes to what you consider your path of personal happiness.

The eclipse is a direct hit on Mars, your love planet, and will test a current relationship and probably bring changes and upheavals in your social circle. The spouse, partner or current love also needs to take stock and re-evaluate his or her self-concept and presentation to others. Perhaps he or she is having some personal drama and this is affecting your relationship. Perhaps your personal dramas are contributing to the testing of the relationship. Most often, long-repressed grievances and annoyances come to the surface so that they can be resolved. A basically healthy relationship will survive this kind of eclipse, but relationships that are fundamentally flawed are in danger.

Since the Sun, the eclipsed planet, rules friendships and friends, we have another indication of upheavals in your social circle. There can be life-changing dramas in the lives of friends. There are shake-ups in trade or professional organizations you are involved with. Computers, software and high-tech gadgetry will get tested and tend to behave erratically. Take common-sense precautions. Back up important files, make sure your antivirus and anti-hacking software is up to date, avoid suspicious websites and avoid opening suspicious attachments.

Mercury, which rules two houses in your Horoscope, the 9th and the 12th, is also directly impacted by this eclipse. There are disturbances and shake-ups in your place of worship. There are dramas in the lives of worship leaders. Your religious, theological and philosophical beliefs will get tested by the events of the eclipse. Some of your beliefs will be dropped completely, some will be refined and amended. This will change how you live your life. College-level students will make important changes to their educational plans, and often will change courses or schools. It's probably not a good idea to be travelling while this eclipse is in effect. If you must travel, and this sometimes happens, try to schedule it around the eclipse.

Alongside this, spiritual changes will be happening, changes in your practice, your teachings and perhaps teachers. Your attitude to spirituality will change. There are personal dramas in the lives of guru figures, and dramas and upheavals in spiritual or charitable organizations you are involved with.

November

Best Days Overall: 7, 8, 9, 16, 17, 25, 26, 27
Most Stressful Days Overall: 5, 6, 12, 13, 18, 19
Best Days for Love: 2, 3, 4, 12, 13, 20, 21, 22, 23, 29, 30
Best Days for Money: 1, 2, 6, 8, 9, 16, 17, 25, 26, 27, 28, 29
Best Days for Career: 1, 2, 10, 11, 18, 19, 22

Finances are much improved over the past few months. Pluto, your financial planet, is now moving forward after many months of retrograde motion. This began on October 12. Also, you are in the midst of a yearly financial peak until the 21st. There is clarity in your financial thinking now and the decisions you make will likely be good ones. You are focused on finance and this focus tends to success. Friends seem to be helpful financially. Many of your fondest financial hopes and dreams will happen this month.

Venus, the ruler of your Horoscope, is out of bounds all month. Thus, you are outside your normal boundaries, in unknown territory. You seem more adventurous. The spouse, partner or current love is also outside his or her normal sphere in financial matters.

The full Moon of the 15th occurs right on Uranus. That should be a fun kind of day. Parents and parent figures should be more mindful on the physical plane.

Mercury is out of bounds from the 7th to December 2. Thus, your urges to travel are to more exotic places outside your usual haunts. We see this in your spiritual life as well. You seem to be exploring teachings and systems that are more exotic and outside your normal boundaries.

Health is good this month. Since your health planet Neptune is still retrograde it is best to postpone medical tests or procedures – elective ones – until next month when she starts to move forward again.

On the 21st the Sun moves into your 3rd house of communication and intellectual interests. This is an excellent transit for students as the mental faculties are much enhanced and learning is easier. They seem successful in their studies. It is also a good time for writers, intellectual workers, teachers, bloggers, sales and marketing people. The gift of the gab is very strong.

Your love planet moves into your 11th house on the 4th and stays there for the rest of the month ahead. Singles can find love opportunities as they get involved with friends, groups, group activities and trade and professional organizations. Friends tend to play Cupid this month. Singles can also find romantic opportunities in the online world, on social media sites.

December

Best Days Overall: 5, 6, 13, 14, 22, 23, 24
Most Stressful Days Overall: 2, 3, 4, 9, 10, 15, 16, 30, 31
Best Days for Love: 2, 3, 4, 9, 10, 13, 14, 17, 18, 19, 22, 23, 24, 27, 28, 29
Best Days for Money: 5, 6, 13, 14, 22, 23, 24, 25, 26
Best Days for Career: 1, 9, 10, 15, 16, 19, 20, 30, 31

Venus has been out of bounds since October 27 and remains so until the 8th. This long period of being outside your normal boundaries, of adventurousness, is almost finished. By the 8th you're back in your normal sphere, your normal comfort zone.

Health and energy are still excellent, but after the 21st will need more watching.

Your health planet finally moves forward again on the 7th, so it is safer now to take those medical tests or procedures, and to make changes to your health regime. Your judgement on health matters is much improved. Enhance the health by getting more rest, as usual, and in the ways mentioned in the yearly report.

Mars, your love planet, rarely goes retrograde. He only does so every two years or so. However, on the 7th he starts to retrograde and will remain so until the end of the month and into next year. This won't stop love, of course. Singles will still go out and attend parties and date. But it slows things down. Your social and romantic judgement is not up to its usual standard. A current relationship can seem to be going backwards instead of forwards. There is nothing wrong with you and you're not being punished. You are as lovable as you always were. It's just cosmic weather. This is not a time to make important love decisions, one way or another. It is good to slow down and see how things develop; there is no need to project too far into the future. This is a good time to review your love and social goals and see where improvements can be made. When Mars starts to move forward next year you can implement your plans.

In the meantime, continue to be involved with friends, groups, group activities, trade and professional organizations as this is where romantic opportunity is most likely. Also, like last month, the online world seems interesting for love.

Finance doesn't seem a major focus this month, but still seems good. Pluto is moving forwards and you have financial clarity. The 7th and 8th, as Venus travels with your financial planet, bring financial increase and opportunity. It seems a fortunate time financially.

Scorpio

♏

THE SCORPION

Birthdays from
23rd October to
22nd November

Personality Profile

SCORPIO AT A GLANCE

Element – Water

Ruling Planet – Pluto
  Co-ruling Planet – Mars
  Career Planet – Sun
  Love Planet – Venus
  Money Planet – Jupiter
  Planet of Health and Work – Mars
  Planet of Home and Family Life – Uranus

Colour – red-violet

Colour that promotes love, romance and social harmony – green

Colour that promotes earning power – blue

Gems – bloodstone, malachite, topaz

Metals – iron, radium, steel

Scents – cherry blossom, coconut, sandalwood, watermelon

Quality – fixed (= stability)

Quality most needed for balance – a wider view of things

Strongest virtues – loyalty, concentration, determination, courage, depth

Deepest needs – to penetrate and transform

Characteristics to avoid – jealousy, vindictiveness, fanaticism

Signs of greatest overall compatibility – Cancer, Pisces

Signs of greatest overall incompatibility – Taurus, Leo, Aquarius

Sign most helpful to career – Leo

Sign most helpful for emotional support – Aquarius

Sign most helpful financially – Sagittarius

Sign best for marriage and/or partnerships – Taurus

Sign most helpful for creative projects – Pisces

Best Sign to have fun with – Pisces

Signs most helpful in spiritual matters – Cancer, Libra

Best day of the week – Tuesday

Understanding a Scorpio

One symbol of the sign of Scorpio is the phoenix. If you meditate upon the legend of the phoenix you will begin to understand the Scorpio character – his or her powers and abilities, interests and deepest urges.

The phoenix of mythology was a bird that could recreate and reproduce itself. It did so in a most intriguing way: it would seek a fire – usually in a religious temple – fly into it, consume itself in the flames and then emerge a new bird. If this is not the ultimate, most profound transformation, then what is?

Transformation is what Scorpios are all about – in their minds, bodies, affairs and relationships (Scorpios are also society's transformers). To change something in a natural, not an artificial way, involves a transformation from within. This type of change is radical change as opposed to a mere cosmetic make-over. Some people think that change means altering just their appearance, but this is not the kind of thing that interests a Scorpio. Scorpios seek deep, fundamental change. Since real change always proceeds from within, a Scorpio is very interested in – and usually accustomed to – the inner, intimate and philosophical side of life.

Scorpios are people of depth and intellect. If you want to interest them you must present them with more than just a superficial image. You and your interests, projects or business deals must have real substance to them in order to stimulate a Scorpio. If they haven't, he or she will find you out – and that will be the end of the story.

If we observe life – the processes of growth and decay – we see the transformational powers of Scorpio at work all the time. The caterpillar changes itself into a butterfly; the infant grows into a child and then an adult. To Scorpios this definite and perpetual transformation is not something to be feared. They see it as a normal part of life. This acceptance of transformation gives Scorpios the key to understanding the true meaning of life.

Scorpios' understanding of life (including life's weaknesses) makes them powerful warriors – in all senses of the word. Add to this their depth, patience and endurance and you have a powerful personality. Scorpios have good, long memories and can at times be quite vindictive

- they can wait years to get their revenge. As a friend, though, there is no one more loyal and true than a Scorpio. Few are willing to make the sacrifices that a Scorpio will make for a true friend.

The results of a transformation are quite obvious, although the process of transformation is invisible and secret. This is why Scorpios are considered secretive in nature. A seed will not grow properly if you keep digging it up and exposing it to the light of day. It must stay buried - invisible - until it starts to grow. In the same manner, Scorpios fear revealing too much about themselves or their hopes to other people. However, they will be more than happy to let you see the finished product - but only when it is completely unwrapped. On the other hand, Scorpios like knowing everyone else's secrets as much as they dislike anyone knowing theirs.

Finance

Love, birth, life as well as death are Nature's most potent transformations; Scorpios are interested in all of these. In our society, money is a transforming power, too, and a Scorpio is interested in money for that reason. To a Scorpio money is power, money causes change, money controls. It is the power of money that fascinates them. But Scorpios can be too materialistic if they are not careful. They can be overly awed by the power of money, to a point where they think that money rules the world.

Even the term 'plutocrat' comes from Pluto, the ruler of the sign of Scorpio. Scorpios will - in one way or another - achieve the financial status they strive for. When they do so they are careful in the way they handle their wealth. Part of this financial carefulness is really a kind of honesty, for Scorpios are usually involved with other people's money - as accountants, lawyers, stockbrokers or corporate managers - and when you handle other people's money you have to be more cautious than when you handle your own.

In order to fulfil their financial goals, Scorpios have important lessons to learn. They need to develop qualities that do not come naturally to them, such as breadth of vision, optimism, faith, trust and, above all, generosity. They need to see the wealth in Nature and in life, as well as in its more obvious forms of money and power. When they develop generosity their financial potential reaches great heights, for Jupiter, the Lord of Opulence and Good Fortune, is Scorpio's money planet.

Career and Public Image

Scorpio's greatest aspiration in life is to be considered by society as a source of light and life. They want to be leaders, to be stars. But they follow a very different road than do Leos, the other stars of the zodiac. A Scorpio arrives at the goal secretly, without ostentation; a Leo pursues it openly. Scorpios seek the glamour and fun of the rich and famous in a restrained, discreet way.

Scorpios are by nature introverted and tend to avoid the limelight. But if they want to attain their highest career goals they need to open up a bit and to express themselves more. They need to stop hiding their light under a bushel and let it shine. Above all, they need to let go of any vindictiveness and small-mindedness. All their gifts and insights were given to them for one important reason – to serve life and to increase the joy of living for others.

Love and Relationships

Scorpio is another zodiac sign that likes committed, clearly defined, structured relationships. They are cautious about marriage, but when they do commit to a relationship they tend to be faithful – and heaven help the mate caught or even suspected of infidelity! The jealousy of the Scorpio is legendary. They can be so intense in their jealousy that even the thought or intention of infidelity will be detected and is likely to cause as much of a storm as if the deed had actually been done.

Scorpios tend to settle down with those who are wealthier than they are. They usually have enough intensity for two, so in their partners they seek someone pleasant, hard-working, amiable, stable and easy-going. They want someone they can lean on, someone loyal behind them as they fight the battles of life. To a Scorpio a partner, be it a lover or a friend, is a real partner – not an adversary. Most of all a Scorpio is looking for an ally, not a competitor.

If you are in love with a Scorpio you will need a lot of patience. It takes a long time to get to know Scorpios, because they do not reveal themselves readily. But if you persist and your motives are honourable, you will gradually be allowed into a Scorpio's inner chambers of the mind and heart.

Home and Domestic Life

Uranus is ruler of Scorpio's 4th solar house of home and family. Uranus is the planet of science, technology, changes and democracy. This tells us a lot about a Scorpio's conduct in the home and what he or she needs in order to have a happy, harmonious home life.

Scorpios can sometimes bring their passion, intensity and wilfulness into the home and family, which is not always the place for these qualities. These traits are good for the warrior and the transformer, but not so good for the nurturer and family member. Because of this (and also because of their need for change and transformation) the Scorpio may be prone to sudden changes of residence. If not carefully constrained, the sometimes inflexible Scorpio can produce turmoil and sudden upheavals within the family.

Scorpios need to develop some of the virtues of Aquarius in order to cope better with domestic matters. There is a need to build a team spirit at home, to treat family activities as truly group activities – family members should all have a say in what does and does not get done. For at times a Scorpio can be most dictatorial. When a Scorpio gets dictatorial it is much worse than if a Leo or Capricorn (the two other power signs in the zodiac) does. The dictatorship of a Scorpio is applied with more zeal, passion, intensity and concentration than is true of either a Leo or a Capricorn. Obviously this can be unbearable to family members – especially if they are sensitive types.

In order for a Scorpio to get the full benefit of the emotional support that a family can give, he or she needs to let go of conservatism and be a bit more experimental, to explore new techniques in childrearing, be more democratic with family members and to try to manage things by consensus rather than by autocratic edict.

Horoscope for 2024

Major Trends

Saturn's move out of Aquarius last year has improved health and energy dramatically. He has moved from a stressful aspect to you, to a harmonious one. Those of you born early in Scorpio, October 22–24, still need to watch your energy as Pluto is making strong adverse aspects to you. More on this later.

Saturn, in your 5th house for all of 2024, shows a need to be more disciplined in your personal creativity. Also, children and children figures in your life seem overly pessimistic, perhaps even depressed. The good news is that they seem to be taking on more responsibility. They seem more serious about life.

Uranus has been in your 7th house for many years now and will be there in the year ahead. This has destabilized the love and social life. There could have been divorces or near divorces in the past few years. This year Jupiter is also moving through your 7th house of love, signifying an important romantic relationship. More on this later.

Pluto's move into Aquarius this year signifies the beginning of a long-term change of personal interests and focus. For the next 30 years home and family will be a major interest. Also, there will be a great interest in psychology and especially depth psychology. This is a great transit for those of you who are therapists or involved with depth psychology.

On May 26 Jupiter will enter your 8th house of regeneration. Thus, eroticism becomes more important and the sex life probably more active. This transit too favours depth psychology. It also has important financial implications which we will deal with later on.

Your most important areas of interest this year are communication and intellectual interest until January 22 and from September 3 to November 20; home, family and emotional well-being from January 22 to September 3 and from November 20 to the end of the year; children, fun, creativity; love and romance; and sex, occult studies and personal transformation from May 26 onwards.

Your paths of greatest fulfilment this year will be health and work; love and romance until May 26; and sex, occult studies and personal transformation after May 26.

Health

(Please note that this is an astrological perspective on health and not a medical one. In days of yore there was no difference, both these perspectives were identical. But these days there could be quite a difference. For a medical perspective, please consult your doctor or health practitioner.)

Most of you, the overwhelming majority, will see improvement in health and energy this year, although – until May 26 – there are two long-term planets in stressful alignment with you. For some of you, those born early in the sign, from October 22 to the 24th, health still needs attention.

The good news is that you seem to be enjoying dealing with health and healthy lifestyles. It is an area of great fulfilment for you. And there is more good news. There is much you can do to enhance the health and prevent problems from developing. Give more attention to the following – the vulnerable areas of your Horoscope this year (the reflex points are shown in the chart opposite):

- The colon, bladder, organs of elimination and sexual organs. These are always important for Scorpio and the reflexes are shown above.
- The head and face. Regular scalp and face massage will not only strength the head and face but the entire body as well. There are reflex points located there and energy meridians that affect the entire body. Craniosacral therapy is also excellent for the head.
- The musculature is another important area for Scorpio. You don't need to be a bodybuilder, you just need good muscle tone. Weak or flabby muscles can knock the spine and skeleton out of alignment. So, vigorous exercise, according to your age and stage in life, is important.
- The adrenals. These too are always important for you, Scorpio. The important thing with the adrenals, as our regular readers know, is to avoid anger and fear – the two emotions that stress them out.
- The heart is important for those of you born early on in Scorpio, October 22–24. The reflex points are shown opposite, and chest massage is also stimulating for the heart. It is important to avoid worry and anxiety, emotions that stress out the heart. Meditation will be a big help for this.

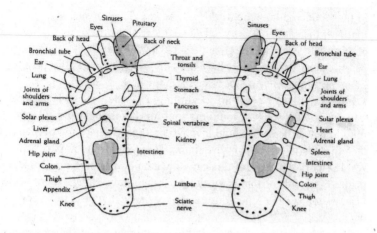

Important foot reflexology points for the year ahead
Try to massage all of the foot on a regular basis – the top of the foot as well as the bottom – but pay extra attention to the points highlighted on the chart. When you massage, be aware of 'sore spots' as these need special attention. It's also a good idea to massage the ankles and, especially, below them.

Mars, your health planet, is a relatively fast-moving planet who over the course of a year moves through eight signs and houses of your horoscope. Thus, there are many short-term health trends that depend on where Mars is and the kinds of aspects he is receiving. These will be dealt with in the monthly reports.

When Jupiter moves away from his stressful aspect on May 26 there will be a further increase in health and energy. This is good news.

Home and Family

Pluto's move into your 4th house this year, while not yet the full-blown transit that begins next year, is nevertheless a harbinger, an announcement, of things to come. Your 4th house of home, family and emotional life will be prominent for many, many years.

First off, your ruling planet's presence in the 4th house shows great personal involvement with home and family. Many of you will adopt the image of the family person. This is how you will present yourself to the world and how the world will see you. The transit also signals that over the coming years you will be undertaking major renovations of the home. There will be great personal involvement with a parent or parent figure. Perhaps there have been disagreements with this parent figure and you are trying to create harmony here.

Most importantly, you are beginning a journey, a psychological journey into the roots of your emotions and emotional habits. As we mentioned earlier, this could involve depth psychology and perhaps lead to the study of past incarnations. There is a desire to purify the whole emotional life, but this can only happen by going deeply into issues. The subconscious world is a huge, huge thing. There are layers upon layers of memories and experience that need to be dealt with.

Pluto moving through your 4th house can indicate deaths, or near-death experiences in the lives of family members. The whole family circle can die and be reborn in another way.

A parent or parent figure seems to have had multiple moves in recent years, and a move could happen this year as well. He or she has been subject to sudden mood changes. He or she has been difficult to handle.

Siblings and sibling figures could have moved last year but this year their home and family life tends to the status quo. Children and children figures seem more serious about life and are taking on more responsibility. A move could happen this year or next year. Female children of childbearing age become more fertile in the year ahead. Grandchildren, if you have them, or those who play that role in your life, are having a stable home and family year. They do seem successful in their career.

If you're planning a major renovation or construction project in the home, February 13 to March 23 would be a good time. If you're redecorating in a cosmetic kind of way or otherwise beautifying the house, February 16 to March 12 would be a good time.

Finance and Career

Your money house is basically empty this year; only short-term planets will pass through there and their impact will only be temporary. This tends to the status quo. Earnings will more or less be the way they were last year. And you seem OK with this.

Jupiter, your financial planet, will be in two signs and houses this year. Until May 26 he will be in your 7th house of love and social relationships. After May 26 he will be in your 8th house of regeneration. Both these positions show a need to be focused on the financial affairs of other people, especially the spouse, partner or current love. To the degree that you prosper other people, your own prosperity will come to you quite naturally. In a certain sense you are like the mutual fund manager or hedge fund manager whose bonus payments grow the more the fund's investors prosper.

Jupiter moving through your 7th house until May 26 shows the importance of social connections in your financial life. Who you know is probably more important than how much you have. This would also indicate a partnership, joint venture or merger in the year ahead. If you are an investor, companies that you own could also be involved in those things. Jupiter in the sign of Taurus gives sound financial judgement – a positive for finance. It favours investments in rural real estate, copper, and companies involved with copper and agricultural products.

On May 26 Jupiter will move into your 8th house, which gives many meanings. Generally, this signals inheritance, but hopefully no one has to actually die. You can be named in someone's will, or to an administrative position in a will. In general, you would profit from estates. Those of you of an appropriate age will probably be doing estate planning. Taxes and tax issues are influencing most of your financial decision-making. Good tax planning and tax efficiency seem unusually important. The financial planet in the 8th house highlights many of your innate strengths, Scorpio. It shows a special ability to see value where others only see death and decay. Thus, you can profit from troubled or even bankrupt companies or properties, turning them around. If you have good business ideas you easily attract outside investors to your projects. In general, you have good access to outside money, either through credit or through investors. You can profit from creative financing. Money can come to you through insurance payments as well. This position is especially good for the finances of the spouse, partner or current love. He or she will have a banner financial year.

The financial planet in the sign of Gemini after May 26 favours earnings from buying, selling, retailing and trading. You have excellent sales and marketing skills from May 26 onwards. Whatever you are doing, good sales, marketing, advertising and PR are very important.

Career doesn't seem a big issue this year. Your 10th house of career is basically empty. Only short-term planets will move through there and their impact will be short term.

The Sun, a fast-moving planet, is your career planet. During the course of the year he will move through every sign and house of your Horoscope, providing many short-term trends in the career that depend on his position at any given time and the kinds of aspects he receives. These are best dealt with in the monthly reports.

Love and Social Life

The love and social life are very active this year, active and basically happy. Uranus has been in your 7th house for many years and this has brought sudden and dramatic change to your love life and relationships. As we mentioned earlier, divorces and break-ups could easily have happened in recent years. For singles, this position is very exciting. Love can happen anywhere at any time, and often when you least expect it. However, the stability of such love is questionable.

Since Uranus is your family planet, this transit signals more socializing from home and with the family. It would also show that family members, and especially a parent or parent figure, are very active in your love life.

Normally, Uranus in the 7th house is not an aspect for marriage. There is a need for much change in love. It is a much better signal for serial love affairs then for serious committed love. But this year could be different because beneficent Jupiter, your money planet, is also moving through your 7th house. This will likely bring serious romance for singles.

Jupiter in your 7th house indicates that a lot of your socializing in the year ahead could be business related. You have the kind of aspects of someone who likes to socialize with the people you do business with and to do business with the people you socialize with. The social compatibility seems important in business. Singles will be attracted to wealthy people. Wealth is a romantic turn-on these days. Probably you're meeting people who are like that.

Self-improvement

Neptune has been in your 5th house of fun and creativity for many, many years now. Spirit, the divine, has been inspiring you in your personal creativity. Spirit is speaking to you in that language. Now with Saturn also in your 5th house this year, it is time to structure these inspirations into good and solid forms. Neptune is the most spiritual of all the planets, so his position in the 5th house is showing that creativity is a valid path to the divine. Through studying the laws of creation, we understand the ways that the great creator works. The same laws that go into a painting or sculpture or story go into the creation of a universe, only the latter is more elaborate and larger. Venus as the ruler of your spiritual 12th house reinforces the above. Venus rules the arts. So, art and creativity are a valid spiritual path for you. Venus, of course, rules love and is your actual love planet too. So, the message of the Horoscope is that when you are in a state of love you are close to the divine.

We mentioned earlier about Pluto's move into your 4th house, where he will stay there for 30 or so more years. Pluto is slow but he is very thorough. There will be all kinds of dramas and upheavals happening in the home and the family life, as we've said. To handle this properly it is important to understand what is behind it. This is not about punishment or about being a bad person, it is about a new birth – a new birth of family and home and a new psychological birth. You will be embarking on a tremendous and interesting journey into your own psyche, your own inner world. This could be compared to visiting an unexplored continent or planet. You are entering the unknown. This new continent within contains many beautiful, wonderful and rapturous places. But it also contains many hidden dangers. As you proceed, and with the help of the divine, you will learn how to handle all this. You will emerge as a new and better person.

For more information on astrology, healing and spiritual topics, please visit my blog at www.spiritual-stories.com.

Month-by-month Forecasts

January

Best Days Overall: 6, 7, 14, 15, 23, 24
Most Stressful Days Overall: 12, 13, 18, 19, 25, 26, 27
Best Days for Love: 8, 9, 18, 19, 27, 28
Best Days for Money: 1, 2, 8, 9, 10, 11, 18, 19, 28, 29
Best Days for Career: 11, 12, 25, 26, 27, 28, 29, 31

You begin the year with tremendous power in your 3rd house of communication and intellectual interests. Thus, the mental powers and communication faculties are very much enhanced. With 60 per cent of the planets either in that house or moving through there this month, your mental faculties are super-charged. This is good news for students, writers, teachers and intellectual workers. It is also an excellent month for sales and marketing people, traders, retailers, advertising and PR people. All these people should have a successful kind of month. The main danger is having too much of a good thing. The mind is so super-charged that it gets easily overstimulated. It can go round and round and round, achieving nothing. This can lead to insomnia or other nervous problems. Scorpios are usually not big talkers but this month is different. You have the gift of the gab these days.

Health needs more attention from the 20th onwards. You can improve the health by learning to turn the mind off when not in use. Undue mental stimulation wastes energy. As always, make sure to get enough rest. Enhance the health in the ways mentioned in the yearly report. In addition, until the 5th thigh massage and massage of the liver reflex will be a help. After the 5th, back and knee massage will be good.

The month ahead should be prosperous as your financial planet is receiving wonderful aspects until the 20th. Prosperity is good after the 20th as well, but you will probably have to work harder for it.

Love is happy and exciting, but also unstable. Marriage is not likely or advisable these days. Venus, your love planet, is in your money house until the 23rd, while Jupiter, your financial planet, is in your 7th house of love. These two planets are in mutual reception until the 23rd. Each is a guest in the house of the other. This shows good cooperation between love and finance. This can show that a lucrative partnership or joint venture is happening. It can show that a focus on your financial goals will lead singles to romantic opportunities. The reverse is also true. The focus on social goals can lead to happy financial opportunities. Singles are likely to find romantic opportunities as they pursue their financial goals, or with people involved in their finances. After the 23rd romantic opportunities happen in educational types of settings, perhaps at school, a lecture, a seminar, the library or bookshop. Romantic opportunities are also found close to home, in the neighbourhood and perhaps with neighbours.

February

Best Days Overall: 1, 2, 3, 10, 11, 19, 20, 29
Most Stressful Days Overall: 8, 9, 14, 15, 21, 22, 23
Best Days for Love: 6, 7, 14, 15, 16, 17, 26, 27
Best Days for Money: 4, 5, 6, 7, 14, 15, 24, 25
Best Days for Career: 8, 9, 18, 19, 21, 22, 23, 29

Health needs serious attention this month. Three long-term planets are in stressful alignment with you and now the short-term planets are joining the party.

As always make sure to get enough rest. Exercise is generally good for you, but this month be more mindful about it. If you feel pain or discomfort while working out, take a break. Try not to push the body beyond its limits. Enhance the health in the ways mentioned in the yearly report. This month give more attention to the back, the knees, the ankles and calves. Also give more attention to the heart. It might be a good idea to schedule some extra massages, reflexology, acupuncture or acupressure treatments. These will boost your energy levels. If you take these precautions, you should sail through the month with relatively good health.

The main headline this month is the incredible power in your house of home and family: over half the planets are either there or moving through there this month. Even your career planet the Sun is in your 4th house until the 19th. So, home and family and your emotional wellness are the real mission this month. This is the career. You can safely let go of your outer ambitions right now and focus on the foundation, which makes outer success possible. Home, family and emotional wellness and understanding are going to be a major focus in your life for the next 30 or so years, and this focus begins now. This would be a good month to enter some formal psychological type of therapy. The conventional therapies will probably not satisfy you, but you need to start somewhere.

The new Moon of the 9th also occurs in your 4th house, further emphasizing its importance. The good news here is that as the days go by and until the next new Moon, many emotional issues will clarify for you.

Venus will travel with Pluto on the 12th and 13th, bringing a happy romantic opportunity. From the 13th onwards Venus will be in your home and family house. Thus, love is found close to home and perhaps happens through the intervention of family and family connections. There will be more socializing from home and with family members. Old flames from the past can reappear. This is generally to resolve old issues.

Health will improve after the 19th but you're still not out of the woods. Health still needs a lot of watching.

March

Best Days Overall: 1, 9, 10, 17, 18, 27, 28
Most Stressful Days Overall: 1, 8, 13, 14, 19, 20, 21
Best Days for Love: 7, 8, 13, 14, 17, 18, 27, 28
Best Days for Money: 2, 3, 4, 5, 13, 14, 22, 23, 28, 30
Best Days for Career: 1, 9, 10, 18, 19, 20, 21, 29, 30

Health and energy are steadily improving. Your health planet Mars is in your 4th house until the 23rd, showing that good health for you means good emotional health – so strive to attain your point of emotional harmony. On the 23rd your health planet moves into Pisces, a positive transit. From the 23rd onwards enhance the health with foot massage and spiritual-healing techniques. If you feel under the weather, see a spiritual healer as you respond well to these things.

The month ahead is much happier than last month as you are in a yearly personal pleasure peak. This began on February 19 and will continue until the 20th of this month. Just enjoying life, taking a vacation from personal cares and worries, will do much for your emotional and physical health. Enjoying life will also boost your career. Though it is counterintuitive, you can make career progress while at the theatre, golf course or party.

With your career planet in your 5th house, you can feel that your children and children figures in your life are your real mission this month.

Love seems happy, especially from the 11th onwards. But this does not seem like serious love, more like a love affair. Love seems like another form of entertainment, like going to the movies or the theatre. Singles are attracted to those who can show them a fun time.

Finances are much improved over the last month. The month ahead seems prosperous. Your social connections and overall social grace play a huge role in your finances. Likeability can be more important than your professional skills.

A lunar eclipse on the 25th is relatively mild in its effects on you, but it won't hurt to take a more relaxed, easy schedule. If this eclipse hits a sensitive point in your personal Horoscope, the one cast especially for you, it can be powerful indeed. So, take it easy while the eclipse is in effect. This eclipse occurs in your 12th house and produces spiritual changes. There will be changes in your practice, teachings, teachers and general spiritual attitudes. If you have a guru, he or she can experience personal dramas. If you are involved in a spiritual or charitable organization, you can expect changes and upheavals there. College-level students experience dramas at their institutions and perhaps change educational plans. Sometimes they even change schools. There are shake-ups in your place of worship and dramas in the lives of worship leaders. Your philosophical and theological concepts will get tested by the events of the eclipse.

April

Best Days Overall: 5, 6, 13, 14, 15, 23, 24, 25
Most Stressful Days Overall: 3, 4, 9, 10, 16, 17, 30
Best Days for Love: 7, 8, 9, 10, 16, 17, 27, 28
Best Days for Money: 1, 2, 9, 10, 18, 19, 26, 27
Best Days for Career: 7, 8, 16, 17, 28, 29

A solar eclipse on the 8th, the strongest eclipse of 2024, is the main headline of the month. This is a total eclipse and one that directly impacts other planets, which makes it unusually powerful. So, use common sense and take normal precautions. Reschedule activities that you can. Stay close to home in a safe environment, watch a movie, read a book and, best of all, meditate. Do your best to stay out of harm's way while the eclipse is in effect and this goes for friends, parents, parent figures and the spouse, partner or current love too.

The eclipse occurs in your 6th house of health and work and thus can bring job changes, changes in the workplace and working conditions and changes in your health regime. There are personal dramas in the lives of aunts, uncles and in-laws. Children and children figures in your life have financial dramas and need to make important changes in this area.

The impact of the eclipse on Venus, your love planet, will test your current relationship. It seems in danger. Love has been unstable for many years and this eclipse adds to the instability. Since Mercury is also directly affected, there can be psychological confrontations with death. Perhaps you personally have a near-death kind of experience or close call. Perhaps you hear of the death of a celebrity that you love or of someone that you know. Perhaps you have dreams of death. But, as our regular readers know, these confrontations with death are not punitive but educational. The cosmos is pushing you to a deeper understanding of death.

Career changes are also happening now. Usually, people don't actually change the career, only the way that they pursue it. But sometimes they do change the actual career, especially if it hasn't been in line with their true life's work. There can be shake-ups and resignations in the hierarchy of your company. The government can change the rules governing your industry or company. Often, there are shake-ups in the company. All these things tend to change the way you pursue your career. There are likely to be personal dramas in the lives of bosses, parents, parent figures and people who are in authority over you.

Computers, software and high-tech gadgetry are likely to behave erratically during this eclipse. Again, take common-sense precautions. Avoid suspicious websites, emails and email attachments. Back up your important files and make sure your antivirus, anti-hacking software is up to date.

The eclipse can bring a health scare. If this happens, God forbid, make sure you get a second opinion.

May

Best Days Overall: 2, 3, 4, 11, 12, 20, 21, 22, 30, 31
Most Stressful Days Overall: 1, 7, 8, 13, 14, 27, 28
Best Days for Love: 7, 8, 15, 16, 27, 28
Best Days for Money: 8, 16, 23, 24, 26, 27
Best Days for Career: 1, 7, 8, 13, 14, 18, 19, 27

The planetary power is mostly in the social Western sector this month. Your 7th house of love is ultra-powerful, while your 1st house of self is basically empty. Only the Moon will move through your own house between the 20th and 22nd. So, the month ahead is a social month, a yearly love and social peak. The focus should be on others and their needs. Pluto, the ruler of your Horoscope, will go retrograde on the 2nd and will be retrograde for the rest of the month ahead. This tends to weaken self-confidence, self-esteem and self-will. Perhaps this is a good thing as these qualities are not so necessary right now. It's your social grace that is important. Your good doesn't come from your personal skills or personal initiative but through others. So, let others have their way, so long as it isn't destructive. Your way is probably not the best way this month.

Parents and parent figures have an uneasy relationship on the 13th and 14th. However, this is a good time to give more attention to the home and family and to emotional wellness. The Sun travels with Jupiter from the 18th to the 20th and this will bring a boost to your career. It is a good financial period as well. A pay rise, official or unofficial, could happen.

On the 26th Jupiter, your money planet, moves into your 8th house and will be there for the rest of the year ahead and into 2025. This strengthens many of your natural gifts. Pursue your natural gifts and inclinations and wealth will increase. On the 20th the Sun also moved into your 8th house, increasing the planetary power there. You have the classic aspects for inheritance, though hopefully no one has to die. You can be named in someone's will or appointed to an administrative position in an estate. In general, you profit from estates and from estate planning. Good tax planning, too, is ultra-important in the year ahead, and especially this month. This is a great month for those of you who need to attract outside investors to your projects – there is much good fortune here. Also a good time for paying down or making debt, depending on your need. There is good access to outside capital and many of you can earn through creative financing. Jupiter is travelling with Uranus early in the month. (The aspect was more exact last month but is still in effect.) This often brings sudden money and large material good.

Health is much improved after the 20th. But before the 20th make sure to get enough rest. Enhance the health in the ways mentioned in the yearly report.

June

Best Days Overall: 7, 8, 17, 18, 26, 27
Most Stressful Days Overall: 3, 4, 9, 10, 11, 24, 25, 30
Best Days for Love: 3, 4, 5, 6, 16, 17, 26, 27, 30
Best Days for Money: 5, 14, 19, 20, 24
Best Days for Career: 5, 6, 9, 10, 11, 14, 15, 26

Health and energy are much improved this month. After the 20th it will improve even further. If you have any pre-existing conditions, they get much easier to manage.

Your health planet will be in two signs this month. Until the 9th Mars will be in Aries, his own sign and house, where he is strong on your behalf. On the 9th he moves into Taurus, your 7th house. Health is in enhanced in the ways mentioned in the yearly report until the 9th. After the 9th neck and throat massage will be beneficial. Exercise regimes will go much better than in previous months.

Your health planet in your 7th house shows that good health for you also means good social health and a healthy love life. If there are problems here, health can be affected. So, if health problems arise, restore harmony in your social life as quickly as possible.

Although home and family issues will be important for many more years, right now, with the planetary power mostly in the upper half of your Horoscope, it is good to shift more attention to the career and your outer goals.

Your 8th house of regeneration is still powerful until the 20th. Keep in mind our discussion of this last month. This is still a good period for attracting outside investors and for paying down or making debt, according to your need. An excellent month for dealing with tax, estate and insurance issues. Most people don't enjoy 8th house issues but you do, Scorpio. So, the month ahead is happy. On the 20th, as the Sun enters your 9th house, there is career expansion, happy love and social experiences, and more good fortune with accessing outside money. There is much progress in your theological, religious and philosophical studies. College-level students are successful in their studies. If you are involved in legal issues, there is good fortune with them. You should get best-case outcomes.

Love seems happy, but complicated. As we have seen for many months now, there is love in your life but it is very unstable. With Mars in your 7th house from the 9th onwards, romantic opportunities can happen at the gym or as you visit the doctor's or therapist's office or with people involved in your health. Co-workers too seem alluring.

Venus will be in your 9th house from the 17th onwards. For singles this shows romantic opportunity at college or religious functions or at your place of worship. Romance can also happen in foreign countries or with foreigners.

July

Best Days Overall: 4, 5, 6, 14, 15, 16, 23, 24
Most Stressful Days Overall: 1, 7, 8, 21, 22, 27, 28
Best Days for Love: 1, 5, 6, 17, 18, 25, 26, 27, 28
Best Days for Money: 2, 3, 12, 13, 17, 18, 21, 22, 29, 30
Best Days for Career: 4, 5, 6, 7, 8, 15, 16, 23

Health is good this month, but after the 20th will need more watching. Until the 20th you can enhance your health in the ways discussed in the yearly report, and also with neck and throat massage. Craniosacral therapy could be beneficial. After the 20th enhance the health with arm and shoulder massage and massage of the lung reflex point. If you feel under the weather after the 20th, get out in the fresh air and do some deep breathing.

Your health planet will travel with Uranus this month, which can signal changes in your health regime and perhaps changes at work and in working conditions. You seem very involved with the health of family members. Family members should be more mindful when driving, and in general.

The planetary power is still mostly in your 9th house until the 22nd. This is a happy, expansive kind of time. It benefits college-level students, and those of you involved in legal issues. Those of you involved in religious and theological studies will also have a good month and you'll see much progress here. Foreign lands seem to call to you and many of you will be travelling abroad – much of this seems career related.

This month the planetary power shifts to your 10th house of career. On the 22nd you begin a yearly career peak. Probably this is the reason why health and energy are less good than normal. The demands of the career are high and you seem very involved here. It is a successful kind of month, on a worldly level. Venus, your love planet, moves into your 10th house on the 11th and stays there for the rest of the month. This indicates that if you pursue your career goals, love will find you. There are loving romantic opportunities with bosses, superiors and people involved in your career. Career is fostered by social means now – your professional skills are important, but your likeability is perhaps equally important. Try attending, or hosting, career-related parties and gatherings.

Mars, your health planet, travels with Jupiter from the 11th to the 14th. This gives many messages. Finances are boosted, and perhaps you are more speculative and risk-taking on those days as well. Perhaps you spend more on health and health issues, but you can also earn from health too. The transit is a very nice signal for your personal health and should bring good news on that score.

August

Best Days Overall: 1, 2, 11, 12, 19, 20, 28, 29
Most Stressful Days Overall: 3, 4, 17, 18, 23, 24, 25, 30, 31
Best Days for Love: 8, 17, 18, 23, 24, 25, 29
Best Days for Money: 8, 9, 13, 14, 17, 18, 27
Best Days for Career: 3, 4, 13, 14, 23, 30, 31

Health, like last month, needs some attention. Make sure to get enough rest. The demands of career are very high just now and the desire for success can tempt you to push the body beyond its limit. This would be a good month to schedule some massages, reflexology or acupuncture treatments. These kinds of therapies tend to boost the energy. With your health planet moving through your 8th house this month, detox regimes also seem good. After the 22nd, you should see dramatic improvement in your health and energy. The short-term planets move away from their stressful aspect with you.

You are still in a yearly career peak until the 22nd. So much success is happening.

Planetary retrograde activity is very near its maximum for the year. From the 4th to the 25th 40 per cent of the planets are in retrograde motion. Although half of them will be retrograde next month for a few days, on a functional level we are at the maximum for the year. You probably can't avoid the delays that will happen, but you can mini-mize them by being more perfect in all that you do. Make sure the details and technicalities of the forms that you fill out and the letters that you send are as perfect as you can make them. Also understand that the delays you experience are not your fault. You're not a bad person and God is not punishing you; it is just the cosmic weather and it will pass.

On the 5th, Venus will move into your 11th house. The love life should be good but becomes more complicated. For singles love and romantic opportunities happen online, through social media, as you involve yourself with friends, groups and organizations. The complications arise from Venus being in the sign of Virgo. This is not her strongest position (in fact, it is her weakest position), and symbolically speaking she is not comfortable in the sign. Social grace and magnetism could be a lot better. The other complication is that there is a tendency to be too critical, analytical and perfectionistic. And, if you yourself are not that way, you are attracting these kinds of people. Avoid this as much as possible. Avoid criticism, especially destructive criticism. This is sure to kill any romantic moment.

Finances are better before the 22nd than after. After the 22nd more work is needed to achieve financial goals.

September

Best Days Overall: 7, 8, 16, 17, 24, 25
Most Stressful Days Overall: 1, 14, 15, 20, 21, 26, 27, 28
Best Days for Love: 4, 5, 14, 15, 20, 21, 23, 24
Best Days for Money: 4, 5, 9, 10, 14, 15, 22, 23
Best Days for Career: 1, 2, 3, 12, 13, 27, 28

Health is good this month, and perhaps this is due to exploring different therapies and perhaps therapists. Mars, your health planet, is out of bounds from the 5th to the 24th. So, when it comes to health, you are exploring outside your normal boundaries, outside your normal sphere. This seems to work for you. Perhaps the demands of work also put you outside your normal sphere.

Although your career peak has passed, career still seems good. You have a good work ethic and superiors take note. Your networking abilities and technological expertise further the career. It is also a very good thing to be more involved with trade and professional organizations.

Children, or children figures in your life, all having a super social month. If they are of an appropriate age they have many romantic opportunities. The problem with the children is that they are not sure of what they want.

There is a lunar eclipse on the 18th which seems relatively mild on you, although if this eclipse hits a sensitive point in your personal Horoscope, the one cast especially for you, it can be rather more powerful. It won't hurt to reduce your schedule while the eclipse is in effect.

This eclipse occurs in your 5th house and impacts very directly on your children and children figures in your life. They definitely should take a more relaxed schedule and stay out of harm's way as much as possible. They have a need to re-define themselves and their self-concept. The events of the eclipse will force this; either they define themselves for themselves or others will do it for them, and this will not be so pleasant. If they haven't been careful in dietary matters, there can be a detox of the physical body.

Those of you involved in the creative arts will make very dramatic changes in your creativity as the months progress. Your tastes and preferences in your hobbies, leisure activities and fun will also change in coming months.

Parents or parent figures need to make important and dramatic changes in their financial lives. A course correction is necessary. This is so for you as well, though it won't be as dramatic. Your financial planet Jupiter is sideswiped by this eclipse. Happily, it is not a direct hit so only minor tweaking and changing of your financial strategy, planning and thinking will be called for.

Every lunar eclipse impacts college-level students, your place of worship, worship leaders, and your religious, philosophical and theological beliefs. With the Moon ruling your 9th house you go through this twice a year and by now you know how to handle it. It is basically a good thing that the cosmos forces you to re-evaluate your religious and theological beliefs on a regular basis. The events of life will show us what is real, what is true, what is partially true and what is false. Thus, we can live our lives on a more realistic basis.

College-level students are likely to change their educational plans, and will sometimes even change schools. Even applicants to college can have dramas with their applications. There are shake-ups and upheavals in your place of worship and personal dramas in the lives of worship leaders.

October

Best Days Overall: 4, 5, 13, 14, 21, 22, 23, 31
Most Stressful Days Overall: 11, 12, 17, 18, 24, 25, 30
Best Days for Love: 4, 5, 13, 14, 17, 18, 24, 25
Best Days for Money: 2, 6, 7, 8, 11, 12, 19, 20, 29, 30
Best Days for Career: 1, 11, 12, 20, 24, 25

A solar eclipse on the 2nd is the main headline this month. Though it is not as powerful as the last solar eclipse in April, it is still pretty strong. It impacts two other planets and so various sectors of your life are affected.

The eclipse occurs in your 12th house of spirituality and brings spiritual changes – changes of practice, teachers, teachings and overall attitudes. A lot of this is very normal and not something to be feared. As one grows spiritually, practices that were once very positive are no longer necessary and perhaps new practices are needed. Teachings that were appropriate at one time are now no longer appropriate due to your spiritual growth. Sometimes it takes a cosmic push, which the eclipse provides, to foster new growth. Guru figures in your life are likely to experience personal dramas. There are shake-ups in spiritual or charitable organizations that you are involved with.

Mars, your health and work planet, is directly impacted by this eclipse. Thus, there can be job changes, changes in the conditions of the workplace, perhaps disruptions in the workplace. Sometimes people change jobs within their present organization, and sometimes with a new organization.

The events of the eclipse tend to signal a need to make changes in your health regime. This will happen over the coming months. Sometimes this kind of eclipse brings a health scare. But your health looks good this month and it is likely to be no more than a scare. Make sure to get a second opinion.

Scorpio has a natural interest in death and understands it better than most. This eclipse, because it impacts on Mercury, the ruler of your 8th house, will deepen your understanding of the subject. This usually happens through psychological encounters with death, perhaps dreams of death, perhaps near-death experiences or close calls.

Generally, it is not a physical death but a psychological encounter with it. (This is another reason to take a more relaxed, easy schedule while the eclipse is in effect.)

Your friends, and social circle in general, are also affected by the eclipse. There are personal dramas in the lives of friends. There are shake-ups in trade and professional organizations that you are involved with. Computers and high-tech gadgetry can behave erratically, and your internet service can be erratic as well. Avoid suspicious websites, emails and attachments.

As the Sun is your career planet, every solar eclipse brings career changes and this one is no different. Usually a person doesn't change the actual career, though it sometimes happens, but the way that they pursue it and their thinking and strategy change.

November

Best Days Overall: 1, 2, 10, 11, 18, 19, 28, 29
Most Stressful Days Overall: 7, 8, 9, 14, 15, 20, 21
Best Days for Love: 3, 4, 12, 13, 14, 15, 22, 23
Best Days for Money: 3, 4, 8, 9, 16, 17, 26, 27, 29, 30
Best Days for Career: 1, 2, 10, 11, 19, 20, 21, 22

A happy and healthy month ahead, Scorpio. Enjoy.

Until the 4th we have a Grand Trine in the Water element – a very positive aspect for you as your native element is Water. You are in a yearly personal pleasure peak until the 21st. The Sun is moving through your own sign which not only helps your career, but your personal appearance as well. You have more charisma, self-confidence and self-esteem. This reflects in your appearance. This is a time for pampering the body and enjoying all the pleasures of the five senses and the flesh. It is a time for getting the body and image in the shape that you want. Happy career opportunities are coming to you this month too. Not only that, but you have the appearance of a successful person. People see you this way, and probably you are dressing the part.

Mars moves into your 10th house of career on the 4th and stays there for the rest of the month ahead. This shows great activity in the career. Career responsibilities and demands are keeping you very busy and active. Your good work ethic is noticed by your superiors.

The new Moon of the 1st occurs in your own sign and is an especially happy day. The personal appearance and charisma are increased even further. It is also an excellent career day. Issues involving your appearance and image will clarify day by day until the next new Moon.

On the 21st the Sun enters your financial 2nd house and you begin a yearly career peak. Earnings are stronger than usual. A pay rise, official or unofficial, is likely. Bosses, parents and parent figures, people in authority over you are boosting earnings and are favourably disposed to your financial goals.

Your love planet Venus is out of bounds all month. This shows that your search for love takes you outside your normal sphere, outside your normal haunts. There are no solutions in your present sphere and you must search outside it. This could also be the case with the beloved, who perhaps sees you as someone outside his or her normal sphere.

Although you'll begin a yearly financial peak on the 21st, Jupiter, your financial planet, is retrograde and has been since October 8. This will not stop earnings, but it could slow things down. Because you are in a yearly financial peak, earnings will be strong but will happen with many delays. Perhaps more work is involved.

December

Best Days Overall: 7, 8, 15, 16, 25, 26
Most Stressful Days Overall: 5, 6, 11, 12, 17, 18, 19
Best Days for Love: 2, 3, 4, 11, 12, 13, 14, 22, 23, 24
Best Days for Money: 1, 6, 14, 23, 24, 27, 28, 29
Best Days for Career: 1, 9, 10, 17, 18, 19, 20, 30, 31

You're still in a yearly financial peak until the 21st. Earnings will increase, assets that you hold will increase in value. Even the retrograde of your financial planet will not stop the prosperity, only slow things down a bit. Major purchases or investments need more research and study, although you still have the financial favour of the authority figures in your life. If a pay rise did not happen last month it can still happen until the 21st. This can be something official or unofficial.

Venus, your love planet, is still out of bounds until the 8th. So, in matters of the heart you are still searching outside your normal boundaries. You are still in strange territory, unfamiliar territory, until the 8th. In addition, Venus in the sign of Capricorn until the 7th makes you more cautious in love matters. And, if this is not true of you, it is true of the people that you attract. Venus is not very comfortable in Capricorn. She is more reserved, cool. She is slow to fall in love and likes to test things to see if they are real. Caution in love is a wonderful thing, but if this becomes fear it is pathology. A thin line separates the two. Venus will be in your 3rd house until the 7th. This shows that love is close to home, in the neighbourhood. Singles can find romantic opportunity at school functions, at lectures, seminars, the library or bookshop. You seem to like intellectual and serious kinds of people these days. Often this transit shows an affinity for older people – not old people per se but older than you. A serious, intellectual kind of conversation is a form of foreplay until the 7th.

After the 7th Venus will be in Aquarius and your 4th house. You are socializing more from the home and with family members now. A romantic evening at home seems preferable to a night out on the town. Venus is less stiff, less formal in the sign of Aquarius than she is in Capricorn. There is more emotional sharing, more emotional intimacy. Both you and the people you meet seem more experimental in love matters.

Health is still good this month. You can enhance it further in the ways mentioned in the yearly report, and by giving more attention to the heart. Chest massage and massage of the heart reflex will be wonderful.

Career still seems very active as Mars will be in your 10th house all month. There is a need to be more aggressive in career matters. Perhaps you need to fend off competitors, either personal or corporate.

Sagittarius

↗

THE ARCHER

Birthdays from
23rd November to
20th December

Personality Profile

SAGITTARIUS AT A GLANCE

Element – Fire

Ruling Planet – Jupiter
  Career Planet – Mercury
  Love Planet – Mercury
  Money Planet – Saturn
  Planet of Health and Work – Venus
  Planet of Home and Family Life – Neptune
  Planet of Spirituality – Pluto

Colours – blue, dark blue

Colours that promote love, romance and social harmony – yellow,
  yellow-orange

Colours that promote earning power – black, indigo

Gems – carbuncle, turquoise

Metal – tin

Scents – carnation, jasmine, myrrh

Quality – mutable (= flexibility)

Qualities most needed for balance – attention to detail, administrative and organizational skills

Strongest virtues – generosity, honesty, broad-mindedness, tremendous vision

Deepest need – to expand mentally

Characteristics to avoid – over-optimism, exaggeration, being too generous with other people's money

Signs of greatest overall compatibility – Aries, Leo

Signs of greatest overall incompatibility – Gemini, Virgo, Pisces

Sign most helpful to career – Virgo

Sign most helpful for emotional support – Pisces

Sign most helpful financially – Capricorn

Sign best for marriage and/or partnerships – Gemini

Sign most helpful for creative projects – Aries

Best Sign to have fun with – Aries

Signs most helpful in spiritual matters – Leo, Scorpio

Best day of the week – Thursday

Understanding a Sagittarius

If you look at the symbol of the archer you will gain a good, intuitive understanding of a person born under this astrological sign. The development of archery was humanity's first refinement of the power to hunt and wage war. The ability to shoot an arrow far beyond the ordinary range of a spear extended humanity's horizons, wealth, personal will and power.

Today, instead of using bows and arrows we project our power with fuels and mighty engines, but the essential reason for using these new powers remains the same. These powers represent our ability to extend our personal sphere of influence – and this is what Sagittarius is all about. Sagittarians are always seeking to expand their horizons, to cover more territory and increase their range and scope. This applies to all aspects of their lives: economic, social and intellectual.

Sagittarians are noted for the development of the mind – the higher intellect – which understands philosophical and spiritual concepts. This mind represents the higher part of the psychic nature and is motivated not by self-centred considerations but by the light and grace of a Higher Power. Thus, Sagittarians love higher education of all kinds. They might be bored with formal schooling but they love to study on their own and in their own way. A love of foreign travel and interest in places far away from home are also noteworthy characteristics of the Sagittarian type.

If you give some thought to all these Sagittarian attributes you will see that they spring from the inner Sagittarian desire to develop. To travel more is to know more, to know more is to be more, to cultivate the higher mind is to grow and to reach more. All these traits tend to broaden the intellectual – and indirectly, the economic and material – horizons of the Sagittarian.

The generosity of the Sagittarian is legendary. There are many reasons for this. One is that Sagittarians seem to have an inborn consciousness of wealth. They feel that they are rich, that they are lucky, that they can attain any financial goal – and so they feel that they can afford to be generous. Sagittarians do not carry the burdens of want and limitation which stop most other people from giving generously. Another reason for their generosity is their religious and philosophical idealism, derived from the higher mind. This higher mind is by nature generous because it is unaffected by material circumstances. Still another reason is that the act of giving tends to enhance their emotional nature. Every act of giving seems to be enriching, and this is reward enough for the Sagittarian.

Finance

Sagittarians generally entice wealth. They either attract it or create it. They have the ideas, energy and talent to make their vision of paradise on Earth a reality. However, mere wealth is not enough. Sagittarians want luxury – earning a comfortable living seems small and insignificant to them.

In order for Sagittarians to attain their true earning potential they must develop better managerial and organizational skills. They must learn to set limits, to arrive at their goals through a series of attainable sub-goals or objectives. It is very rare that a person goes from rags to riches overnight. But a long, drawn-out process is difficult for Sagittarians. Like Leos, they want to achieve wealth and success quickly and impressively. They must be aware, however, that this over-optimism can lead to unrealistic financial ventures and disappointing losses. Of course, no zodiac sign can bounce back as quickly as Sagittarius, but only needless heartache will be caused by this attitude. Sagittarians need to maintain their vision – never letting it go – but they must also work towards it in practical and efficient ways.

Career and Public Image

Sagittarians are big thinkers. They want it all: money, fame, glamour, prestige, public acclaim and a place in history. They often go after all these goals. Some attain them, some do not – much depends on each individual's personal horoscope. But if Sagittarians want to attain public and professional status they must understand that these things are not conferred to enhance one's ego but as rewards for the amount of service that one does for the whole of humanity. If and when they figure out ways to serve more, Sagittarians can rise to the top.

The ego of the Sagittarian is gigantic – and perhaps rightly so. They have much to be proud of. If they want public acclaim, however, they will have to learn to tone down the ego a bit, to become more humble and self-effacing, without falling into the trap of self-denial and self-abasement. They must also learn to master the details of life, which can sometimes elude them.

At their jobs Sagittarians are hard workers who like to please their bosses and co-workers. They are dependable, trustworthy and enjoy a challenge. Sagittarians are friendly to work with and helpful to their colleagues. They usually contribute intelligent ideas or new methods that improve the work environment for everyone. Sagittarians always look for challenging positions and careers that develop their intellect, even if they have to work very hard in order to succeed. They also work well under the supervision of others, although by nature they would rather be the supervisors and increase their sphere of influence. Sagittarians excel at professions that allow them to be in contact with many different people and to travel to new and exciting locations.

Love and Relationships

Sagittarians love freedom for themselves and will readily grant it to their partners. They like their relationships to be fluid and ever-changing. Sagittarians tend to be fickle in love and to change their minds about their partners quite frequently.

Sagittarians feel threatened by a clearly defined, well-structured relationship, as they feel this limits their freedom. The Sagittarian tends to marry more than once in life.

Sagittarians in love are passionate, generous, open, benevolent and very active. They demonstrate their affections very openly. However, just like an Aries they tend to be egocentric in the way they relate to their partners. Sagittarians should develop the ability to see others' points of view, not just their own. They need to develop some objectivity and cool intellectual clarity in their relationships so that they can develop better two-way communication with their partners. Sagittarians tend to be overly idealistic about their partners and about love in general. A cool and rational attitude will help them to perceive reality more clearly and enable them to avoid disappointment.

Home and Domestic Life

Sagittarians tend to grant a lot of freedom to their family. They like big homes and many children and are one of the most fertile signs of the zodiac. However, when it comes to their children Sagittarians generally err on the side of allowing them too much freedom. Sometimes their children get the idea that there are no limits. However, allowing freedom in the home is basically a positive thing – so long as some measure of balance is maintained – for it enables all family members to develop as they should.

Horoscope for 2024

Major Trends

Saturn's move into Pisces last year put an added stress on your physical energy. So, health needs more attention these days as Saturn remains in adverse aspect to you for the rest of the year ahead. On May 26 Jupiter will also move into adverse aspect with you, so health really needs keeping a close eye on after that date. More on this later.

Saturn will be in your 4th house for the entire year. This shows that home and family are a kind of burden to you. You deal with family and the home in a dutiful kind of way, it doesn't seem joyous. Spiritual Neptune has been in your 4th house for many years now and will remain there in the year ahead, signalling an emotional sensitivity and a spiritual agenda behind your family relationships. More details later.

Jupiter has been in your 6th house of health and work since May of last year. He will be there until May 26, which is a positive for health. It shows focus and a tendency to get best-case outcomes with any health problems that might arise. Uranus has been in your 6th house for a long time and is still there in the year ahead. Thus, there have been many job changes over the years and changes in the health regime. More on this later.

On May 26 Jupiter, the ruler of your Horoscope, will enter your 7th house of love and stays there for the rest of the year. This shows a happy and active romantic life. You seem very socially popular from May 26 onwards. Details later.

Pluto, the planet of transformation, has been in your money house for over 30 years. This year he is getting ready to move into your 3rd house of communication and intellectual interests. He moves there briefly this year, but in 2025 he moves in for the long haul. The focus on finance will start to get less and less this year, while there will be a greater focus on your intellectual and mental life.

Your most important areas of interest in the year ahead are finance to January 22 and from September 3 to November 20; communication and intellectual interests from January 22 to September 3 and from November 20 to the end of the year; home and family; health and work until May 26; and love, romance and social life from May 26 to the end of the year.

Your paths of greatest fulfilment this year are children, creativity and leisure activities; health and work until May 26; and love, romance and social activities from May 26 onwards.

Health

(Please note that this is an astrological perspective on health and not a medical one. In days of yore there was no difference, both these perspectives were identical. But these days there could be quite a difference. For a medical perspective, please consult your doctor or health practitioner.)

As we've already said, health needs more attention this year. The good news is that, with your 6th house very strong, you are on the case. You are giving your health the attention that's necessary. This is a positive.

With Saturn in stressful aspect to you, you might not be able to jog or cycle the same distances as you would normally. So, if you are working out and feel any pain or discomfort, take a break. Try not to force things.

As our regular readers know, there is much that can be done to enhance the health and prevent problems from developing. Give more attention to the following – the vulnerable areas of your Horoscope this year (the reflex points are shown in the chart overleaf):

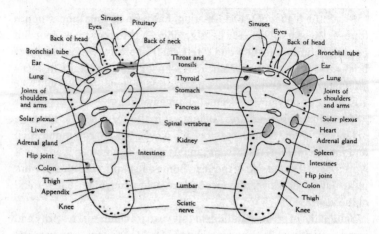

Important foot reflexology points for the year ahead

Try to massage all of the foot on a regular basis – the top of the foot as well as the bottom – but pay extra attention to the points highlighted on the chart. When you massage, be aware of 'sore spots' as these need special attention. It's also a good idea to massage the ankles especially, and below them.

- The liver and thighs. These areas are always important for Sagittarius. Regular thigh massage will not only strengthen the thighs and the liver but the lower back as well.
- The ankles and calves. These have been important for the past six or seven years and remain so this year. These areas should be regularly massaged and, if you are exercising, give the ankles more support.
- The neck and throat are another two areas that are always important for Sagittarius. Regular neck and throat massage will be very beneficial, especially if you feel tightness or tension in these areas. Craniosacral therapy is excellent for the neck.
- The kidneys and hips. Regular hip massage will not only strengthen the hips and kidneys but the lower back as well.
- The heart. This became important last year when Saturn moved into stressful alignment with you. The important thing with the heart is to avoid worry and anxiety, the two emotions that stress it out. The good news is that Sagittarians are not big worriers.

However, if you catch yourself in such a state change it immediately: replace worry with faith. Meditation will be a big help here. Chest massage will also help and stimulate the heart.

Venus, your health planet, is a very fast-moving planet, and in any given year will move through every sign and house of your Horoscope. Thus, there are many short-term trends in health that depend on where Venus is and the kinds of aspects that she receives. These short-term trends are best discussed in the monthly reports.

Uranus has been in your 6th house for the past six years or so. This shows a more experimental approach to health than usual. It would show a tendency to gravitate to alternative therapies rather than orthodox medicine. But even if you go with orthodox medicine, you would favour the new and cutting-edge technologies here.

Uranus's long transit through your health and work house has a deeper message. The cosmos is urging you to learn about how you personally function. This is everybody's job in life but for you it is especially important these days. The rule books on health should be seen merely as guidelines and not written in stone. Things that affect others do not affect you. Things that affect you do not affect others. You are a unique individual wired up in a unique way. Therapies that work for others might not work for you, and therapies that work for you might not work for others. We learn how we function personally through trial, error and experiment. In the long run it is well worth undergoing the effort.

Home and Family

With Saturn in your 4th house for the rest of the year ahead, family life could be a lot happier. As it is, you deal with it as a duty, an obligation, a discipline. The joy is not there.

There is a feeling of pessimism in the family. Perhaps it is you, perhaps it is in family members, especially a parent or parent figure. You need to be careful about depression this year. Don't stay in it as it can negatively impact your health. Meditation will help you conquer depression. (There is more on this in the 'Self-improvement' section below.)

On the purely physical, material level there is a sense that you are cramped in the home; that there is not enough space. However, a move is not advisable this year and you would be better off making creative use of the space that you have. If you re-order things in the home, rearrange things, you should have all the space that you need.

Saturn is your financial planet, and his move through your 4th house shows someone who is earning money from home. Perhaps you are setting up a home office or a home-based business. (This could be the cause of the feeling of being cramped.) Although family life doesn't seem that happy, the family do seem financially supportive.

There are some good things about this Saturn transit. By the time he is finished with you, you'll have more control over your moods and your emotions. We are not meant to be victims of our moods and emotions but the masters of them. This will happen for many of you in the year ahead.

Neptune, the most spiritual of the planets, has been in your 4th house for many, many years, signalling increased spirituality in the family as a whole and among family members. Spirituality will help you deal with family issues this year.

A parent or parent figure could move in the year ahead and it seems like a happy move. He or she also needs to be careful of depression: he or she seems pessimistic about life, and there is a tendency for him or her to feel older than their years. Their health and energy could also be better. A sibling or sibling figure is beginning a long-term cycle of personal transformation. Many personal dramas will happen over the next 30 years, but the purpose is not punishment but only to purify. He or she is likely to move in the year ahead and perhaps to renovate the existing home. If this sibling is a woman of childbearing age, she is more fertile than usual.

Children and children figures in your life are having a stable home and family year. A move is more likely next year than this. Grandchildren, if you have them, or those who play that role in your life, are likely to be making major renovations to the home. More importantly, they are entering a cycle of major psychological change and study. This will go on for many years.

If you're planning house renovations or construction work around the home, February 19 to March 20 would be a good time. If you are redecorating in a cosmetic kind of way or otherwise beautifying the home, March 12 to April 5 would be a good time.

Finance and Career

Pluto has been in your money house for the past 30 or so years. This year he is starting to leave, but this is a slow process. However, by next year he will be completely out of your 2nd house. This long transit produced many financial adventures and dramas over the decades. Perhaps there were near-death financial experiences. Actual bankruptcies in some cases. But none of these events was a punishment, only a purification. The cosmos was leading you to the financial life of your dreams, the ideal financial life. By now you are starting to experience this, and Pluto can move on to another job.

Pluto is your spiritual planet. His move through your money house enhanced the financial intuition, and by now this is a tool of great power. Many of you explored the spiritual laws of affluence over the past 30 years. By now you are operating these laws and in a successful way.

Your financial planet Saturn has been in the spiritual sign of Pisces since May of last year – he will be there for the rest of the year ahead. This also favours good use of financial intuition and application of the spiritual laws of affluence.

The financial planet in Pisces favours investments in oil, natural gas, water utilities, water bottles, ship-building and the shipping business, and certain kinds of pharmaceuticals, such as mood enhancers and anaesthetics.

Saturn in your 4th house favours residential real estate, restaurants, the food business, hotels and motels and companies and industries that cater to the homeowner. You spend more on the home and family this year but can also earn from there. Family support seems good. Family and family connections are playing an important role in the financial life.

Though finances are good, career doesn't seem a big issue this year. You don't seem especially ambitious these days; you seem more concerned with home and family and emotional issues. Most of the long-term planets are below the horizon of your chart – in the night side of the chart. Your 4th house of home and family is very strong while your 10th house of career is basically empty – only fast-moving planets will move through there and their effect is temporary. So, the message of the Horoscope is: get the home and family life in order, and especially the emotional life, and you will build the foundations for future career advancement.

With Mercury, one of the fastest moving of all the planets, as your career planet, there are many short-term career trends that depend on where Mercury is at any given time and the kinds of aspects he receives. These are best dealt with in the monthly reports.

Love and Social Life

Until May 26 the love situation seems rather quiet. It will be more or less the same as last year. But, come May 26, as Jupiter, the ruler of your Horoscope, enters your 7th house it starts to become active and happy. Love and social goals, whether you are single or married, will tend to be attained. Jupiter's move into your 7th house shows that you are proactive in love. You go after what you want rather aggressively. If you like someone, that person will know it. You're not into playing games. You are actively involved in shaping the love and social life the way that you want it.

More importantly, with Jupiter in your 7th house you are very much there for others. You put the interest of others ahead of your own. If you are in a relationship or a friendship you are totally behind the current love or friend. Totally supportive. This attitude makes you personally more popular in the year ahead. People sense that you are there for them and they respond to it. You're a very good friend to have these days.

Your love planet is Mercury, and as our regular readers know he is a very fast-moving planet, moving through all the signs and houses of your Horoscope in a year. Thus, there are many short-term trends in love that depend on where Mercury is and the aspects he receives, which are best dealt with in the monthly reports.

Mercury does double duty in your Horoscope. He is your love planet and your career planet. Thus, there is a strong connection between love and career. When love is going well, the career tends to go well.

This signals that love tends to be high on your priorities. In many cases it is seen as the actual mission in life, and especially in the year ahead. There is a need to be there for the current love, spouse or partner and for your friends. This focus on love also tends to success.

With Mercury as your love planet and with Jupiter in the sign of Gemini from May 26 onwards, you are attracted to intellectual types of people. The gift of the gab is very important in love. You like people who are easy to talk to and with whom you can share ideas. You need to fall in love with a person's mind as much as with their body.

Love opportunities will arise in school or at school functions, at lectures or seminars, bookstores or the library. You would also tend to be attracted to people of high status and power. People involved in your career would also be interesting love prospects.

Self-improvement

Saturn in your 4th house, as we mentioned, shows tendencies to depression. It shows a tendency to repress feelings. Perhaps you feel unsafe about expressing how you really feel about things and you tend to hold them in. Of course, this cannot go on for very long. Eventually these feelings will be expressed and probably in a completely out-of-proportion way to whatever triggered them. Thus, you need a method of expressing your true feelings, especially the negative ones, without dumping them on other people or family members. You need a safe way of expressing these feelings, a harmless way. This is a great year for practising the 'touch and let go' exercise described in my book *A Technique for Meditation*.

Regular use of this technique will not only enable you to clear your negative feelings but will also be a safeguard against depression. Negative feelings will not have a chance to accumulate. Also, as you do this exercise, the mind will clear and solutions to your problems will often reveal themselves. Talking it out with a professional therapist might also work well for many of you. The point is, you don't want to hold these things in as it can be detrimental to your health.

Pluto is at the beginning of a long-term, 30-year transit through your 3rd house. As time goes on your whole thought process, taste in reading and verbal expression will be transformed. It is good to understand what is really happening here, to understand the spiritual agenda behind this. The cosmos has decreed that you are to give birth to a new mind and a new intellect. To the mind and intellect of your dreams, your ideal. Thus, the old mental habits and patterns need to be expunged and eliminated. This is not usually pleasant while it's happening. Like any new birth there can be much pain and drama involved. But as with a new birth the end result is good and eminently worth it.

As you change your thought process and mental patterns, your whole life will start to improve, for most of your problems in life originated in these patterns. Eventually, there will be a feeling of 'good riddance'. Pluto will deepen your mind. You will not be satisfied with superficial knowledge. You'll have the urge to delve deep into any subject that you study, to understand it thoroughly. This can slow down learning, but it will be more effective.

For more information on astrology, healing and spiritual topics, please visit my blog at www.spiritual-stories.com.

Month-by-month Forecasts

January

Best Days Overall: 8, 9, 16, 17, 25, 26, 27
Most Stressful Days Overall: 1, 2, 14, 15, 21, 22, 28, 29
Best Days for Love: 1, 2, 8, 9, 18, 19, 21, 22, 27, 28
Best Days for Money: 1, 2, 6, 10, 11, 14, 18, 19, 23, 28, 29
Best Days for Career: 1, 2, 9, 18, 19, 28, 29, 30, 31

With two long-term planets in stressful alignment with you, health will need more attention all year. This month, however, with the short-term planets either helping you or leaving you alone, health should be good. You can enhance it further with massage of the liver reflex and the thighs until the 23rd and with back and knee massage after the 23rd.

The main headline this month is finance. This is a very prosperous kind of month. Your money house is chock-full of planets: 60 per cent of the planets are either there or moving through there this month. So the focus is on finance and earnings, and this focus will lead to success. Focus, in my opinion, is more important than easy aspects. With so many planets in your money house, earnings can happen in many ways and through many people. For those of you who invest this indicates a diversified kind of portfolio. You have been in a yearly financial peak since the 21st of last month, and this will go on until the 20th of this month. The new Moon of the 11th, which occurs in your money house, is an especially good financial day. It is also good for college-level students, or those applying to college, and for those of you involved in legal issues. This new Moon's effects will last long after it has happened. As the days go by, and until the next new Moon next month, financial matters will clarify for you. All the information you need to make good financial decisions will come to you, normally and naturally.

The Sun travels with Pluto on the 20th and 21st, and this will bring spiritual insights and perhaps enhanced ESP.

On the 20th the Sun leaves your money house and enters your 3rd house of communication and intellectual interests. The focus on finance is still ultra-powerful but now you want to enlarge your store of knowledge. Intellectual pursuits interest you.

Love seems happy this month, especially after the 14th. You are attracted to wealthy people. You have romantic or social opportunities as you pursue your financial goals and perhaps with people who are involved with your finances. A lot of your socializing after the 14th seems business-related.

The spouse, partner or current love seems actively involved in your finances and is helpful.

The planetary momentum is overwhelmingly forward this month. Until the 27th 90 per cent of the planets are moving forward, while after the 27th they are *all* moving forward. So, this is a month of fast-paced events. This is how you like things. There is fast progress towards your goals.

February

Best Days Overall: 4, 5, 12, 13, 21, 22, 23
Most Stressful Days Overall: 10, 11, 17, 18, 24, 25
Best Days for Love: 6, 7, 8, 9, 17, 18, 26, 27, 29
Best Days for Money: 6, 7, 10, 19, 14, 15, 24, 25, 29
Best Days for Career: 8, 9, 18, 24, 25, 29

Your money house is still strong until the 17th, so there is good prosperity this month. By the 17th your short-term financial goals have most likely been achieved and you can start to focus on your intellectual life. The power this month will be in your 3rd house, and the intellectual and communication faculties are very much enhanced this month. It is a good month for teachers, students, writers, sales and marketing people, and intellectual workers in general. Students should do well in school.

Where last month 60 per cent of the planets were moving through your money house, this month this situation is with your 3rd house of communication: 60 per cent of the planets are either there or moving through that house. So, a good month to attend lectures and seminars, and to read books on subjects that interest you. It is the time to feed the mental body.

Siblings and sibling figures in your life are having an excellent month, and prosperous as well.

The new Moon of the 9th will occur in your 3rd house and further strengthen your communication and intellectual skills. But the new Moon will have effects long after it occurs, and as the days go by it will help clarify educational goals, relations with siblings and neighbours and many intellectual issues.

On the 19th the Sun enters your 4th house and moves into a stressful alignment with you. It is good that your 6th house of health is very powerful, as it shows a focus on health that will be needed after the 19th. As always, make sure to get enough rest. Low energy tends to weaken the immune system and makes a person vulnerable to all kinds of opportunistic infections. Enhance the health with back and knee massage until the 13th. After the 13th ankle and calf massage will be helpful. Enhance the health in the ways mentioned in the yearly report, too.

Your house of home and family has been strong for over a year now and becomes even stronger this month. Time to focus more on the home, family and your emotional wellness and to let career issues go for a while. The family base, and your emotional wellness, are the foundation for a successful career. This focus on home will lead to career success later on.

Love and romantic opportunities are found in your own neighbourhood from the 4th to the 23rd. Pursue your intellectual goals and love will find you. Romantic opportunities also happen in school and at school functions, at lectures, seminars, the library or bookshop.

On the 23rd your love planet moves into your 4th house, again indicating that love is close to home. There will be more socializing from home and with family members. Family members seem involved in your love life.

With Mercury's entry into your 4th house on the 23rd, the home, family and your emotional wellness become your career. They become your mission after the 23rd.

March

Best Days Overall: 2, 3, 11, 12, 19, 20, 21, 29, 30
Most Stressful Days Overall: 9, 10, 15, 16, 22, 23
Best Days for Love: 1, 7, 8, 9, 11, 15, 16, 17, 18, 19, 20, 27, 28, 29, 30
Best Days for Money: 4, 5, 6, 9, 10, 13, 14, 17, 18, 22, 23, 27, 28
Best Days for Career: 1, 9, 11, 19, 20, 22, 23, 29, 30

All the planets are moving forward this month. Your personal solar cycle is waxing, so this is an excellent time to launch new projects or products into the world. If you can do this from the 10th to the 25th when the Moon is also waxing, you'll have the best possible time to launch a new product or venture. You will have maximum cosmic support.

Your 4th house, which was very strong last month, becomes even stronger in the month ahead. Keep in mind our discussion of this last month.

Health and energy are stressed this month, so continue to rest when you are tired and enhance the health in the ways mentioned in the yearly report. Until the 11th ankle and calf massage will be helpful. After the 11th foot massage would be excellent and you will respond well to spiritual-healing techniques. So, if you feel under the weather, see a spiritual type of healer. The good news is you will see dramatic improvement in health from the 20th onwards.

A lunar eclipse on the 25th is relatively mild in its effect on you, but it won't hurt to take a more relaxed schedule anyway. If this eclipse hits a sensitive point in your personal horoscope, cast especially for you, it can be powerful indeed.

This eclipse occurs in your 11th house and brings dramas to the lives of friends, and to trade and professional organizations that you are involved with. The eclipse will also impact computers, software and high-tech gadgetry in general. Internet service can be patchy or erratic. Take some normal common-sense precautions. Back up important files, avoid suspicious emails or websites and especially avoid suspicious attachments. The eclipsed planet, the Moon, is the ruler of your 8th house. Thus the spouse, partner or current love will need to make important financial changes. This is so for friends and trade or professional organizations you're involved with, as well.

This kind of eclipse brings psychological encounters with death. These can happen in many ways. Perhaps you have a near-death experience or a close call. Perhaps you read of the death of a celebrity that you admire or of someone you know. Perhaps you have dreams of death. All of this is the cosmos's way of reminding you that life is short and death can happen at any time. So, be about the business that you were born to do. Also, this is the cosmos's way of giving you a deeper understanding of death.

Be more mindful on the physical plane from the 1st to the 8th. Be more patient with children and children figures during that period too.

April

Best Days Overall: 7, 8, 16, 17, 26, 27
Most Stressful Days Overall: 5, 6, 11, 12, 18, 19, 20
Best Days for Love: 7, 8, 11, 12, 16, 17, 26, 27, 28
Best Days for Money: 1, 2, 5, 6, 9, 10, 13, 14, 18, 19, 23, 24, 28, 29
Best Days for Career: 7, 8, 16, 17, 18, 19, 20, 26, 27

A total solar eclipse on the 8th is the main headline of the month. Of all the eclipses in 2024 this one is easily the strongest. So, take it nice and easy while this eclipse is in effect. Whatever needs to be done should be done, but anything else – especially if it's stressful – is best rescheduled for another time. This advice applies not just to you, but to children and children figures in your life, parents and parent figures and the spouse, partner or current love. Let them all stay out of harm's way while the eclipse is in effect.

This eclipse occurs in your 5th house of creativity and children – hence the need for children and children figures to stay out of harm's way – and it signals a need to re-define themselves, re-define the self-concept, the image they project to others and the way they want others to see them. The events of the eclipse will show why this is necessary. They need to define themselves for themselves or others will do it for them, and this will not be pleasant.

The same is true for the spouse, partner or current love and for parents or parent figures. Sometimes, especially if they haven't been careful in dietary matters, this kind of eclipse will bring a detox of the physical body. The symptoms can seem like disease or sickness, but it is really not so. The body is just getting rid of material that doesn't belong there.

For those of you involved in the creative arts this eclipse brings important changes to your creativity. Also, all of you will change your notions of what fun is, and the kinds of leisure activities that you like.

Since Mercury is also impacted, this eclipse will test your current relationship. Long-suppressed grievances can surface that need to be dealt with, or it can bring some drama, a personal drama in the life of the beloved. A good relationship, something that is fundamentally sound, will weather this crisis, but a flawed relationship is in danger. Since Mercury is also your career planet, this eclipse will bring important career changes. Rarely do people actually change the career, though sometimes it happens. Usually there is a need to change the way the career is pursued or the career strategies. Bosses, parents and parent figures, people who are in authority over you, will experience dramas. There are likely to be shake-ups in your corporate hierarchy which will change the way you pursue your career. There can even be changes in government rules and regulations.

You love to travel, Sagittarius, but it's not a good time for this while the eclipse is in effect. If you must travel, especially to foreign countries, try to schedule your trip around the eclipse. College students are forced to make important changes in their educational plans. Perhaps there are dramas and disruptions at school. Perhaps they change courses or even change schools. There are dramas and disruptions at your place of worship, and dramas in the lives of worship leaders. Your religious, theological and philosophical beliefs will get tested, and severely so, by this eclipse. Many of your deeply held beliefs will be dropped, or changed. The end result is that you will live your life in a different way over the coming months.

May

Best Days Overall: 5, 6, 13, 14, 23, 24
Most Stressful Days Overall: 2, 3, 4, 9, 10, 15, 16, 30, 31
Best Days for Love: 5, 6, 7, 8, 9, 10, 14, 15, 16, 25, 26, 27, 28
Best Days for Money: 3, 4, 8, 11, 12, 15, 16, 21, 22, 25, 26, 27, 28, 30, 31
Best Days for Career: 5, 6, 14, 15, 16, 25, 26

The planetary momentum is still overwhelmingly forward this month, with 90 per cent of the planets moving forward. The pace of life is fast, just the way you like things, and quick progress is made to your goals.

Most of the planets are now in the Western, social sector of your Horoscope. Even Jupiter, the ruler of your Horoscope, is in the West and will be even further West after the 26th. So, the month ahead is more about other people and their needs. Personal happiness will come as you put others first. Your way is probably not the best way these days, and you should let others have their way so long as it isn't destructive.

This month is basically a preparation for love and romance that will be happening very shortly. Jupiter moves into your 7th house of love on the 26th and will remain there for the rest of the year. This shows that you are putting others first, putting them ahead of your own personal interest. You are there for your friends and for the spouse, partner or current love. You might feel as if you are in exile, far away from home, for Jupiter is very far from his natural home in your own sign.

Until the 20th the power this month is in your 6th house of health and work. This is a positive for health. After the 20th health will need more watching, and you seem to be on the case. As always, make sure to rest more, especially after the 20th. Don't allow yourself to get over-tired. Enhance the health with neck and throat massage until the 23rd. After the 23rd arm and shoulder massage will be powerful. Tension tends to collect in the shoulders and needs to be released. After the 23rd you have a good connection with the healing powers of the Air element. If you feel under the weather get out in the fresh air and just breathe deeply.

Venus, your health planet, travels with Uranus on the 18th and 19th, signalling that in health matters you want to be more open to alternative therapies and to experimental kinds of therapies. An unexpected job opportunity can come to you. Your high-tech gadgetry and perhaps your internet service can be more erratic those days.

On the 13th and 14th the Sun travels with Uranus, and this can bring a sudden travel opportunity. More opportunities for travel will come as the Sun journeys with Jupiter from the 18th to the 20th. This will also be a good time for college students or those applying to college.

Finances are better before the 20th than after. After the 20th there will be more work involved to attain your financial goals.

June

Best Days Overall: 1, 2, 9, 10, 11, 19, 20, 28, 29
Most Stressful Days Overall: 5, 6, 12, 13, 26, 27
Best Days for Love: 5, 6, 15, 16, 17, 26, 27
Best Days for Money: 5, 7, 8, 14, 17, 18, 21, 22, 23, 24, 26, 27
Best Days for Career: 5, 6, 12, 13, 15, 16, 17, 26, 27

Health and energy could be a lot better, but nevertheless many nice things are happening. The main headline is your loving social life which is both active and very happy. There is much romantic opportunity for singles, much dating and attending of parties and gatherings.

Romance is definitely in the air. You are taking a proactive approach to romance. You are taking charge of your romantic life. You're not just sitting around waiting for the phone to ring. If you like someone you approach them directly. There is no game playing with you these days. People know where they stand with you.

Health still needs watching until the 20th. Keep in mind our discussion of this last month. The good news is that health and energy will improve from the 20th as the short-term planets move away from their stressful aspects with you. Meanwhile, enhance the health with arm and shoulder massage, massage of the lung reflex, and with exposure to the Air element. After the 17th diet seems more of an issue. Make sure to eat right. Massage of the stomach reflex and abdominal massage should also be helpful, as will detox regimes.

From the 20th onwards you are in a more erotic kind of month. (Perhaps this is just a natural consequence of a strong romantic period.) Whatever your age or stage in life, the libido will be stronger than usual. With your health planet Venus in your 8th house from the 17th onwards, sexual moderation is called for. Neither too much, nor too little. Your body will tell you when enough is enough.

Finances will be much improved from the 20th.

With so much going on in the love life, it would be normal for singles to have a lot of questions about it. The new Moon of the 6th occurs in your 7th house and will, in due course, bring you the answers you need. The 6th is also a great romantic and erotic day.

July

Best Days Overall: 7, 8, 17, 18, 25, 26
Most Stressful Days Overall: 2, 3, 9, 10, 11, 23, 24, 29, 30, 31
Best Days for Love: 2, 3, 5, 6, 7, 8, 17, 18, 25, 26, 27, 28, 29, 30, 31
Best Days for Money: 2, 3, 4, 5, 6, 12, 13, 14, 15, 16, 19, 20, 21, 22, 23, 24, 29, 30
Best Days for Career: 7, 8, 9, 10, 11, 17, 18, 27, 28

Health still needs attention this month. On the 20th Mars moves into stressful alignment with you, joining Jupiter, Saturn and Neptune in stressful alignments. This is more or less balanced out with the Sun's harmonious aspect with you from the 22nd. Diet still seems important until the 11th. Give more attention to the stomach reflex point as well. Women should massage the reflexes to the breasts which are located on top of the foot. After the 11th massage of the heart reflex and chest massage will also be helpful.

With your 8th house very strong until the 22nd the spouse, partner or current love is having a very good financial time – a time of peak earnings. Your financial planet Saturn is receiving wonderful aspects this month so your personal earnings should also be good. But because Saturn is retrograde, earnings can happen slower than usual, with some delays. This is a good month for tax and insurance planning and, for those of appropriate age, for estate planning. It is also good for detox regimes on all levels, physical, emotional and mental. Like last month it is a more sexually active kind of month. Libido is stronger than usual.

The new Moon of the 5th occurs in your 8th house. This is an especially erotic kind of day. It is also an especially good financial day for the spouse, partner or current love. More importantly, as the days go by, until the next new Moon next month the beloved's financial life will clarify itself.

Mars moves into your 7th house on the 20th and starts to travel with Jupiter. This favours love affairs rather than serious committed love. On the other hand, if you are involved in a serious relationship – and many of you are – it is a good time to have fun with the beloved. For singles, there are mixed emotions about love. A part of you prefers a love affair, A non-serious kind of fling. Another part of you wants serious committed love. So, you waver between the two.

On the 22nd the Sun enters your 9th house. Foreign lands call to you and, being a Sagittarius, all you need is the slightest excuse to pack your bags and travel. It is a good month for college students and for those applying to college. These things seem fortunate.

August

Best Days Overall: 3, 4, 13, 14, 21, 22, 30, 31
Most Stressful Days Overall: 5, 6, 7, 19, 20, 26, 27
Best Days for Love: 5, 6, 7, 8, 17, 18, 21, 22, 26, 27, 29, 30, 31
Best Days for Money: 8, 9, 11, 12, 15, 16, 17, 18, 19, 20, 27, 28, 29
Best Days for Career: 5, 6, 7, 21, 22, 30, 31

Health is reasonable this month – there are ups and downs but they basically balance each other out. Still, it won't hurt to pay more attention to the health – especially from the 22nd onwards. Until the 5th chest massage and massage of the heart reflex are beneficial still. After the 5th abdominal massage and massage of the small intestine reflex will be good.

Love is still active and happy, but from the 4th to the 25th it becomes more complicated with your love planet Mercury's retrograde. The social life can slow down a bit. You and the current love are not sure what you want. Doubts have entered into the picture. After the 25th, however, social and romantic clarity return and love is once again happy and active. Don't make any important love decisions, one way or another, between the 4th and the 25th. This is a time for gaining clarity. Actions can happen after the 25th.

The power this month remains in your beneficent 9th house until the 22nd. It is basically a happy and optimistic kind of time.

On the 22nd, the Sun crosses your Mid-heaven and enters your 10th house. You begin a yearly career peak. This is where the focus needs to be. Family issues are still important, but you can shift some attention to your career. The demands of both home and career are very strong, so focus on the truly essential things in your life and drop all the frivolities. This alone will increase your energy. It might be good to schedule in some massages, reflexology, acupressure or acupuncture treatments from the 22nd onwards. These treatments tend to boost the energy levels. Make sure to get enough rest from the 22nd onwards.

September

Best Days Overall: 1, 9, 10, 18, 19, 26, 27, 28
Most Stressful Days Overall: 2, 3, 16, 17, 22, 23, 29, 30
Best Days for Love: 1, 4, 5, 12, 13, 14, 15, 21, 22, 23, 24
Best Days for Money: 4, 5, 7, 8, 12, 13, 14, 15, 16, 17, 22, 23, 24, 25
Best Days for Career: 1, 2, 12, 13, 21, 28, 30

A lunar eclipse on the 18th in your 4th house affects you and your family strongly. So, it would be a good idea for you and them to take a nice, relaxed schedule while the eclipse is in effect.

Passions will run high at home, so be more patient with family members. The dream life is likely to be hyper-active and perhaps unpleasant. But don't give it much weight as much of what you are dreaming is merely psychic garbage stirred up by the eclipse. There are personal dramas in the lives of parents and parent figures, and family members in general. Often, with this kind of eclipse hidden flaws are discovered in the home. The eclipse brings these flaws to your attention so you can make corrections.

The spouse, partner or current love has financial dramas and is forced to make important financial changes. The financial thinking or planning has not been realistic, as the events of the eclipse will show, and a course correction is necessary.

With the Moon the ruler of your 8th house, every lunar eclipse brings psychological encounters with death. Rarely is this physical death. After all, you go through this twice a year and you're still around. What usually happens is that you hear of the death of someone that you know, or you have dreams of death. The dark angel is letting you know that he is around. Sometimes, you or people close to you have near-death experiences, close calls. All of this is meant to give you a deeper understanding of death.

Health still needs watching until the 22nd, and especially around the time of the eclipse. As always, make sure to get enough rest. Health will improve dramatically after the 22nd, but in the meantime schedule in more massages or other natural therapies – therapies that boost the overall energy level.

Career is still very successful this month and there is probably career-related travel happening. The new Moon of the 3rd occurs in your 10th house, making this an excellent career day. It will also, almost as a side effect, clarify career issues and doubts as the days go by. All the information that you need to make a good decision will come to you very naturally and normally.

October

Best Days Overall: 6, 7, 8, 15, 16, 24, 25
Most Stressful Days Overall: 13, 14, 19, 20, 26, 27, 28
Best Days for Love: 1, 4, 5, 12, 13, 14, 19, 20, 21, 22, 24, 25, 31
Best Days for Money: 2, 4, 5, 9, 10, 11, 12, 13, 14, 19, 20, 21, 22, 23, 29, 30, 31
Best Days for Career: 1, 12, 13, 21, 22, 26, 27, 28, 31

A solar eclipse on the 2nd, while not as strong as the one in April, is still pretty strong as it impacts other planets and other people in your life. So take common-sense precautions, do what needs to be done and reschedule anything else.

This eclipse impacts very strongly on your social circle and brings many changes there. It occurs in your 11th house of friends and affects Mercury, your love planet. So, your friendships and your current relationship are getting tested. It would be a good idea for your friends, and the beloved, to reduce their schedules and to stay out of harm's way. The upheavals in your relationship and social circle are not necessarily the fault of the relationships themselves, but more about personal dramas going on in the lives of your friends and the current love. These dramas can often be life changing.

Since Mars is directly impacted too, children and children figures in your life are also experiencing dramas and should stay out of harm's way while the eclipse is in effect. Children and children figures, the current love and friends are all re-defining themselves these days. They are re-defining their image, personality and the impression that they make on others. This will lead to future changes of wardrobe, hairstyle and overall presentation. If they have been negligent in dietary matters, they can experience detoxes of the body.

Those of you involved in the creative arts will make important changes in your creativity. Your taste in fun activities will also change in the coming months. What you thought of as fun will not seem like so much fun down the road.

The impact on Mercury also indicates career changes. This is usually not an actual change of career, though sometimes that does happen, but a change in the way you think about it and the way you pursue it. Bosses, parents, parent figures and authority figures in your life all have personal dramas now. Government intervention can change the regulations of your company or industry and this will also create change. Parents and parent figures are forced to make important financial changes.

Because this eclipse occurs in your 11th house, computers and high-tech gadgetry in general can behave erratically. Internet services can be erratic. Back up your important files. Avoid suspicious emails, attachments and websites. Sometimes repairs to such equipment are necessary.

Every solar eclipse affects college students, and those applying to college. This can bring disruption to educational plans and sometimes brings a change of school. There are dramas and upheavals at your place of worship and in the lives of worship leaders. More importantly, this eclipse will test your religious, theological and philosophical beliefs. Every six months the cosmos gives you the opportunity to refine and purify your religious and theological beliefs, and to change how you live your life. In the coming months you'll have a new attitude to life. You will shed old, limiting beliefs and perhaps amend some of your beliefs.

November

Best Days Overall: 3, 4, 12, 13, 20, 21, 29, 30
Most Stressful Days Overall: 10, 11, 16, 17, 22, 23, 24
Best Days for Love: 3, 4, 12, 13, 16, 17, 20, 21, 22, 23, 29, 30
Best Days for Money: 1, 2, 5, 6, 8, 9, 10, 11, 16, 17, 18, 19, 26, 27, 28, 29
Best Days for Career: 3, 12, 13, 20, 21, 22, 23, 24, 29, 30

Health and energy are vastly improved compared to the past few months, and will get even better from the 21st onwards. If you want to enhance health further, massage of the liver reflex and thighs is beneficial until the 11th, and after the 11th back and knee massage is helpful.

This is a happy month, Sagittarius. It starts off a little slow, as your spiritual 12th house is very powerful. Your spiritual growth during this time will lead to material happiness later on. This is a good month to delve into the mystical aspects of your own native religion. Every religion has this mystical, supernatural side and it would be good to explore this.

On the 21st, as the Sun enters your own sign, you begin a yearly personal pleasure peak. Time to pamper the body and rewarded it for its years of yeoman service. The Sun's move into your sign improves the personal appearance and gives charisma to the image. And because Venus is in your sign until the 11th there is beauty, grace and glamour to the image as well.

The planetary power is now mostly in the East, the sector of self. You are in the most independent part of your year. So, your happiness is up to you. Choose to make the changes that will make you happy or enlarge your happiness. This is the time to have things your way. Your way is the best way. Your way is receiving cosmic support.

Sagittarius is a born traveller, and this month – especially after the 21st – even more so than usual. A foreign trip would not be a surprise. You will need to watch your weight more from the 21st onwards: this is the price we pay for personal pleasure and the good life.

Love seems very happy. Your love planet moves into your sign on the 12th and stays there for the rest of the month, signalling that love is seeking you out and you have love on your own terms. But this is not a one-sided deal. Your beloved is there for you and you are there for him or her. You both seem devoted to each other. Both Mercury (the beloved) and Jupiter (you) are retrograde, so neither you nor the beloved are sure of what you want. Important love decisions should not be made after the 26th.

Finances are improving as Saturn, your financial planet, starts to move forward on the 5th after many months' retrograde motion. Thus, the financial judgement is good and trustworthy this month. You're starting to move forward in your financial life.

Venus, your health planet, will spend the month out of bounds and outside her normal orbit. This is how you are in health matters: you seek therapies and therapists that are outside your normal boundaries. It seems to work for you this month because health is good. The obligations of work could also be pulling you outside your normal boundaries.

December

Best Days Overall: 1, 9, 10, 17, 18, 19, 27, 28, 29
Most Stressful Days Overall: 7, 8, 13, 14, 20, 21
Best Days for Love: 2, 3, 4, 9, 10, 13, 14, 17, 18, 19, 22, 23, 24
Best Days for Money: 2, 3, 4, 6, 7, 8, 14, 15, 16, 23, 24, 25, 26, 30, 31
Best Days for Career: 7, 8, 16, 26

Another happy month ahead. Enjoy. This month will be more prosperous than last month. Your financial planet is moving forward and on the 21st you enter a yearly financial peak. There is excellent financial intuition now and it is trustworthy. In your Horoscope, the Sun behaves like a mini-Jupiter. He expands and enlarges whatever he touches. So, earnings are increased and happy financial opportunities come to you.

You're still in a yearly personal pleasure peak until the 21st. So, like last month, time to enjoy all the pleasures of the five senses and to pamper the body. This is still a great period for getting the body and image in the shape that you want. Continue to watch the weight.

You're still in a very independent part of your year. You can easily create the conditions of your own happiness. The problem is, with Jupiter retrograde you might not be sure of where personal happiness lies. But once you are sure, make the changes that need to be made. You are having life on your own terms right now and again the problem is you're not sure what your terms are.

The new Moon of the 1st occurs in your own sign and raises the libido way above normal. It is an erotic kind of day. Self-esteem and self-confidence are boosted. As the days go by and well into next month, issues involving the body and image, and your path of personal happiness, will become clearer.

Love is still happy, and you definitely have love in your life and the devotion of the beloved. The only problem right now is that you are not sure what you want. You have doubts about love.

You and the beloved are seeing things from opposite perspectives, but this does not interfere with the good cooperation between you. Jupiter (you) and Mercury (the beloved) are in mutual reception. Each is a guest in the house and sign of the other. This denotes good cooperation.

Health is still excellent this month, and any pre-existing conditions seem much less severe. You can enhance the health even further with back and knee massage until the 7th, and with ankle and calf massage from the 7th onwards.

Capricorn

♑

THE GOAT

Birthdays from
21st December to
19th January

Personality Profile

CAPRICORN AT A GLANCE

Element – Earth

Ruling Planet – Saturn
  Career Planet – Venus
  Love Planet – Moon
  Money Planet – Uranus
  Planet of Communications – Neptune
  Planet of Health and Work – Mercury
  Planet of Home and Family Life – Mars
  Planet of Spirituality – Jupiter

Colours – black, indigo

Colours that promote love, romance and social harmony – puce, silver

Colour that promotes earning power – ultramarine blue

Gem – black onyx

Metal – lead

Scents – magnolia, pine, sweet pea, wintergreen

Quality – cardinal (= activity)

Qualities most needed for balance – warmth, spontaneity, a sense of fun

Strongest virtues – sense of duty, organization, perseverance, patience, ability to take the long-term view

Deepest needs – to manage, take charge and administrate

Characteristics to avoid – pessimism, depression, undue materialism and undue conservatism

Signs of greatest overall compatibility – Taurus, Virgo

Signs of greatest overall incompatibility – Aries, Cancer, Libra

Sign most helpful to career – Libra

Sign most helpful for emotional support – Aries

Sign most helpful financially – Aquarius

Sign best for marriage and/or partnerships – Cancer

Sign most helpful for creative projects – Taurus

Best Sign to have fun with – Taurus

Signs most helpful in spiritual matters – Virgo, Sagittarius

Best day of the week – Saturday

Understanding a Capricorn

The virtues of Capricorns are such that there will always be people for and against them. Many admire them, many dislike them. Why? It seems to be because of Capricorn's power urges. A well-developed Capricorn has his or her eyes set on the heights of power, prestige and authority. In the sign of Capricorn, ambition is not a fatal flaw, but rather the highest virtue.

Capricorns are not frightened by the resentment their authority may sometimes breed. In Capricorn's cool, calculated, organized mind all the dangers are already factored into the equation – the unpopularity, the animosity, the misunderstandings, even the outright slander – and a plan is always in place for dealing with these things in the most efficient way. To the Capricorn, situations that would terrify an ordinary mind are merely problems to be managed, bumps on the road to ever-growing power, effectiveness and prestige.

Some people attribute pessimism to the Capricorn sign, but this is a bit deceptive. It is true that Capricorns like to take into account the negative side of things. It is also true that they love to imagine the worst possible scenario in every undertaking. Other people might find such analyses depressing, but Capricorns only do these things so that they can formulate a way out – an escape route.

Capricorns will argue with success. They will show you that you are not doing as well as you think you are. Capricorns do this to themselves as well as to others. They do not mean to discourage you but rather to root out any impediments to your greater success. A Capricorn boss or supervisor feels that no matter how good the performance there is always room for improvement. This explains why Capricorn supervisors are difficult to handle and even infuriating at times. Their actions are, however, quite often effective – they can get their subordinates to improve and become better at their jobs.

Capricorn is a born manager and administrator. Leo is better at being king or queen, but Capricorn is better at being prime minister – the person actually wielding power.

Capricorn is interested in the virtues that last, in the things that will stand the test of time and trials of circumstance. Temporary fads and fashions mean little to a Capricorn – except as things to be used for profit or power. Capricorns apply this attitude to business, love, to their thinking and even to their philosophy and religion.

Finance

Capricorns generally attain wealth and they usually earn it. They are willing to work long and hard for what they want. They are quite amenable to forgoing a short-term gain in favour of long-term benefits. Financially, they come into their own later in life.

However, if Capricorns are to attain their financial goals they must shed some of their strong conservatism. Perhaps this is the least desirable trait of the Capricorn. They can resist anything new merely because it is new and untried. They are afraid of experimentation. Capricorns need to be willing to take a few risks. They should be more eager to market new products or explore different managerial techniques. Otherwise, progress will leave them behind. If necessary, Capricorns must be ready to change with the times, to discard old methods that no longer work.

Very often this experimentation will mean that Capricorns have to break with existing authority. They might even consider changing their present position or starting their own ventures. If so, they should be willing to accept all the risks and just get on with it. Only then will a Capricorn be on the road to highest financial gains.

Career and Public Image

A Capricorn's ambition and quest for power are evident. It is perhaps the most ambitious sign of the zodiac – and usually the most successful in a worldly sense. However, there are lessons Capricorns need to learn in order to fulfil their highest aspirations.

Intelligence, hard work, cool efficiency and organization will take them a certain distance, but will not carry them to the very top. Capricorns need to cultivate their social graces, to develop a social style, along with charm and an ability to get along with people. They need to bring beauty into their lives and to cultivate the right social contacts. They must learn to wield power gracefully, so that people love them for it – a very delicate art. They also need to learn how to bring people together in order to fulfil certain objectives. In short, Capricorns require some of the gifts – the social graces – of Libra to get to the top.

Once they have learned this, Capricorns will be successful in their careers. They are ambitious hard workers who are not afraid of putting in the required time and effort. Capricorns take their time in getting the job done – in order to do it well – and they like moving up the corporate ladder slowly but surely. Being so driven by success, Capricorns are generally liked by their bosses, who respect and trust them.

Love and Relationships

Like Scorpio and Pisces, Capricorn is a difficult sign to get to know. They are deep, introverted and like to keep their own counsel. Capricorns do not like to reveal their innermost thoughts. If you are in love with a Capricorn, be patient and take your time. Little by little you will get to understand him or her.

Capricorns have a deep romantic nature, but they do not show it straight away. They are cool, matter of fact and not especially emotional. They will often show their love in practical ways.

It takes time for a Capricorn – male or female – to fall in love. They are not the love-at-first-sight kind. If a Capricorn is involved with a Leo or Aries, these Fire types will be totally mystified – to them the Capricorn will seem cold, unfeeling, unaffectionate and not very spontaneous. Of course none of this is true; it is just that Capricorn likes to take things slowly. They like to be sure of their ground before making any demonstrations of love or commitment.

Even in love affairs Capricorns are deliberate. They need more time to make decisions than is true of the other signs of the zodiac, but given this time they become just as passionate. Capricorns like a relationship to be structured, committed, well regulated, well defined, predictable and even routine. They prefer partners who are nurturers, and they in turn like to nurture their partners. This is their basic psychology. Whether such a relationship is good for them is another issue altogether. Capricorns have enough routine in their lives as it is. They might be better off in relationships that are a bit more stimulating, changeable and fluctuating.

Home and Domestic Life

The home of a Capricorn – as with a Virgo – is going to be tidy and well organized. Capricorns tend to manage their families in the same way they manage their businesses. Capricorns are often so career-driven that they find little time for the home and family. They should try to get more actively involved in their family and domestic life. Capricorns do, however, take their children very seriously and are very proud parents – particularly should their children grow up to become respected members of society.

Horoscope for 2024

Major Trends

Pluto has been in your own sign for over 30 years now. This has brought about a complete transformation of your image, body and self-concept. You had many personal dramas, and perhaps surgeries and even near-death experiences. Happily, this is about over for the overwhelming majority of you. Those of you born late in the sign of Capricorn, from January 18–20, are still feeling some of this, though, and you late-born Capricorns still need to watch the heart. This year Pluto will be moving into Aquarius, your money house, and this will have a strong impact on your finances. More on this later. For most of you, overall health and energy is greatly improved in the year ahead. More on this later on.

Saturn, the ruler of your Horoscope, moved into your 3rd house last year and remains there for this year. This shows a great focus on your intellectual life. You are more bookish these days. You seem more involved with your neighbourhood and neighbours in general. This will be a great year for students, teachers and writers. Rationality is a great thing, but this year you have an intuitive kind of rationality, which is even better.

Jupiter entered your 5th house in May of last year and remains until May 26 this year. This shows a more fun and creative kind of year. Time to relax a bit and smell the roses.

Uranus has been in your 5th house for many years, signalling luck in speculations and, for those of you in the creative arts, greater income from your creativity. This will be even more pronounced in the year ahead with Jupiter also in the 5th house. More details later.

Jupiter enters your 6th house of health on May 26 and spends the rest of the year there. This is another positive health signal. Should health problems arise, Jupiter will bring best-case outcomes. There should be good news about pre-existing conditions as well. More on this later.

Jupiter in the 6th house indicates very beautiful job opportunities will be coming to you – dream job opportunities. This could be within your present situation or with another company.

Your most important areas of interest in the year ahead are the body, image and self-concept until January 22 and from September 3 to November 20; finance from January 22 to September 3 and from November 20 to the end of the year; communication and intellectual interests, neighbours and siblings; children, creativity and fun until May 26; and health and work from May 26 onwards.

Your paths of greatest fulfilment in the year ahead are home and family; children, creativity and fun until May 26; and health and work from May 26 onwards.

Health

(Please note that this is an astrological perspective on health and not a medical one. In days of yore there was no difference, both these perspectives were identical. But these days there could be quite a difference. For a medical perspective, please consult your doctor or health practitioner.)

As we mentioned above, the overwhelming majority of you will have a good health year. There are no long-term planets in stressful alignment with you. Only those of you born late in Capricorn, January 18–20, need to watch the health – especially the heart.

Of course, there will be times in the year when health and energy are less easy than usual, and perhaps even stressful. But these are not trends for the year, only temporary blips caused by short-term transits. When they pass your naturally good health and energy return.

Good though your health is, you can make it better. Give more attention to the following – the vulnerable areas of your Horoscope this year (the reflex points are shown in the chart overleaf):

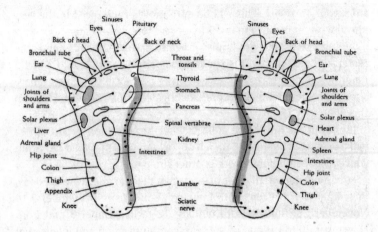

Important foot reflexology points for the year ahead

Try to massage all of the foot on a regular basis – the top of the foot as well as the bottom – but pay extra attention to the points highlighted on the chart. When you massage, be aware of 'sore spots' as these need special attention. It's also a good idea to massage the ankles and below them.

- The spine, knees, bones, skin and overall skeletal alignment are always important for Capricorn and this year is no different. Back and knee massage should be part of your regular health regime, and remember to give the knees more support when exercising or working out. Regular visits to a chiropractor or osteopath would also be a good thing. The vertebrae need to be kept in right alignment. Therapies such as Feldenkrais, Alexander Technique, Rolfing and yoga are excellent for the spine. Make sure to get enough calcium for the bones. If you're out in the sun make sure to use a good sunscreen.

- The arms, shoulders, lungs and respiratory system. These too are always important areas for you, Capricorn. Arms and shoulders should be regularly massaged. Tension tends to collect in the shoulders and needs to be released. Hand reflexology (not shown here) is a powerful therapeutic tool for you. If you feel under the weather, get out into the fresh air and just do some deep breathing.

- The liver and thighs become important this year from May 26 and the reflex points are shown above. Regular thigh massage will not only strengthen the thighs and liver but also the lower back.
- The heart is important for those of you born late in the sign, from January 18–20, and could be problematic until January 22 and from September 3 to November 20, the times when Pluto is in your sign this year. The reflex is shown above. The important thing with the heart is to avoid worry and anxiety, the two emotions that stress it out. Replace worry with faith. Regular chest massage will also stimulate and strengthen the heart.

Fast-moving Mercury is your health planet, and over the course of any given year he will move through every sign and house of your Horoscope. Thus, there are many short-term trends in health that depend on where Mercury is and the kinds of aspects he is receiving. These short-term trends are best dealt with in the monthly reports.

Mercury will be retrograde four times this year. Technically it is four times but practically speaking it is really only three times – his retrograde on January 1 only lasts for one day. He will be in full-blown retrograde motion from April 2–24; August 5–26; and from November 26 to December 14. In general, these are not times for undergoing procedures or taking medical kinds of tests – especially if they are elective kinds of things. Try to schedule such things around Mercury's retrograde periods if you can. These are also not good times to make dramatic changes in your health regime. Things need to be studied more.

Home and Family

A move, a happy one, could have happened last year. This year home and family life tends to the status quo. You seem satisfied with things as they are. Not only that but dealing with home and family brings you great satisfaction. The north node of the Moon will be in your 4th house all year. Capricorns are generally career oriented and take pleasure in career activities and in pursuing their ambitions. But this year there is satisfaction to be found in the simple pleasures of home and hearth.

There is pleasure and fulfilment too in psychological studies and activities. Those of you involved in formal types of therapy should make a lot of progress in the year ahead. But even if you're not involved in formal therapy you should see psychological progress. The cosmos has its ways of therapizing the past. Perhaps old memories arise that need to be looked at from your present state of consciousness. Perhaps you'll come across a book that explains a certain emotional pattern. Perhaps a parent or parent figure will, probably inadvertently, illuminate a past memory or pattern.

Women of childbearing age were very fertile last year, and this continues in the year ahead, until May 26. Pregnancy would not be a surprise.

There is pleasure from children and the children figures in your life. They seem to be having a good year, a prosperous year. They do need to watch their weight as they seem to be living the high life. Children and children figures in your life of childbearing age also seem very fertile this year. Though there is nothing against a move in the year ahead, there is nothing especially supporting it either. The year ahead is probably stable for them.

Parents and parent figures seem happy this year. A move is not likely – more likely next year. Siblings and sibling figures could move in the year ahead, and if they are of childbearing age they are more fertile than usual. Grandchildren, if you have them, or those who play that role in your life, can have multiple moves this year. Perhaps they are living in different places for long periods of time.

If you are planning a major renovation to the home, April 30 to June 9 seems a good time. If you're redecorating in a cosmetic kind of way or otherwise beautifying the home, April 5–29 would be a good time.

Finance and Career

The year ahead looks like a prosperous year. Jupiter, the planet of abundance and good fortune, is travelling with your financial planet Uranus early in the year. April and May seem especially prosperous as the aspect will be more exact. This indicates a large payday, perhaps unexpected, good fortune in speculations and a fabulous financial intuition. Your hunches are good in April and May.

Uranus has been in Taurus, your 5th house, for many years now. Thus, in general you have been more speculative. This would also show that you spend more on children and children figures in your life and can earn from them too. If they are very young they can inspire you to earn more. Often, the children can have profitable ideas. If the children are older and more settled, they can be financially supportive in a material way.

Uranus as your financial planet favours investments in technology, the online world and in companies involved in new inventions and new innovations. It favours tech start-ups as well. Your money planet in Taurus favours investments in rural real estate, farmland and agricultural commodities, while Uranus in your 5th house of fun and creativity favours investments in music, entertainment and in companies and industries that cater to the youth market. You have a good feeling for all these kinds of companies and industries.

Although you are by nature a conservative, traditional type of person, when it comes to finance you are much more experimental. You're willing to try new things, to go outside the normal rule book and learn what works for you through trial and error and experimentation. Not every experiment works out, of course, but real and lasting knowledge comes from it. This is knowledge that works for you personally.

Pluto is beginning to make a move into your money house this year. This is not yet the full-blown transit (that happens next year), but it is an announcement of things to come. So, there will be a great focus on finance not only this year but in many future years. This focus tends to bring success.

Pluto in your money house often signals inheritance (though hopefully no one has to die), trust funds, and perhaps being named in someone's will or being appointed to some administrative position in an estate. In general, you would profit from estates. Pluto in the money house would show that you are doing estate planning these days. It would also show the importance of tax efficiency and good tax planning. Tax issues are influencing many of your financial decisions these days. You are also likely to profit, this year and in future years, from creative financing. If you have good business ideas, there are investors out there willing to invest in you. This aspect also shows good access to outside money, to banks and credit. This ease of access needs to be kept in check, otherwise you could be deluged in debt.

With Pluto in your 2nd house you will also find that you have a good innate feeling for value where others see only death and decay. Thus you can profit from troubled or even bankrupt companies or properties. In the coming years you will be quite the turnaround artist.

Career does not seem a big issue this year. Capricorns are always ambitious but this year less so than usual. Your 10th house of career is basically empty. Only short-term planets will move through there and their effect will be temporary. So, as we mentioned earlier, this is a good year to enjoy the simple pleasures of hearth and home. Find and occupy your personal point of emotional harmony and career will take care of itself in the future.

Venus is your career planet and she is a fast-moving planet, moving through every sign and house of your Horoscope in any given year. So, there are many short-term career trends which depend on where Venus is at any given time and the kinds of aspects she receives. These are best dealt with in the monthly reports.

Love and Social Life

Your 7th house of love and romance is not prominent this year, not a house of power. Next year it will be a different story, but right now only short-term planets will move through there and their effects will be short term. This tends to the status quo. You seem satisfied with your current relationship and with the social life as it is. Those who are married will tend to stay married and singles will tend to stay single.

Your love planet the Moon is the fastest moving of all the planets. Where the other fast-moving planets travel through your Horoscope in a year, the Moon will do this every month. Thus, there are many short-term trends in love that depend on where the Moon is and the kinds of aspects she receives. These are best dealt with in the monthly reports.

In general, the new Moon and the full Moon tend to be strong love and social days. The social magnetism is stronger as the Moon is waxing or growing. There is also more energy and enthusiasm for social activities during the waxing Moon. If you're looking to break off a relationship, waning Moon periods are best.

The Moon as your love planet tends to make you moody in love. And if you are not like that yourself, you attract these kinds of people.

Pluto, your planet of friends, makes a major move from Capricorn, your own sign, into Aquarius. This is not yet the full-blown transit, but an announcement of things to come. The full-blown transit will happen next year. This move signals the importance of friends and social connections in your financial life, and it indicates that you gravitate to wealthy people. A lot of your socializing seems business related.

For singles, this is a year of preparation. Major love is likely next year. In the meantime, you need to get prepared for it. Since the Moon is your love planet, two lunar eclipses in the year ahead will shake up and test the existing relationship. The first lunar eclipse is on March 25 and the second is on September 18. You go through these things every year and by now you know how to handle them. Fundamentally sound relationships will tend to survive and even thrive. It is the essentially flawed relationships that are in danger.

Self-improvement

With your ruling planet Saturn travelling with Neptune in your 3rd house, this is a good year to increase your intellectual knowledge, for taking courses in subjects that interest you and attending lectures, seminars and workshops. If you are an expert on a subject, this would be a good year for teaching it to others.

Jupiter as your spiritual planet favours the exploration of the mystical traditions of your own native religion, whatever it is. There's no need to travel far and wide to explore the exotic forms of spirituality – although there's nothing wrong with doing that, by the way, and perhaps you are already doing so. But spiritual growth is right there at hand, in the ground beneath your feet. Go deeper into your native religion.

Jupiter will travel with your financial planet Uranus this year, as we have mentioned, and especially closely in April and May. This not only brings enhanced financial intuition but also will lead you into the spiritual laws of wealth. You should read up as much as you can on this subject.

Your spiritual planet will move into Gemini, your 6th house, on May 26. This will show a great interest in spiritual healing. You will tend to get good results with it. Good to read all you can on this subject. There is a very strong relationship between the spiritual body and the physical body. They are not the same thing, but one controls the other.

For more information on astrology, healing and spiritual topics, please visit my blog at www.spiritual-stories.com.

Month-by-month Forecasts

January

Best Days Overall: 1, 2, 10, 11, 18, 19, 28, 29
Most Stressful Days Overall: 5, 6, 16, 17, 23, 24, 30, 31
Best Days for Love: 8, 9, 11, 12, 18, 19, 21, 23, 24, 27, 28
Best Days for Money: 1, 2, 10, 11, 12, 13, 18, 19, 28, 29
Best Days for Career: 5, 6, 8, 9, 27, 28, 30, 31

A happy and prosperous month ahead, Capricorn. Enjoy. You start 2024 in the midst of a yearly personal pleasure peak. This will go on until the 20th, and perhaps even afterwards. Your own house is chockfull of planets: 60 per cent of the planets are either in your 1st house or moving through there. This brings a lot of physical energy. It is excellent for health. The personal appearance shines and the opposite sex certainly takes notice. However, this is not an especially strong social or romantic month. It is a me-oriented kind of month. The focus is on yourself, your image and personal appearance. The focus is more on your personal path to personal happiness. This is not selfish, as many people think. It is just a response to the cosmic energy cycle.

Personal independence is at its maximum for the year ahead. This is the time to create the conditions for your own personal happiness and you should make the changes that need to be made. The new Moon of the 11th also occurs in your own sign. It is an especially good day for you as it increases your energy and social appeal. It is an excellent romantic day for singles. Furthermore, as the days go by, the Moon will clarify any issues involving the body, the image and your path of personal happiness. This will go on well into next month, until the next new Moon.

This is an excellent month for getting the body and image into the shape that you want. It is also good for weight loss regimes. As we said, health is good this month, and with Mars in your own sign you have the energy of 10 people.

Your money house also becomes powerful this month, although still only a prelude to what will happen next month when the 2nd house becomes really powerful. But we see the beginnings of it now. On the 22nd Pluto will move into your money house, while on the 20th the Sun will move into your money house and you begin a yearly financial peak.

Love is not a big issue this month and will probably be stable.

February

Best Days Overall: 6, 7, 14, 15, 24, 25
Most Stressful Days Overall: 12, 13, 19, 20, 26, 27, 28
Best Days for Love: 6, 7, 8, 9, 17, 18, 19, 20, 26, 27, 29
Best Days for Money: 6, 7, 8, 9, 14, 15, 16, 24, 25
Best Days for Career: 6, 7, 17, 26, 27, 28

The main headline this month is the tremendous power in your financial life. Your money house is more powerful this month than at any other time during the year: 60 per cent of the planets are either there or moving through there. This is a lot of financial power. The cosmic genii are conspiring to enrich you. With so many different planets in the money house, money can come to you from a variety of people and in a variety of ways. For those of you who invest, this favours a well-diversified portfolio. You might spend more this month as well, but you will have the wherewithal to spend.

The new Moon of the 9th also occurs in the money house and it is an excellent financial day. It can also bring romantic opportunities with people involved in your finances or a business-type partnership or joint venture. The new Moon of the 9th will not only enrich you but it will also clarify the financial picture. Day by day, well into next month, all the information you need to make good financial decisions will come to you, naturally and normally.

Your 3rd house of communication and intellectual interests has been very powerful for over a year now. On the 19th it becomes even more powerful as the Sun moves into that house and stays there for the rest of the month ahead.

Your personal solar cycle is waxing this month. So is the cosmic solar cycle. All the planets are moving forward, so this is a great month for launching new products into the world or launching new projects. You have a lot of cosmic momentum behind you. If you can launch your product or venture from the 9th to the 24th, as the Moon waxes, you will have even more cosmic momentum behind you.

March

Best Days Overall: 4, 5, 6, 7, 14, 15, 24, 25
Most Stressful Days Overall: 11, 12, 17, 18, 24, 25, 26
Best Days for Love: 1, 9, 10, 17, 18, 27, 28, 29, 30
Best Days for Money: 4, 5, 7, 8, 13, 14, 22, 23
Best Days for Career: 7, 8, 17, 18, 24, 25, 26, 27, 28

By now, your financial goals, the short-term ones at least, have been achieved and it is time to shift your focus to other things – to your intellectual life. The mental and communication faculties are much stronger now than usual. This is a good month for students, especially below college level. They should be successful in their studies.

It is a good month for those of you who write, sell, teach or work on the intellectual level. The mental body, the invisible body, is real and has its needs. This is a good time to give your mental body what it needs. It is an excellent month for attending lectures or seminars – and for giving them.

Beneficent Jupiter travels with your financial planet on the 29th and 30th. These are excellent financial days. The financial intuition is super and there should be a nice payday.

The lunar eclipse of the 25th impacts you pretty strongly, so as always, relax and take it nice and easy over the eclipse period. Do what you have to do but reschedule anything else for another time.

This eclipse occurs in your 10th house of career and brings career changes to you. Generally, people don't change their actual career, although sometimes it happens, but they change their thinking, planning and strategizing about it. Sometimes these changes happen because of changes in the corporate hierarchy; sometimes the government body in charge of regulating your company or industry changes the rules. You're still in the same career but you're following it in a different way. There can be personal dramas in the lives of parents, parent figures and those in authority over you. The eclipse can also bring changes and turmoil in the government, both local and national.

Every lunar eclipse tests your current relationship, and this one is no different. You go through this twice a year, so you know how to handle it by now. Sometimes the eclipse brings up long-repressed grievances, perhaps things you were not even aware of, and now you get a chance to fix things. Sometimes it is not the fault of the relationship itself, but more about personal dramas in the life of the beloved.

Good relationships will survive these things and will get even better. But flawed ones are in danger.

April

Best Days Overall: 1, 2, 9, 10, 18, 19, 20, 28, 29
Most Stressful Days Overall: 7, 8, 13, 14, 15, 21, 22
Best Days for Love: 7, 8, 13, 14, 15, 16, 17, 27, 28, 29
Best Days for Money: 1, 2, 3, 4, 9, 10, 18, 19, 29, 30
Best Days for Career: 7, 8, 16, 17, 21, 22, 27, 28

A very powerful solar eclipse on the 8th is the main headline of the month. This eclipse is the strongest one of the entire year, so take a very nice easy and relaxed schedule during the eclipse period. It is not something to panic about, as that never helps, but it would be good to take normal and natural precautions. Common-sense precautions. If you don't need to drive or travel, then don't. Stay close to home, read a book, watch a movie, or (best of all) meditate. You don't need to involve yourself in stressful, daredevil-type activities. Reschedule them for another time. This advice applies also to parents and parent figures, and to family members.

The eclipse occurs in your 4th house of home and family and can bring dramas at home. Perhaps major repairs need to be made at home.

Since Venus, your career planet, is directly impacted by this eclipse, there are more changes in the career, and perhaps more upheavals in your corporate hierarchy this month. Job changes are also afoot. This can be within your present situation or with a new one. If you employ others there will be unusual amounts of turnover among employees in the coming months.

Your health regime will change dramatically in coming months.

College-level students experience disruptions at school, changes in their educational plans and perhaps even changes of institution. There are dramas and disruptions at your place of worship and in the lives of worship leaders. Your religious, theological and philosophical beliefs will get tested by this eclipse. Some beliefs will be discarded, some will be amended. Your theological beliefs need to be kept in line with reality.

May

Best Days Overall: 7, 8, 15, 16, 25, 26
Most Stressful Days Overall: 5, 6, 11, 12, 17, 18, 19
Best Days for Love: 1, 7, 8, 11, 12, 15, 16, 18, 19, 27, 28
Best Days for Money: 1, 8, 15, 16, 26, 27, 28
Best Days for Career: 7, 8, 15, 16, 17, 18, 19, 27, 28

Now that the dust is settling from April's monster eclipse, the job changes of last month are likely to be very good ones and better than what you had before. Jupiter's move into your 6th house on the 26th signals a very happy job opportunity coming to you. In addition, it indicates that the changes in the health regime caused by last month's eclipse are also very positive.

Last month brought career changes and we see this in the coming month as well, on the 18th and 19th. These changes are likely to be good ones. They can lead to pay rises, official or unofficial, and earnings that come from your good career reputation.

The spouse, partner or current love was forced to make important financial changes last month and they seem to pay off on the 18th and 19th. These are excellent financial days for the beloved.

With all the craziness and upheavals of last month's eclipse it is a good idea to indulge more in leisure activities this month. You are in the midst of a yearly personal pleasure peak, so enjoy your life as much as possible. You're not ignoring your challenges but taking a break from them to face them with a fresh perspective.

Health is improved over the last month. Jupiter's move into your 6th house on the 26th shows that you benefit from spiritual-healing techniques. If you feel under the weather, see a spiritual type of healer. Jupiter's presence in your health house for the rest of the year indicates that if there are health problems you receive best-case outcomes.

Love doesn't seem a big issue in the month ahead. Your 7th house is basically empty with only the Moon moving through there on the 11th and 12th. This tends to the status quo. In general, love and social issues will go better from the 10th to the 23rd, as the Moon waxes. You will have more energy and enthusiasm for these things.

Mars, your home and family planet, will be in his own sign and house all month, so this is a good time to undertake any renovations in the home, if you are planning these things.

June

Best Days Overall: 3, 4, 12, 13, 21, 22, 23, 30
Most Stressful Days Overall: 1, 2, 7, 8, 14, 15, 16, 28, 29
Best Days for Love: 5, 6, 7, 8, 14, 15, 16, 17, 26, 27
Best Days for Money: 4, 5, 13, 14, 22, 23, 24, 25
Best Days for Career: 5, 6, 14, 15, 16, 17, 26, 27

Health needs more attention this month, especially from the 20th onwards. As always, make sure to get enough rest. Never allow yourself to get overtired. Any issues don't seem to be major health problems, though, just short-term blips caused by the transit of short-term planets. Enhance the health with arm and shoulder massage, and massage of the lung reflex, from the 3rd to the 17th. After the 17th diet becomes more important. Good to massage the reflex to the stomach, too.

The main headline this month is the love and social life. It sparkles, Capricorn. For singles, there are many romantic opportunities. While marriage will probably not happen this month, or even this year, next year is a different story. All of you, whether single or in a relationship, will be going out more and attending more parties and gatherings.

You work hard this month but also socialize and party hard.

Saturn, the ruler of your Horoscope, starts to retrograde on the 29th. This tends to weaken self-confidence and self-esteem. Personal initiative is less than usual. But this is a good thing. With so many planets in the Western, social sector of your chart, and with your 7th house very powerful, the month ahead is more about others and their needs. It is about cultivating your social skills, not personal initiative. Let others have their way so long as it isn't destructive. Your good will come to you through others, and quite naturally.

The new Moon of the 6th occurs in your 6th house, making it an especially good day for job-seekers or those who hire others. It is also a good day to deal with health issues. As the days go by the new Moon will clarify health and work issues, as well as the financial situation of children and children figures in your life.

The month ahead should be prosperous as Jupiter is still travelling near your financial planet Uranus.

Mercury will be out of bounds from the 11th to the 29th and Venus will be out of bounds from the 13th to the 29th. Thus, in health matters and in your religious life you are going outside your usual spheres, and perhaps your job situation also pulls you out of your normal comfort zone. Children and children figures are also outside their usual sphere.

July

Best Days Overall: 1, 9, 10, 11, 19, 20, 27, 28
Most Stressful Days Overall: 4, 5, 6, 12, 13, 25, 26
Best Days for Love: 4, 5, 6, 15, 16, 17, 18, 23, 25, 26
Best Days for Money: 1, 2, 3, 10, 12, 13, 20, 21, 22, 28, 29, 30
Best Days for Career: 5, 6, 12, 13, 17, 18, 25, 26

Health still needs more watching until the 22nd. As always, make sure to get enough rest. Until the 2nd enhance the health with right diet, massage of the stomach reflex and abdominal massage. After the 2nd give more attention to the heart. Massage of the heart reflex and chest massage in general should be helpful. Health will improve from the 22nd onwards. From the 25th, enhance the health with abdominal massage and with massage of the small intestine reflex.

On the 22nd the Sun will move into your 8th house, where he is very strong. Thus, your 8th house of regeneration is where the planetary power is to be found from the 22nd. A very sexually active kind of month, therefore. The libido is strong – whatever your age or stage in life, it is stronger than usual. Perhaps this focus on eroticism is merely the natural side-effect of a very strong love and social time. But this is good for other things too. The theme of the month is about getting rid of the extraneous in your life, the things that no longer serve you. These can be physical possessions, or mental and emotional patterns that are no longer useful. This is the kind of month where you expand by getting rid of what doesn't belong in your life. It's not so much about adding things to your life.

Mars enters your 6th house on the 20th so vigorous physical exercise should be helpful health-wise: you need good muscle tone. And since Mars is your home and family planet it shows a need for emotional harmony and harmony with the family. Mars travels with Uranus on the 13th and 14th. This can show spending more on the home and family and good family support.

Power in your 8th house from the 22nd onwards makes this an excellent month for dealing with tax, estate and insurance issues. Those of you of an appropriate age will probably be doing some estate planning.

August

Best Days Overall: 5, 6, 7, 15, 16, 23, 24, 25
Most Stressful Days Overall: 1, 2, 8, 9, 21, 22, 28, 29
Best Days for Love: 1, 2, 3, 4, 8, 13, 14, 17, 18, 23, 28, 29
Best Days for Money: 6, 7, 8, 9, 15, 16, 17, 18, 24, 25, 27
Best Days for Career: 8, 9, 17, 18, 29

The power is still very much in your 8th house until the 22nd, so keep in mind our discussion of this last month. Everything we said then is still very much in effect. But there is more that needs to be said about the 8th house. Power in this house makes it a good period to use spare cash to pay down debt, if possible, but it's also good to take on debt if that is your need. You can earn through creative kinds of financing. This is also a good month to attract outside investors to your projects, if you have good ideas. Your access to outside capital is especially good now. The spouse, partner or current love is having a strong financial month, a financial peak this month too.

Mars travels with Jupiter on the 11th to the 14th. This brings financial increase to the family as a whole and to a parent and parent figure. Women of childbearing age are much more fertile at this time as well.

On the 22nd the Sun moves into your 9th house – a happy house and time for you. The 9th house is expansive and happy, which makes this still a good time to attract outside investors to projects and to access outside capital.

This transit is especially good for college-level students and shows focus and success in their studies. They are taking their studies seriously and seem successful. When there is power in the 9th house our thoughts tend to wander to foreign countries and foreign locations. We have the urge to travel. But with retrograde activity among the planets very high this month, and with both Mercury and Jupiter in retrograde motion, the month ahead is better for planning a foreign trip rather than actually taking it.

For those of you interested in religion, theology and philosophy, your interest is stronger in the month ahead. Small talk, inane conversation bores you these days. You would prefer a juicy, meaty, theological or philosophical discussion any day of the week.

September

Best Days Overall: 2, 3, 12, 13, 20, 21, 29, 30
Most Stressful Days Overall: 4, 5, 6, 18, 19, 24, 25
Best Days for Love: 2, 3, 4, 5, 12, 13, 14, 15, 22, 23, 24, 25
Best Days for Money: 2, 3, 4, 5, 13, 14, 15, 21, 22, 23
Best Days for Career: 4, 5, 6, 14, 15, 23, 24

Health and energy are still excellent, and better than last month.

Many of you have important decisions to make about college and higher education, and these questions will be answered by the new Moon of the 3rd which occurs in your 9th house. Day by day, as the month progresses, all the information that you need to make a right decision will come to you. You can also expect clarification on any nagging religious and philosophical issues.

A lunar eclipse on the 18th is a relatively mild one for you, but it won't hurt to reduce your schedule anyway. For if the eclipse hits a sensitive point in your personal horoscope, the one cast especially for you, it can be very strong indeed.

The eclipse occurs in your 3rd house and impacts directly on the ruler of that house, Neptune. Siblings and sibling figures in your life are strongly affected. There are dramas in your neighbourhood and with neighbours. Cars and communication equipment will get tested and can behave erratically. Best to avoid unnecessary driving or short trips while the eclipse is in effect. The eclipse impacts very strongly on students below college level. There are many scenarios here. There can be drama or disruptions at school. Dramatic changes in educational plans. Sometimes people even change schools.

This eclipse sideswipes Jupiter, your spiritual planet, although happily it is not a direct hit. There are minor changes in your spiritual practice, teachings and teachers. There can be minor disruptions in spiritual or charitable organizations that you are involved with and dramas in the lives of guru figures.

Every lunar eclipse will test your current relationship and this one is no different. Dirty laundry in the relationship can surface, so you become aware of it and can resolve the problem. Perhaps the beloved experiences some personal drama and this causes the disruption. As we have mentioned many times, you go through this twice a year and by now you know how to handle it.

Every lunar eclipse will tend to activate the dream life, and not in a pleasant way. You need not give these dreams any notice. Most of the time it is merely psychological waste stirred up by the eclipse.

October

Best Days Overall: 9, 10, 17, 18, 26, 27, 28
Most Stressful Days Overall: 1, 2, 3, 15, 16, 21, 22, 23, 29, 30
Best Days for Love: 1, 4, 5, 11, 12, 13, 14, 20, 21, 22, 23, 24, 25
Best Days for Money: 2, 10, 11, 12, 18, 19, 20, 28, 29, 30
Best Days for Career: 1, 2, 3, 4, 5, 13, 14, 24, 25, 29, 30

A solar eclipse on the 2nd, which impacts you strongly, is the main headline of the month ahead. While it is not as strong as the solar eclipse in April, it is still pretty strong so, as always, take some common-sense precautions. Stay close to home, avoid unnecessary driving or unnecessary travelling and spend some quiet time at home. Read a book, watch a movie, or meditate. What needs to be done should be done, but unnecessary things, especially if they are stressful, are better off being rescheduled.

This eclipse occurs in your 10th house of career. So, career changes are afoot. It also impacts both Mars and Mercury. So job changes are also happening. This could be within your present situation or with another one. Those of you who hire others will experience employee turnover in the coming months. The events of the eclipse will show why it is necessary to make important changes to your health regime. With Mars impacted too, both sets of parents or parent figures go through personal dramas, and repairs could be needed in the home. There are personal dramas in the lives of family members as well as in the lives of people in authority over you. There can be changes and upheavals in government nationally or locally.

Generally, when any solar eclipse impacts on the career it doesn't usually change the actual career, though sometimes it happens. It usually shows that you need to pursue the career in a different way and perhaps think and plan about it in a different way.

The spouse, partner or current love needs to make important financial changes. The events of the eclipse will reveal where his or her financial thinking was not realistic. A course correction will be necessary.

Every solar eclipse brings psychological encounters with death and this one is no different. The cosmos is urging you to a deeper understanding of death. It is possible that you or people you know have near-death kinds of experiences, close calls. Sometimes you read of the death of some celebrity or hear of the death of someone you know. The dark angel has his ways of letting you know that he is around.

November

Best Days Overall: 5, 6, 14, 15, 22, 23, 24
Most Stressful Days Overall: 12, 13, 18, 19, 25, 26, 27
Best Days for Love: 1, 2, 3, 4, 10, 11, 12, 13, 18, 19, 22, 23, 28, 29
Best Days for Money: 6, 7, 8, 9, 16, 17, 26, 27
Best Days for Career: 3, 4, 12, 13, 22, 23, 24

Health and energy show some improvement over the previous months. They will improve further on the 20th when Pluto finally moves out of your own sign and into Aquarius. However, Mercury, your health planet, starts to retrograde on the 26th, so health still needs attention. Enhance the health by massage of the heart reflex until the 20th – especially those of you born later in Capricorn – and in the ways detailed in the yearly report.

Pluto, the generic ruler of the 8th house of regeneration, makes his long-drawn-out move into your money house on the 20th, where he'll remain for the next 30-odd years. Your finances will be transformed – shaken and stirred – over the decades to come. You begin to get an inkling of this through the rest of this year.

The Eastern sector of self is growing stronger now. After months of backward travel Saturn, the ruler of your Horoscope, begins to move forward on the 5th. Personal independence and initiative are getting stronger day by day. You have confidence and self-esteem. You no longer need to adapt to others or put others first. You can and should begin to create the conditions for your own happiness.

Your 11th house of friends is powerful this month. The sun is in Scorpio for most of this month, until the 21st. Mercury starts the month in the 11th house, and the new Moon of the 1st occurs in this house too. Your love planet in the 11th house of friends signals a social kind of time. Romance doesn't seem a big issue, but friendships, groups and group activities are. You will feel the effects of this new Moon well into next month too, until the next new Moon.

Mercury's move into your 12th house on the 2nd shows spiritual healing becoming important. He's also out of bounds from the 7th until December 12, signalling that health matters are taking you into unconventional places. You are searching for answers outside your comfort zone and are likely exploring more esoteric healing systems.

Your career planet Venus is in Sagittarius until the 11th and is out of bounds all month. Your career is taking you outside your normal haunts. Or you are pursuing career goals in unconventional ways. You can further your career through involvement with charities and altruistic causes.

December

Best Days Overall: 2, 3, 4, 11, 12, 20, 21, 30, 31
Most Stressful Days Overall: 9, 10, 15, 16, 22, 23, 24
Best Days for Love: 1, 2, 3, 4, 9, 10, 13, 14, 15, 16, 19, 20, 22, 23, 24, 30, 31
Best Days for Money: 3, 5, 6, 12, 14, 21, 23, 24, 31
Best Days for Career: 1, 9, 10, 17, 18, 19, 20, 30, 31

The planetary power has made full circle and is back where it was at the beginning of the year. So, you are more independent than usual. Your happiness is up to you. The cosmos wants you to be happy and is supporting this, and so if there are changes that need to be made that will increase your personal happiness, by all means make them now. Later, in a few months' time when the planets are less supportive, such changes will be more difficult to make.

There is still much power in your 12th house of spirituality until the 21st. So, continue with your spiritual practice.

On the 21st, as the Sun enters your own sign and your 1st house, you begin a yearly personal pleasure peak. A time to enjoy all the pleasures of the five senses and to get your body and image into the shape you want. From the 21st onwards it is a very good period for weight-loss regimes, if you need them.

Finances are much improved over the last month. Money is earned through hard work and productivity, but also from your good career reputation. This can bring pay rises, official or unofficial, and the financial favour of parents, parent figures, bosses and those in authority over you.

Love tends to the status quo this month with your 7th house basically empty of planets. This shows a kind of contentment with things as they are. However, the full Moon of the 15th, which occurs exactly on Jupiter, is a very powerful romantic transit, especially for singles.

Health is good all month but especially from the 21st onwards. Mercury, your health planet starts to move forward on the 15th and this will improve health even more. You can enhance the health even further in the ways mentioned in the yearly report and with massage of the liver reflex and thighs.

Aquarius

~~~

THE WATER-BEARER

Birthdays from
20th January to
18th February

Personality Profile

AQUARIUS AT A GLANCE

Element – Air

Ruling Planet – Uranus
   Career Planet – Pluto
   Love Planet – Sun
   Money Planet – Neptune
   Planet of Health and Work – Moon
   Planet of Home and Family Life – Venus
   Planet of Spirituality – Saturn

Colours – electric blue, grey, ultramarine blue

Colours that promote love, romance and social harmony – gold, orange

Colour that promotes earning power – aqua

Gems – black pearl, obsidian, opal, sapphire

Metal – lead

Scents – azalea, gardenia

Quality – fixed (= stability)

Qualities most needed for balance – warmth, feeling and emotion

Strongest virtues – great intellectual power, the ability to communicate and to form and understand abstract concepts, love for the new and avant-garde

Deepest needs – to know and to bring in the new

Characteristics to avoid – coldness, rebelliousness for its own sake, fixed ideas

Signs of greatest overall compatibility – Gemini, Libra

Signs of greatest overall incompatibility – Taurus, Leo, Scorpio

Sign most helpful to career – Scorpio

Sign most helpful for emotional support – Taurus

Sign most helpful financially – Pisces

Sign best for marriage and/or partnerships – Leo

Sign most helpful for creative projects – Gemini

Best Sign to have fun with – Gemini

Signs most helpful in spiritual matters – Libra, Capricorn

Best day of the week – Saturday

Understanding an Aquarius

In the Aquarius-born, intellectual faculties are perhaps the most highly developed of any sign in the zodiac. Aquarians are clear, scientific thinkers. They have the ability to think abstractly and to formulate laws, theories and clear concepts from masses of observed facts. Geminis might be very good at gathering information, but Aquarians take this a step further, excelling at interpreting the information gathered.

Practical people – men and women of the world – mistakenly consider abstract thinking as impractical. It is true that the realm of abstract thought takes us out of the physical world, but the discoveries made in this realm generally end up having tremendous practical consequences. All real scientific inventions and breakthroughs come from this abstract realm.

Aquarians, more so than most, are ideally suited to explore these abstract dimensions. Those who have explored these regions know that there is little feeling or emotion there. In fact, emotions are a hindrance to functioning in these dimensions; thus Aquarians seem – at times – cold and emotionless to others. It is not that Aquarians haven't got feelings and deep emotions, it is just that too much feeling clouds their ability to think and invent. The concept of 'too much feeling' cannot be tolerated or even understood by some of the other signs. Nevertheless, this Aquarian objectivity is ideal for science, communication and friendship.

Aquarians are very friendly people, but they do not make a big show about it. They do the right thing by their friends, even if sometimes they do it without passion or excitement.

Aquarians have a deep passion for clear thinking. Second in importance, but related, is their passion for breaking with the establishment and traditional authority. Aquarians delight in this, because for them rebellion is like a great game or challenge. Very often they will rebel strictly for the fun of rebelling, regardless of whether the authority they defy is right or wrong. Right or wrong has little to do with the rebellious actions of an Aquarian, because to a true Aquarian authority and power must be challenged as a matter of principle.

Where Capricorn or Taurus will err on the side of tradition and the status quo, an Aquarian will err on the side of the new. Without this virtue it is doubtful whether any progress would be made in the world. The conservative-minded would obstruct progress. Originality and invention imply an ability to break barriers; every new discovery represents the toppling of an impediment to thought. Aquarians are very interested in breaking barriers and making walls tumble – scientifically, socially and politically. Other zodiac signs, such as Capricorn, also have scientific talents, but Aquarians are particularly excellent in the social sciences and humanities.

Finance

In financial matters Aquarians tend to be idealistic and humanitarian – to the point of self-sacrifice. They are usually generous contributors to social and political causes. When they contribute it differs from when a Capricorn or Taurus contributes. A Capricorn or Taurus may expect some favour or return for a gift; an Aquarian contributes selflessly.

Aquarians tend to be as cool and rational about money as they are about most things in life. Money is something they need and they set about acquiring it scientifically. No need for fuss; they get on with it in the most rational and scientific ways available.

Money to the Aquarian is especially nice for what it can do, not for the status it may bring (as is the case for other signs). Aquarians are neither big spenders nor penny-pinchers and use their finances in practical ways, for example to facilitate progress for themselves, their families, or even for strangers.

However, if Aquarians want to reach their fullest financial potential they will have to explore their intuitive nature. If they follow only their financial theories – or what they believe to be theoretically correct – they may suffer some losses and disappointments. Instead, Aquarians should call on their intuition, which knows without thinking. For Aquarians, intuition is the short-cut to financial success.

Career and Public Image

Aquarians like to be perceived not only as the breakers of barriers but also as the transformers of society and the world. They long to be seen in this light and to play this role. They also look up to and respect other people in this position and even expect their superiors to act this way.

Aquarians prefer jobs that have a bit of idealism attached to them – careers with a philosophical basis. Aquarians need to be creative at work, to have access to new techniques and methods. They like to keep busy and enjoy getting down to business straight away, without wasting any time. They are often the quickest workers and usually have suggestions for improvements that will benefit their employers. Aquarians are also very helpful with their co-workers and welcome responsibility, preferring this to having to take orders from others.

If Aquarians want to reach their highest career goals they have to develop more emotional sensitivity, depth of feeling and passion. They need to learn to narrow their focus on the essentials and concentrate more on the job in hand. Aquarians need 'a fire in the belly' – a consuming passion and desire – in order to rise to the very top. Once this passion exists they will succeed easily in whatever they attempt.

Love and Relationships

Aquarians are good at friendships, but a bit weak when it comes to love. Of course they fall in love, but their lovers always get the impression that they are more best friends than paramours.

Like Capricorns, they are cool customers. They are not prone to displays of passion or to outward demonstrations of their affections. In fact, they feel uncomfortable when their other half hugs and touches them too much. This does not mean that they do not love their partners. They do, only they show it in other ways. Curiously enough, in relationships they tend to attract the very things that they feel uncomfortable with. They seem to attract hot, passionate, romantic, demonstrative people. Perhaps they know instinctively that these people have qualities they lack and so seek them out. In any event, these relationships do seem to work, Aquarian coolness calming the more passionate partner while the fires of passion warm the cold-blooded Aquarius.

The qualities Aquarians need to develop in their love life are warmth, generosity, passion and fun. Aquarians love relationships of the mind. Here they excel. If the intellectual factor is missing in a relationship an Aquarian will soon become bored or feel unfulfilled.

Home and Domestic Life

In family and domestic matters Aquarians can have a tendency to be too non-conformist, changeable and unstable. They are as willing to break the barriers of family constraints as they are those of other areas of life.

Even so, Aquarians are very sociable people. They like to have a nice home where they can entertain family and friends. Their house is usually decorated in a modern style and full of state-of-the-art appliances and gadgets – an environment Aquarians find absolutely necessary.

If their home life is to be healthy and fulfilling Aquarians need to inject it with a quality of stability – yes, even some conservatism. They need at least one area of life to be enduring and steady; this area is usually their home and family life.

Venus, the generic planet of love, rules the Aquarian's 4th solar house of home and family, which means that when it comes to the family and child-rearing, theories, cool thinking and intellect are not always enough. Aquarians need to bring love into the equation in order to have a great domestic life.

Horoscope for 2024

Major Trends

Since Saturn moved out of your sign in 2023, the overwhelming majority of you are experiencing increased health and energy. Life seems brighter and more optimistic these days. Those of you born early in the sign of Aquarius, January 20–21, still need to watch the health, though, and especially the heart. The same is true for your significant other. More on this later.

Saturn has been in your money house since May last year and will be there for all of 2024. This shows a need to reorganize and reshuffle your investments and financial affairs. For those of you who have been responsible in your financial dealings, this transit will lead to greater and long-term wealth. For those of you who have been irresponsible in these things, this transit can be quite traumatic. More on this later.

Uranus has been in your 4th house of home and family for many years now and he will be there for the year ahead as well. This continues a trend of sudden changes in the family situation, perhaps multiple moves or multiple renovations in the home. Passions in the home have been quite high, both in a good sense and a negative sense. Last year Jupiter entered your 4th house and will be there until May 26. This is a very positive transit for the home and family and the changes and upheavals should be good ones. More details later.

On May 26 Jupiter will enter your 5th house and will stay there for the rest of the year. This too is a positive for your health and energy. It brings more joy into your life and more personal creativity.

Pluto begins to move into your own sign this year. This is not yet the full-blown transit, which will happen next year, but is the beginning of it, a harbinger of things to come. A long-term transformation of your body, image and self-concept is beginning. Your career will start to become more prominent and important and more successful too. More on this later.

Your most important areas of interest this year are spirituality until January 22 and from September 3 to November 20; the body, image and personal appearance from January 22 to September 3 and from November 20 to the end of the year; finance; home and family; and children, creativity and fun from May 26 onwards.

Your paths of greatest fulfilment this year are communication and intellectual interests; home and family until May 26; and children, fun and creativity from May 26 onwards.

Health

(Please note that this is an astrological perspective on health and not a medical one. In days of yore there was no difference, both these perspectives were identical. But these days there could be quite a difference. For a medical perspective, please consult your doctor or health practitioner.)

As we mentioned above, health and energy are much improved for most of you now that Saturn has left your sign. Still, health needs keeping an eye on, especially until May 26, as there are still two long-term planets in stressful alignment with you. Also, as we said, those born early in the sign, January 20–21, need to be more careful of the heart. Jupiter's move into Gemini on May 26, a harmonious aspect, will improve the health even further. Overall, as the year progresses health and energy will keep improving.

As our regular readers know, there is much that can be done to enhance the health and make it even better than it is. Give more attention to the following – the vulnerable areas of your Horoscope this year (the reflex points are shown in the chart opposite):

- The stomach and breasts are always important for Aquarius, and you can send energy to the breasts by massaging the top of the foot (not shown here). Diet is always important for you, and there is a need to eat right. What you eat is important and should be checked with a professional. But how you eat is just as important. You have a special need to elevate the act of eating from mere animal appetite to an act of worship. Make your meal a ritualistic act. Where possible have nice soothing, harmonious music playing in the background. Grace should be said and food should be blessed, in your own words. These practices will not only elevate the energy vibrations of the food you eat but also the vibrations of the digestive system and the whole body. You will not only get the highest and best from your food but it will also digest better. Ever since Uranus has been in your 4th house, the digestion has been erratic. These practices will help smooth it out and stabilize it.

- The heart. This has become important over the past seven years and remains so this year, especially until May 26 and most especially for those born early in Aquarius. The reflex point is shown above. The important thing with the heart is to avoid worry and anxiety, the two emotions which stress it out. Replace worry with faith; meditation will be a big help. Regular chest massage will also strengthen the heart.

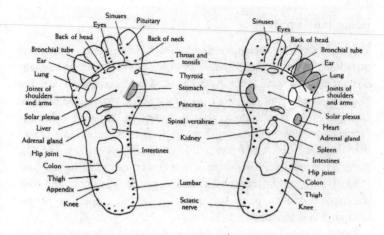

Important foot reflexology points for the year ahead

Try to massage all of the foot on a regular basis – the top of the foot as well as the bottom – but pay extra attention to the points highlighted on the chart. When you massage, be aware of 'sore spots' as these need special attention. It's also a good idea to massage the ankles and below them.

Your health planet, the Moon, is the fastest moving of all the planets and goes through your entire chart each and every month. Thus, there are many short-term trends in health that depend on where the Moon is and the kinds of aspects she receives. These are best dealt with in the monthly reports.

In general, you will feel healthier and more energetic on the new and full Moon and as the Moon grows and waxes. The waning Moon is good for weight-loss and detox regimes.

Two lunar eclipses in the year ahead, one on March 25 and the second on September 18, could produce health scares and bring important changes to the health regime and the diet. If they bring a health scare, don't take it at face value but get second and third opinions.

Home and Family

This area of life has been important for many years and has been a very tumultuous area. Uranus's move through your 4th house has basically destabilized the family circle, the lives of family members and the physical home itself. So, the past six or seven years have brought changes in the family circle, dramatic changes. In some cases the family could have split apart. There could have been multiple moves over the years, and sometimes multiple renovations of the home. The home has been a work in progress, and every time you think you have things right a new idea comes to you and you change again. You have the aspects of someone who upgrades the home the way people upgrade their computers and software.

This year the changes seem happier. Your many years of attention on the home and family seem to be paying off. Jupiter has been in your 4th house since May of last year and will be there until May 26 this year. The family circle is growing and expanding. Usually this happens by birth or marriage, but not always. You can meet people who are like family to you, who fulfil that role in your life. A move could have happened last year, but if not, it can happen in the year ahead. This is a happy move.

There could be the fortunate sale or purchase of a home. Some of you will be purchasing additional homes. Some of you will discover that you have access to other homes. Women of childbearing age have been extra fertile since May of last year and this will continue for this year. Yes, dramatic changes are still happening in the home and family situation, but these look like good ones.

A parent or parent figure has been restless for many years now and has a need for personal freedom. He or she is prospering in the year ahead and is living at a higher standard. He or she will be travelling more, but a move is not likely, though there is nothing against it. The other parent figure seems very devoted to you but perhaps a bit over-controlling. Children and children figures in your life are making important spiritual breakthroughs this year but a move is not likely, the home seems stable.

Siblings and sibling figures seem happy this year and they also seem to have a status quo home and family year. A move is not likely, though there is nothing against it. Grandchildren, if you have them, or those who play that role in your life, can have a move from May 26 onwards.

If you're planning any renovations, all year is good but especially from June 9 to July 21. If you're redecorating or otherwise beautifying the home, April 29 to May 24 would be a good time.

Finance and Career

With Saturn firmly entrenched in your money house finances are more complicated. More challenging. This transit will produce many different effects. First off, as we mentioned, there is a need to re-order, and rearrange your investments, savings and financial strategy in general. Generally, when Saturn moves into the money house it signals a need for good financial management. This is perhaps just as important as increasing the earnings. Often with this kind of transit it shows taking on an extra financial burden, something that you can't avoid. This extra expense often produces a feeling of lack, even when there is no real lack in reality. However, the feeling is there. You'll find that as you rearrange things, shift things around here and there, you'll have all the resources that you need.

Neptune, your financial planet, has been in your money house for many, many years now. While this is basically a good thing, in some cases it could have produced an unrealistic attitude to wealth. Saturn is now straightening that out. The outlook will be more realistic and more practical. Saturn is not out to punish you; on the contrary, he wants to give enduring, long-term wealth. Stable wealth. So he is forcing the moves that you need to make this happen.

The two planets that govern spirituality in your Horoscope are both in the money house this year. Neptune is the generic spiritual planet and Saturn is your actual spiritual planet. Thus, there is a spiritual agenda behind all your financial adventures and challenges. For one thing, it is going to make you more reliant on the spiritual laws of affluence, and more practical in their application.

Saturn in the money house favours earning through your management skills and through the corporate world. It favours commercial real estate and blue-chip companies. It favours conservative-type investments. Like last year, this is a good year to establish long-term savings and investment plans. Wealth is really a long-term project and is attained in a step-by-step methodical kind of way. Although you will become more speculative from May 26 onwards, Saturn does not favour this. He will reward careful, well-thought-out and well-hedged risks but not casino-type speculations.

Though your 10th career house is basically empty this year – only short-term planets will move through there with short-term effects – career is becoming increasingly important and will be for many years to come. Those born early in Aquarius will feel the career urge more strongly this year, but eventually all of you will feel it. Pluto, your career planet, is moving into your own sign and will be there for the next 30 years. This shows greater than usual ambition. It shows that career opportunities will chase you rather than vice versa. Just go about your business and career opportunities will find you. You will be adopting the image of success and dressing the part. People will see you as a successful person. This career focus will cause many and deep changes in your image, body and concept of yourself.

Another way to read this transit is that your career, your mission, is really your body and image, getting that into the shape that you want. This is not as selfish as it seems, as many people are suffering from poor self-image. Your insights and knowledge can help heal others.

Love and Social Life

Your 7th house of love is not prominent this year. Basically, it is empty. Only short-term planets will move through there and their impact will be short term. This tends to the status quo. The love and social life will basically be as it was last year. Those of you who are married will tend to stay married and singles will tend to stay single. This empty 7th house shows a basic contentment with things as they are and there is no need to make dramatic and important changes.

However, there will be two solar eclipses in the year ahead that can shake up your present relationship and the love life in general. The first, and the strongest, is a total solar eclipse on April 8 and the second is a solar eclipse on October 2. These will test your existing relationships. Generally, dirty laundry, old grievances, come to the surface and need to be resolved. Good relationships tend to survive these things, but it is the faulty ones that are in danger. With the Sun as your love planet you go through these testings every year and by now you know how to handle them.

While singles are not likely to marry in the year ahead, we do see much dating and love affair types of relationships, especially from May 26 onwards.

Friendships, Platonic-type relationships, seem happy this year, especially in April and May. New and significant friendships are happening.

A parent or parent figure has love this year. The only question is the stability of this relationship. In general, he or she is having an exciting kind of social life. Children and children figures also have love this year. If they are of an appropriate age it could even lead to marriage. Grandchildren, if you have them, or those who play that role in your life, experienced a serious relationship last year and this could still be ongoing. In general, their social life seems happy.

There are many short-term trends in love as your love planet is a fast-moving planet. During the year the Sun will move through all the signs and houses of your Horoscope, and these short-term trends will depend on where the Sun is at any given time and the kinds of aspects that he receives. They are best dealt with in the monthly reports.

Self-improvement

Neptune, the most spiritual and idealistic of all the planets, has been in your money house for many years now. This has brought outstanding financial intuition, and also a deepening of your understanding of the spiritual laws of affluence, as we've mentioned. Most of you have advanced in your understanding of this. However, for many of you this transit could have given you financial goals that were larger than life and perhaps unrealistic. Sure, most of you felt that your wealth would be used for good and idealistic purposes. But perhaps with these high goals you skipped many of the intermediate steps to get to them. Perhaps you expected it to happen all at once. Saturn, your actual spiritual planet, in your money house is going to show you that even the highest concepts of wealth are attainable if you take a step-by-step approach. It is good to have larger-than-life financial goals, but you need to take the practical steps that lead to their achievement. This will be Saturn's revelation to you in the year ahead.

As long as you are making progress towards your goals, as long as you are richer today than you were yesterday, you are on the road to your goals even though they seem far from attainment. As the Buddhists say, you must learn to love the way as much as the goal. You must learn to love the process that takes you to your goal as much as the goal itself.

Pluto's move into your own sign this year initiates a long-term, 30-year process through which you will be giving birth to the ideal you, the ideal body and image. This process can bring surgeries, perhaps cosmetic types of surgery, detox regimes and perhaps near-death experiences. Rest assured the cosmos will not send you more than you can handle at any given time, for this process is not punitive. How will you manifest your ideal body and image without letting go of the old patterns? Sometimes these old patterns can be dropped and transformed in the natural, normal way. But sometimes these things are so deep and ingrained that stronger measures might be necessary. Pluto will supply the stronger measures. A new birth tends to be a messy business, with much blood and gore and pain involved. But the end result is always good. So it is with the new body you are giving birth to.

For more information on astrology, healing and spiritual topics, please visit my blog at www.spiritual-stories.com.

Month-by-month Forecasts

January

Best Days Overall: 3, 4, 12, 13, 21, 22, 30, 31
Most Stressful Days Overall: 6, 7, 18, 19, 25, 26, 27
Best Days for Love: 8, 9, 11, 12, 18, 19, 21, 25, 26, 27, 28, 29
Best Days for Money: 1, 2, 7, 10, 11, 14, 15, 18, 19, 24, 28, 29
Best Days for Career: 3, 6, 7, 11, 12, 19, 20, 31

The immense power in your 12th house of spirituality is the main headline of the month ahead. It is a very spiritual month. The new Moon of the 11th is especially so, as it occurs in your spiritual 12th house.

This is a month for increased ESP and synchronistic-type experiences. The invisible world is very active and letting you know that it is around. The dream life will be very active and revelatory. Dreams should be written down as you will see their meaning later on. The effects of the new Moon of the 11th go on long after it actually happens and will bring clarity to the spiritual experiences you've been having.

On the 20th the Sun will move into your own sign, initiating a yearly personal pleasure peak. More important than that is Pluto's move into your sign on the 22nd. This brings happy career opportunities to you. There's nothing much that you need to do to find them, just go about your business and these opportunities will find you.

Health is good this month and improves further from the 20th onwards. The new Moon of the 11th is especially good for healing, and especially for spiritual healing. The full Moon of the 25th is also an excellent day for healing.

Love is happy this month. Until the 20th love is found in spiritual type of settings – at the yoga studio, the meditation lecture or seminar, the charity or spiritual event. Spiritual compatibility seems a very important factor in romance.

On the 20th love pursues you. It is probably unavoidable. All you need to do is just show up. This is the kind of month where you have love on your own terms. The beloved is very eager to please and puts your interest ahead of his or her own.

February

Best Days Overall: 8, 9, 17, 18, 26, 27, 28
Most Stressful Days Overall: 1, 2, 3, 14, 15, 21, 22, 23, 29
Best Days for Love: 6, 7, 8, 9, 17, 18, 19, 21, 22, 23, 26, 27, 29
Best Days for Money: 2, 3, 6, 7, 10, 11, 14, 15, 20, 24, 25, 29
Best Days for Career: 1, 2, 3, 8, 17, 26, 29

A happy, healthy and prosperous month ahead, Aquarius. Enjoy.

The main headline is the incredible power in your own sign: 60 per cent of the planets are either there or moving through there this month. This is a lot of power. It shows great energy. The personal appearance shines and the opposite sex takes notice.

Health is great this month. The only danger is hyperactivity. You might be overdoing things.

Personal independence is probably at a multi-year high right now. This definitely is a time to have your way in things: your way is the best way, so pursue your path of personal happiness. Make the changes that need to be made to enhance this.

This is still a great month to enjoy all the physical pleasures of the five senses. Like last month it is an excellent time for getting the body and image into the shape that you want.

Love continues to be good, and like last month it pursues you. If you are single there is nothing much that you need to do to attract love, it will find you. If you are already in a relationship the beloved goes out of his or her way to please you; you come first.

When it comes to personal happiness you seem to have many options this month and perhaps you are confused about it. The new Moon of the 9th, which occurs in your own sign, is not only a great personal pleasure day but will also clarify issues involving your personal happiness. It will clarify issues involving the image and personal appearance, too. Day by day all the information that you need to make good decisions will come to you, naturally and normally. This will go on until the next new Moon.

On the 19th the Sun moves into your money house and you begin a yearly financial peak. There is prosperity now. Social connections are playing a big role in finance. The spouse, partner or current love seems very active in your financial life, in a good kind of way. You have had wonderful financial intuition for many years now and this month it is even better. Perhaps an opportunity for a business partnership or joint venture will come your way.

With the Sun moving into your money house on the 19th the needs and attitudes in love will change. You seem more interested in material prosperity. Singles gravitate to rich people. Love is expressed in material ways, through gift-giving and material support. Romantic opportunities happen as you pursue your financial goals and perhaps with people involved in your finances.

March

Best Days Overall: 7, 8, 13, 14, 15, 16, 24, 25, 26
Most Stressful Days Overall: 1, 13, 14, 19, 20, 21, 27, 28
Best Days for Love: 1, 7, 8, 9, 10, 17, 18, 19, 20, 21, 27, 28, 29, 30
Best Days for Money: 1, 4, 5, 9, 10, 13, 14, 18, 22, 23, 28
Best Days for Career: 1, 7, 15, 24, 27, 28

All the planets are moving forward this month, which is highly unusual. Your personal solar cycle is waxing, as is the universal solar cycle. You are in an excellent time for launching new products or ventures into the world. If you can do this from the 10th to the 25th, while avoiding the lunar eclipse of the 25th, you will have the best of the best. There is much cosmic support for your new ventures or products.

Even the lunar eclipse of the 25th seems relatively mild in its effect on you, as far as eclipses go. However, keep in mind that if this eclipse hits something sensitive in your personal Horoscope, the one cast especially for you, it can be strong indeed. So it won't hurt to reduce your schedule while the eclipse is in effect.

This eclipse occurs in your 9th house and will affect college-level students or those applying to college. It can cause changes in educational plans or even changes of school. There can be dramas and disruptions at their institutions. There can be dramas at your place of worship and in the lives of worship leaders. Most importantly, however, your religious, theological and philosophical beliefs will get tested by the events of the eclipse. While, in the long term, this is a good thing, it is usually not so pleasant while it is happening. Some beliefs will get changed or amended and some will be dropped altogether. In the end you will live your life in a whole different way.

Every lunar eclipse affects health and work because the eclipsed planet, the Moon, is the ruler of these areas. This one is no different. There can be job changes, either in your present situation or with a new one. There can be dramas at the workplace. If you employ others there can be employee turnover in the coming months.

The events of the eclipse will show you that there need to be important changes in your health regime over the next few months, and this will happen. However, health is good this month.

The month ahead is very prosperous, as you are still in the midst of a yearly financial peak, and the money house is very strong. The new Moon of the 10th will add to the prosperity but will also bring clarity to your financial life as the days go by.

April

Best Days Overall: 3, 4, 11, 12, 21, 22, 30
Most Stressful Days Overall: 9, 10, 16, 17, 23, 24, 25
Best Days for Love: 7, 8, 16, 17, 27, 28, 29
Best Days for Money: 1, 2, 5, 6, 9, 10, 14, 15, 18, 19, 24, 25
Best Days for Career: 7, 15, 23, 24, 25

A very strong solar eclipse on the 8th is the big headline of the month. This eclipse will not only impact you but various other people and areas of life that are important to you. So, as always, take a nice, easy, relaxed schedule while the eclipse is in effect. There is no need for panic, this never helps, but common-sense precautions should be taken. Do you really need to take that short drive out that period? Do you need to take that trip? Do you need to schedule an appointment that day? Best to take the day off, stay close to home and watch a movie, read a book or, best of all, meditate. Things that need to be done should be done, of course, but anything else, especially if it's stressful, should be rescheduled.

This eclipse occurs in your 3rd house and impacts siblings and sibling figures in your life. They have personal dramas, and should also reduce their schedule while the eclipse is in effect. There can be dramas and upheavals in your neighbourhood. Students below college level are also affected here. Perhaps there are dramas and disruptions at school, perhaps there are changes in educational plans, perhaps – as sometimes happens – they change schools.

Mercury and Venus are both directly impacted by this eclipse. Venus is your home and family planet and your planet of creativity and children. Thus there are dramas in the lives of family members, a parent or parent figure and in the lives of children and children figures. They should be kept out of harm's way as much as possible. Repairs could be needed in the home.

Those of you involved in the creative arts will make important changes to your creativity.

Every solar eclipse impacts your love life, your current relationship and your social circle in general, as we mentioned earlier. However, because this eclipse is a total eclipse, it is probably much stronger than the ones you have faced before. Even good relationships will be stressed out by this eclipse. But they will survive. It is the flawed ones that are in danger.

The spouse, partner or current love feels the impact of this eclipse very strongly and should also take an easy, relaxed schedule. Perhaps there are personal dramas happening in his or her life. Be more patient with him or her these days.

May

Best Days Overall: 1, 9, 10, 17, 18, 19, 27, 28
Most Stressful Days Overall: 7, 8, 13, 14, 20, 21, 22
Best Days for Love: 1, 7, 8, 13, 14, 15, 16, 18, 19, 27, 28
Best Days for Money: 2, 3, 4, 8, 12, 15, 16, 22, 26, 27, 28, 30, 31
Best Days for Career: 1, 9, 17, 20, 21, 22, 27

Health is a bit stressful until the 20th, but afterwards you will see dramatic improvement, not just for the month but for the entire year ahead. In the meantime, enhance the health in the ways mentioned in the yearly report. Most of all, make sure to maintain high energy levels and don't let yourself get overtired.

The planetary power this month is in your 4th house of home and family. This is where the focus should be. With your career planet Pluto retrograde, career issues need more time to resolve. You may as well focus on the home and family and, of course, your emotional life.

The home situation has seemed relatively happy for the past year, with Jupiter in the 4th house. He has been expanding the family circle and brings optimism to the family life. Women of childbearing age have been fertile all year, but especially so this month. The home is being beautified and modernized. There is more entertaining from home and with family members.

The Sun will travel with Uranus on the 13th and 14th and this should bring a happy romantic opportunity. If you are in a relationship there is more closeness with the beloved.

Love seems especially excellent from the 18th to the 20th as the Sun, your love planet, travels with Jupiter.

On the 20th the Sun will enter your 5th house and you will begin a yearly personal pleasure peak. You have personal pleasure peaks every year but this one will be stronger than most for, on the 26th, Jupiter will also move into your 5th house. This is a time for enjoying leisure activities and exploring the rapture side of life. This will be an interest for the rest of the year ahead, but especially intensely this month. Even love is more about fun and games than about personal commitment. Singles are attracted to people who can show them a good time. Those who are already in a relationship are having more fun with their partners.

Your personal creativity is very strong from the 20th onwards and for the rest of the year ahead.

June

Best Days Overall: 5, 6, 14, 15, 16, 24, 25
Most Stressful Days Overall: 3, 4, 9, 10, 11, 17, 18, 30
Best Days for Love: 4, 5, 6, 9, 10, 11, 13, 14, 15, 16, 17, 22, 23, 26, 27
Best Days for Money: 5, 8, 14, 24, 18, 26, 27
Best Days for Career: 5, 14, 17, 18, 23, 24

You're still very much in a party kind of month until the 20th. After the 20th, however, you seem a bit more serious and work oriented. You will work hard and play hard.

Health is excellent this month and I can only presume that the power in your 6th house is not so much a focus on health but more a focus on work. Job-seekers have many job opportunities available, and they will not be unemployed for too long. Even those of you who are employed will have opportunities for overtime and second jobs.

Venus and Mercury are both out of bounds this month. Mercury is out of bounds from the 11th to the 29th and Venus is out of bounds from the 13th to the 29th. This indicates that a parent or parent figure is venturing outside his or her natural boundaries, perhaps exploring new territory, perhaps spending more time educating him- or herself.

Children and children figures in your life are also outside their usual boundaries. This seems to involve finance but could involve other things as well. They are having a very strong financial month. There is serious romance for children and children figures on the 3rd and 4th.

Mars moves into your 4th house on the 9th and stays there for the rest of the month ahead. This would be a good time for renovating the home or doing construction work around the house. However, this transit can make family members more combative so be more patient with them.

The new Moon of the 6th is an especially happy day and also a very creative kind of day. More importantly, this new Moon will have effects long after it actually happens. Day by day until the next new Moon next month, issues involving children, children figures, pregnancies and creative issues will be clarified as the days progress. All the information you need for making a right decision in these areas will come to you normally and naturally.

July

Best Days Overall: 2, 3, 12, 13, 21, 22, 29, 30, 31
Most Stressful Days Overall: 1, 7, 8, 14, 15, 16, 27, 28
Best Days for Love: 4, 5, 6, 7, 8, 15, 16, 17, 18, 23, 25, 26
Best Days for Money: 2, 3, 6, 12, 13, 16, 21, 22, 23, 24, 29, 30
Best Days for Career: 2, 12, 14, 15, 16, 29

Health is basically good this month, but after the 22nd will need more watching. As always make sure to get enough rest. There is nothing serious afoot, only short-term stresses caused by short-term planets. But if you allow yourself to get overtired, all kinds of things can happen. Enhance the health in the ways discussed in the yearly report.

Your powerful 6th house shows that job-seekers still have many opportunities to find work. Even those of you already employed will have opportunities for overtime and side jobs. You're in the mood for work and it is an excellent time to do all those boring detail-oriented jobs that you keep putting off.

On the 22nd the Sun enters your 7th house and you begin a yearly love and social peak. Singles are dating more and attending more parties and gatherings. Even those of you already in relationships are attending more parties and gatherings.

Mars travels with Uranus on the 13th and 14th. A good idea to drive more carefully and to be more mindful on the physical plane. Watch the temper and avoid rush.

Siblings and sibling figures seem prosperous this month, especially from the 11th to the 14th. Children and children figures have a very strong romantic month. Much depends on their age. Marriage or a relationship that is like marriage can happen.

The new Moon of the 5th occurs in your 6th house, which makes the day an especially good one for job-seekers. And as the days progress the Moon will continue to clarify health and work issues. This will go on until the next new Moon in August.

From the 22nd onwards there are many planets in your 7th house of love. For singles this shows many different romantic interests. It shows an attraction to different types of people. Your problem can be too much of a good thing – but have no fear, next month's new Moon will help clarify your love life.

August

Best Days Overall: 8, 9, 17, 18, 26, 27
Most Stressful Days Overall: 3, 4, 11, 12, 23, 24, 25, 30, 31
Best Days for Love: 3, 4, 8, 13, 14, 17, 18, 23, 29, 30, 31
Best Days for Money: 2, 8, 9, 12, 17, 18, 19, 20, 27, 28, 29
Best Days for Career: 8, 11, 12, 17, 18, 26

Continue to be more mindful about your health and energy until the 22nd. Make sure to get enough rest and enhance the health in the ways mentioned in the yearly report. There is no need to be overly concerned about health as it is just short-term stresses caused by short-term planetary transits. By the 22nd most of the issues will have resolved themselves. You are still in the midst of a yearly love and social peak. This will go on until the 22nd. Singles are dating more and have multiple love interests. All of you will be attending more parties and gatherings; your social energy is much stronger than usual.

The new Moon of the 4th occurs in your 7th house of love and makes it an especially strong social day. With so many romantic opportunities open to you it would be natural to have many questions about who is who, and what is what. The new Moon cycle beginning on the 4th will start to clarify these issues for you. All the information you need to make a good social decision will come to you normally and naturally.

Children and children figures in your life have also been having an active and happy social life. If they are of marriageable age, marriage can happen. (Or relationships that are like marriage.) They also seem more involved with friends, groups and group activities.

Finances are more stressful than usual from the 22nd onwards, as Neptune receives challenging aspects. You will probably have to work harder for earnings. Like last month, little things, little omissions, can delay or complicate earnings. So, handle all the details of finance in a more perfect way.

With 40 per cent of the planets retrograde from the 4th to the 25th, very near the maximum for the year, life is slowing down and you are dealing with more delays. This is not your fault, generally, just the cosmic weather.

On the 22nd, as the Sun enters your 8th house of regeneration, you begin a more erotic kind of month. This is just the natural consequence of the strong social months you've had. But power in the 8th house has other meanings as well. First of all, though your personal finances could be a lot better, it shows that the finances of the spouse, partner or current love seem excellent this month. He or she will probably make up the difference. Power in the 8th house also shows that good financial management is important this month. This is an excellent time to deal with tax, estate and insurance issues. But, best to wait until after the 25th before making any specific moves. The same is true for those of you involved in estate planning.

Mars travels with Jupiter from the 11th to the 14th and this brings prosperity to siblings, or sibling figures in your life. Students below college level seem to have success in school. Writers, teachers and marketing people have a good financial period.

September

Best Days Overall: 4, 5, 6, 14, 15, 22, 23
Most Stressful Days Overall: 1, 7, 8, 20, 21, 26, 27, 28
Best Days for Love: 1, 2, 3, 4, 5, 12, 13, 14, 15, 23, 22, 24, 27, 28
Best Days for Money: 4, 5, 8, 14, 15, 16, 17, 22, 23, 25
Best Days for Career: 3, 4, 7, 8, 13, 14, 21

Retrograde activity is, for practical purposes, at its maximum extent for the year. Technically, the maximum happens next month but only briefly, for three days. So, the month ahead is about learning patience. You probably won't be able to avoid all delays but you will be able to minimize them by striving to be perfect in all that you do. Pay attention to all the little details of life. You're still in an excellent month for dealing with tax, insurance and estate issues, and now that Mercury is moving forward the decisions here will be a lot better.

A lunar eclipse on the 18th is relatively mild on you, as far as eclipses go, but it won't hurt to reduce your schedule. If this eclipse hits an important point in your personal Horoscope, the one cast especially for you, it can have a powerful effect indeed.

This eclipse not only occurs in your money house but is a direct hit on your money planet. So important financial changes and shifts need to happen. Most likely your financial thinking and planning have not been realistic, as the events of the eclipse will show, and now you must make the appropriate changes. There can be personal dramas in the lives of the money people in your life as well.

Jupiter, your planet of friends, is sideswiped by this eclipse, although happily it is not a direct hit. There are minor dramas in the lives of friends and minor dramas with your computers, software and high-tech gadgetry in general. Your internet service could be much better. Take the normal common-sense precautions with your online activities. Every lunar eclipse affects your work and health issues and this one is no different. So, there can be dramas at the workplace, job changes and changes in your health regime in the coming months. If you employ others there are dramas in the lives of employees and probably employee turnover in the next few months. Since your health is basically good these days, this eclipse is probably indicating merely a need to change your health regime.

Children and children figures in your life need to make important financial changes, too.

Mars will be out of bounds from the 5th through the 24th, signalling that in your intellectual life you are exploring subjects outside your normal interests. Your taste in reading is outside your norm. You have a yen to explore or visit places outside your usual haunts.

On the 22nd, the Sun enters your 9th house and you'll begin a more or less happy kind of period. Singles will find love and social opportunities at university or university functions, at religious functions, at the place of worship, in foreign lands or with foreigners. Your current relationship can be enhanced with a foreign trip.

Health looks excellent from the 22nd onwards.

October

Best Days Overall: 1, 2, 3, 11, 12, 19, 20, 29, 30
Most Stressful Days Overall: 4, 5, 17, 18, 24, 25, 30
Best Days for Love: 1, 4, 5, 11, 12, 13, 14, 20, 24, 25
Best Days for Money: 2, 4, 5, 11, 12, 13, 14, 19, 20, 23, 29, 30, 31
Best Days for Career: 4, 5, 10, 18, 28, 31

There are two main headlines this month. The first is that planetary retrograde activity reaches the maximum limit of the year, albeit briefly, from the 9th to the 11th.

The other headline is the solar eclipse of the 2nd. This is not as strong as the last solar eclipse in April but is still pretty strong as it impacts other planets in the Horoscope. So, as always, take sensible precautions: avoid unnecessary driving, reschedule any activities you can (especially those that are stressful) and spend more quiet time at home.

The eclipse occurs in your 9th house but directly impacts Mercury, the ruler of your 5th house of children, and so affects children and children figures in your life. They should also take a relaxed and easy schedule; they don't need to be involved in daredevil-type activities. They experience personal dramas with this eclipse, and if they haven't been careful in dietary matters they can experience a physical detox. The eclipse also impacts grandchildren, if you have them, or those who play that role in your life.

Students at college level are affected by this eclipse. There are dramas at college, there are changes in educational plans and sometimes even a change of establishment. There are dramas in your place of worship too, and in the lives of worship leaders. Big changes going on in your place of worship.

Because Mars is directly impacted here, students below college level are also affected. They too will experience changes in educational plans, disruptions at school and perhaps even a change of school.

As we said earlier, best to avoid unnecessary driving altogether, but if you must do so, drive in a more mindful and careful manner. Cars and communication equipment will tend to get tested and sometimes need repair or replacement.

There can be personal drama in the lives of siblings, sibling figures and neighbours. There can be disruptions and upheavals in your neighbourhood as well.

Because Mercury is directly impacted, this eclipse can bring encounters with death, although most often this is not about physical death but psychological encounters. There can be near-death experiences, and often people have dreams of death. The dark angel is letting you know that he is around and can strike at any time. The purpose here is not punitive but educational. The purpose is to bring a deeper understanding of what death is.

Every solar eclipse affects your current relationship and this one is no different. The spouse, partner or current love has financial dramas and probably personal dramas as well. He or she is experiencing career changes. So, you need to be more patient with him or her. The problem might not be with your relationship per se but with the dramas that are going on in the life of the beloved.

On the 22nd the Sun moves into your 10th house and you begin a yearly career peak. Career should be successful now. Your career planet Pluto is moving forward now and your 10th house is strong.

November

Best Days Overall: 7, 8, 9, 16, 17, 25, 26, 27
Most Stressful Days Overall: 1, 2, 14, 15, 20, 21, 28, 29
Best Days for Love: 1, 2, 3, 4, 10, 11, 12, 13, 19, 20, 21, 22, 23
Best Days for Money: 2, 8, 9, 10, 11, 16, 17, 19, 26, 27, 29
Best Days for Career: 1, 2, 6, 16, 25, 28, 29

Career is still very strong this month and you are making excellent progress here, and with Mercury, the ruler of your 5th house, in your career house until the 2nd you seem to be enjoying the career as well. Children and children figures also seem more successful these days. Career will improve even further when Pluto moves back into your own sign on the 20th.

Though your financial planet is still retrograde, finances are much improved this month as Neptune is receiving very positive aspects.

Still, important purchases and investments still need more research and due diligence.

Health needs more attention until the 21st. This doesn't seem very serious, only short-term stresses caused by short-term planets, but it's still a good idea to make sure you get enough rest. Enhance the health in the ways mentioned in the yearly report. The full Moon of the 15th, which occurs right on Uranus, the ruler of your Horoscope, should bring healing to you, either spontaneously or through a therapist. In general, the 1st to the 15th, as the Moon waxes, is good for taking things that build up the body, while from the 15th to the end of the month is good for detox regimes of all kinds.

Love should be happy this month. It seems very high on your list of priorities. There is great focus here and focus is 90 per cent of success. You are attracted to successful people, people above you in status and power. Love and social opportunities will happen as you involve yourself in your career, or with people involved in your career.

On the 21st the Sun will enter your 11th house and the love attitude will change. Singles will want a more equitable kind of relationship. A relationship of peers, of equals. There is a need for friendship with the beloved as well as romance. The good news is that with the Sun in the beneficent 11th house, fondest hopes and wishes in love tend to happen.

For singles it would be good to be more involved with friends, groups and group activities. These will bring romantic opportunities. The online world also seems a good venue for romance.

December

Best Days Overall: 5, 6, 13, 14, 22, 23, 24
Most Stressful Days Overall: 11, 12, 17, 18, 19, 25, 26
Best Days for Love: 1, 2, 3, 4, 9, 10, 13, 14, 17, 18, 19, 20, 22, 23, 24, 30, 31
Best Days for Money: 6, 7, 8, 14, 16, 23, 24, 26
Best Days for Career: 5, 13, 22, 25, 26

Basically a happy month ahead, Aquarius. Enjoy.

Many nice things are happening. Your financial planet Neptune starts to move forward on the 7th after many months of retrograde motion. The financial thinking and judgement are much improved now. There is more clarity in finance and your decisions should be good ones. Also, the financial intuition is much more trustworthy from the 7th. It began to improve on November 15 but now it improves even further.

The power in your 11th house until the 21st is also happy for you. The cosmos impels you to do the things that you most love to do. It strengthens your already strong gifts of networking, innovation and invention. When the 11th house is strong people often have their Horoscopes done, and this aspect is also a good one to pursue your interests in science and technology. If you need to buy any high-tech equipment, this is a good month to do it.

Venus is out of bounds from the 1st to the 8th. This shows that parents, parent figures, children and children figures are outside their normal spheres. Outside their normal boundaries. They are in unknown territory for a while.

From the 6th to the end of the year Mars will make one of his rare retrogrades, which only happens every two years or so. This can bring delays in communication, delays at the post office, problems with your phones. It is advisable to make sure that you are saying what you mean and that you are hearing what others mean. This can save a lot of heartache later on. Miscommunication is a problem this period.

If you're buying a car or new communication equipment study the issues more carefully. It is better to do your homework on these kinds of purchases during a Mars retrograde, rather than making them – that can be done later.

Like last month, there is an active social life on two fronts, romantically and in terms of friendships and Platonic kinds of relationships. You seem equally happy with either. Those of you interested in romance should get more involved with friends, groups, organizations and group activities. Like last month the online world seems a venue for romance.

Your spiritual planet, Saturn, has been moving forward since November 15. This month, on the 21st the Sun enters your 12th house of spirituality. The spiritual life becomes more active and happy. It is a time for spiritual breakthroughs, and when they happen they are most joyous events. It is a time for peak spiritual experiences. With the love planet in the 12th house from the 21st onwards, the message is, 'Take care of your spiritual life, your connection with the divine, and love will take care of itself.' From the 21st onwards romantic opportunities happen at spiritual types of venues: the prayer meeting, the meditation seminar, the *satsang*, the spiritual lecture or seminar, or the charity event.

Health is good this month. If there are problems, the full Moon of the 15th brings healing.

Venus will be in your own sign from the 7th onwards, bringing beauty, grace and charm to the image. You dress beautifully and fashionably. Pluto, now in your sign for the long term, brings sex appeal to the image.

Pisces

THE FISH

Birthdays from
19th February to
20th March

Personality Profile

PISCES AT A GLANCE

Element – Water

Ruling Planet – Neptune
  Career Planet – Jupiter
  Love Planet – Mercury
  Money Planet – Mars
  Planet of Health and Work – Sun
  Planet of Home and Family Life – Mercury
  Planet of Love Affairs, Creativity and Children – Moon

Colours – aqua, blue-green

Colours that promote love, romance and social harmony – earth tones, yellow, yellow-orange

Colours that promote earning power – red, scarlet

Gem – white diamond

Metal – tin

Scent – lotus

Quality – mutable (= flexibility)

Qualities most needed for balance – structure and the ability to handle form

Strongest virtues – psychic power, sensitivity, self-sacrifice, altruism

Deepest needs – spiritual illumination, liberation

Characteristics to avoid – escapism, keeping bad company, negative moods

Signs of greatest overall compatibility – Cancer, Scorpio

Signs of greatest overall incompatibility – Gemini, Virgo, Sagittarius

Sign most helpful to career – Sagittarius

Sign most helpful for emotional support – Gemini

Sign most helpful financially – Aries

Sign best for marriage and/or partnerships – Virgo

Sign most helpful for creative projects – Cancer

Best Sign to have fun with – Cancer

Signs most helpful in spiritual matters – Scorpio, Aquarius

Best day of the week – Thursday

Understanding a Pisces

If Pisces have one outstanding quality it is their belief in the invisible, spiritual and psychic side of things. This side of things is as real to them as the hard earth beneath their feet – so real, in fact, that they will often ignore the visible, tangible aspects of reality in order to focus on the invisible and so-called intangible ones.

Of all the signs of the zodiac, the intuitive and emotional faculties of the Pisces are the most highly developed. They are committed to living by their intuition and this can at times be infuriating to other people – especially those who are materially, scientifically or technically orientated. If you think that money, status and worldly success are the only goals in life, then you will never understand a Pisces.

Pisces have intellect, but to them intellect is only a means by which they can rationalize what they know intuitively. To an Aquarius or a Gemini the intellect is a tool with which to gain knowledge. To a well-developed Pisces it is a tool by which to express knowledge.

Pisces feel like fish in an infinite ocean of thought and feeling. This ocean has many depths, currents and undercurrents. They long for purer waters where the denizens are good, true and beautiful, but they are sometimes pulled to the lower, murkier depths. Pisces know that they do not generate thoughts but only tune in to thoughts that already exist; this is why they seek the purer waters. This ability to tune in to higher thoughts inspires them artistically and musically.

Since Pisces is so spiritually orientated – though many Pisces in the corporate world may hide this fact – we will deal with this aspect in greater detail, for otherwise it is difficult to understand the true Pisces personality.

There are four basic attitudes of the spirit. One is outright scepticism – the attitude of secular humanists. The second is an intellectual or emotional belief, where one worships a far-distant God-figure – the attitude of most modern church-going people. The third is not only belief but direct personal spiritual experience – this is the attitude of some 'born-again' religious people. The fourth is actual unity with the divinity, an intermingling with the spiritual world – this is the attitude of yoga. This fourth attitude is the deepest urge of a

Pisces, and a Pisces is uniquely qualified to pursue and perform this work.

Consciously or unconsciously, Pisces seek this union with the spiritual world. The belief in a greater reality makes Pisces very tolerant and understanding of others – perhaps even too tolerant. There are instances in their lives when they should say 'enough is enough' and be ready to defend their position and put up a fight. However, because of their qualities it takes a good deal to get them into that frame of mind.

Pisces basically want and aspire to be 'saints'. They do so in their own way and according to their own rules. Others should not try to impose their concept of saintliness on a Pisces, because he or she always tries to find it for him- or herself.

Finance

Money is generally not that important to Pisces. Of course they need it as much as anyone else, and many of them attain great wealth. But money is not generally a primary objective. Doing good, feeling good about oneself, peace of mind, the relief of pain and suffering – these are the things that matter most to a Pisces.

Pisces earn money intuitively and instinctively. They follow their hunches rather than their logic. They tend to be generous and perhaps overly charitable. Almost any kind of misfortune is enough to move a Pisces to give. Although this is one of their greatest virtues, Pisces should be more careful with their finances. They should try to be more choosy about the people to whom they lend money, so that they are not being taken advantage of. If they give money to charities they should follow it up to see that their contributions are put to good use. Even when Pisces are not rich, they still like to spend money on helping others. In this case they should really be careful, however: they must learn to say no sometimes and help themselves first.

Perhaps the biggest financial stumbling block for the Pisces is general passivity – a *laissez faire* attitude. In general Pisces like to go with the flow of events. When it comes to financial matters, especially, they need to be more aggressive. They need to make things happen, to create their own wealth. A passive attitude will only cause loss and missed opportunity. Worrying about financial security will not provide that security. Pisces need to go after what they want tenaciously.

Career and Public Image

Pisces like to be perceived by the public as people of spiritual or material wealth, of generosity and philanthropy. They look up to big-hearted, philanthropic types. They admire people engaged in large-scale undertakings and eventually would like to head up these big enterprises themselves. In short, they like to be connected with big organizations that are doing things in a big way.

If Pisces are to realize their full career and professional potential they need to travel more, educate themselves more and learn more about the actual world. In other words, they need some of the unflagging optimism of Sagittarius in order to reach the top.

Because of all their caring and generous characteristics, Pisces often choose professions through which they can help and touch the lives of other people. That is why many Pisces become doctors, nurses, social workers or teachers. Sometimes it takes a while before Pisces realize what they really want to do in their professional lives, but once they find a career that lets them manifest their interests and virtues they will excel at it.

Love and Relationships

It is not surprising that someone as 'otherworldly' as the Pisces would like a partner who is practical and down to earth. Pisces prefer a partner who is on top of all the details of life, because they dislike details. Pisces seek this quality in both their romantic and professional partners. More than anything else this gives Pisces a feeling of being grounded, of being in touch with reality.

As expected, these kinds of relationships – though necessary – are sure to have many ups and downs. Misunderstandings will take place because the two attitudes are poles apart. If you are in love with a Pisces you will experience these fluctuations and will need a lot of patience to see things stabilize. Pisces are moody, intuitive, affectionate and difficult to get to know. Only time and the right attitude will yield Pisces' deepest secrets. However, when in love with a Pisces you will find that riding the waves is worth it because they are good, sensitive people who need and like to give love and affection.

When in love, Pisces like to fantasize. For them fantasy is 90 per cent of the fun of a relationship. They tend to idealize their partner, which can be good and bad at the same time. It is bad in that it is difficult for anyone to live up to the high ideals their Pisces lover sets.

Home and Domestic Life

In their family and domestic life Pisces have to resist the tendency to relate only by feelings and moods. It is unrealistic to expect that your partner and other family members will be as intuitive as you are. There is a need for more verbal communication between a Pisces and his or her family. A cool, unemotional exchange of ideas and opinions will benefit everyone.

Some Pisces tend to like mobility and moving around. For them too much stability feels like a restriction on their freedom. They hate to be locked in one location for ever.

The sign of Gemini sits on the cusp of Pisces' 4th solar house of home and family. This shows that Pisces likes and needs a home environment that promotes intellectual and mental interests. They tend to treat their neighbours as family – or extended family. Some Pisceans can have a dual attitude towards the home and family – on the one hand they like the emotional support of the family, but on the other they dislike the obligations, restrictions and duties involved with it. For Pisces, finding a balance is the key to a happy family life.

Horoscope for 2024

Major Trends

Like last year, the main headline in the year ahead is Saturn's sojourn in your sign. He will be there for all of 2024. It is time to get serious about life, to take on more responsibility, to become more practical about the body and your path to personal happiness. Overall energy is not up to its usual standard. This can impact on health. On the other hand, this is a very good transit for weight-loss regimes. Also, it will enhance your management skills. More on this later. However, self-esteem and self-confidence could be a lot better.

Uranus has been in your 3rd house of intellectual interests for many years now, and he remains there this year. For students, especially below college level, this would tend to show many changes of schools over the years and many changes of educational plans. Now, with Jupiter also in your 3rd house until May 26, these changes seem to be fortunate this year. Students are doing much better in school, and there is good focus on the studies and good success there. It is a very good year for writers, teachers, bloggers, traders and retailers. The intellectual and communication faculties are unusually strong. This is a year, especially until May 26, to take courses in subjects that interest you, to attend more lectures and workshops and to otherwise increase your knowledge. It is a year to feed the mind.

Pluto will begin to move into your 12th house of spirituality this year. This is only the bare beginning of this transit, which will go on for 30 years and begins in earnest next year. Your whole spiritual life and practice is being transformed. There will also be major transformations in your charitable giving and in charitable or spiritual organizations that you are involved with.

Your major areas of interest this year are friends, groups and group activities until January 22 and from September 3 to November 20; spirituality from January 22 to September 3 and from November 20 to the end of the year; the body, image and personal appearance; communication, intellectual interests, siblings, neighbours and the neighbourhood in general until May 26; and home and family from May 26 onwards.

Your paths of greatest fulfilment this year are finance; communication, intellectual interests, siblings, neighbours and your neighbourhood until May 26; and home and family from May 26 onwards.

Health

(Please note that this is an astrological perspective on health and not a medical one. In days of yore there was no difference, both these perspectives were identical. But these days there could be quite a difference. For a medical perspective, please consult your doctor or health practitioner.)

Though Saturn's position in your sign tends to lower your overall energy, health should be good this year. This is because the other long-term planets are either in harmonious aspect or leaving you alone. Saturn by himself is not enough to cause disease. However, when Jupiter moves into Gemini – a stressful aspect for you – health will start to need more attention. With Saturn in your sign, don't be alarmed if you can't jog or cycle as far as you usually can. This is very natural under this transit. Saturn is teaching you about your physical limits, and it is good to respect that. So, if you are cycling, jogging or otherwise working out, rest when you are tired. Try not to force things. Listen to the messages that your body is sending you.

The fact that your 6th house is basically empty this year is another positive for overall health. You don't need to overly focus here as there is nothing really wrong. Of course, there will be times in the year when health and energy are less easy than usual. This is normal and nothing to be alarmed about. These are blips caused by the short-term planetary transits and their effects are temporary. When the challenging transits pass, your normal health and energy return.

Also, there is much you can do to enhance your health and prevent problems from developing. Give more attention to the following – the vulnerable areas of your Horoscope this year (the reflex points are shown in the chart opposite):

- The feet. These are always important for Pisces as the feet are ruled by your sign. Regular foot massage should be part and parcel of your normal health regime. You not only strengthen the feet themselves but the entire body as well. There are gadgets that give foot massages, not very expensive, and this might be a good investment for you. There are also gadgets that give foot whirlpool treatments and these would be very good for you, too.
- The heart is another area that is always important for Pisces. The Sun, the planet that rules the heart, is your health planet and the reflex point is shown opposite. The important thing with the heart is to avoid worry and anxiety, the two emotions that stress it out. Pisceans tend to be worriers, so this is very important. Meditation will help you replace worry with faith. Regular chest massage will also strengthen the heart.

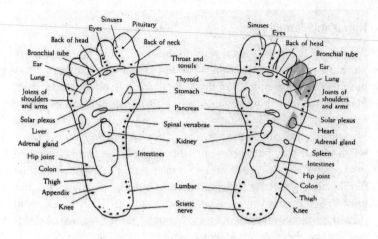

Important foot reflexology points for the year ahead

Try to massage all of the foot on a regular basis – the top of the foot as well as the bottom – but pay extra attention to the points highlighted on the chart. When you massage, be aware of 'sore spots' as these need special attention. It's also a good idea to massage the ankles and below them.

Your health planet is a fast-moving planet, and in any given year he will move through every sign and house of your Horoscope. This shows that your needs in health are always changing. Effective therapies also change constantly. So, there are many short-term health trends that depend on the position of the Sun at any given time and the kinds of aspects he receives. These will be dealt with in the monthly reports.

Jupiter's move into your 4th house on May 26 impacts women of childbearing age. They become more fertile. But this transit will also counteract some of the pessimism that comes from Saturn's position in your sign. Saturn in your own sign can give a tendency to depression, but Jupiter in your 4th house counteracts this. In some cases, this could show a person who seesaws from depression to optimism. Neither side dominates.

Home and Family

For many years now, Pisces, your 4th house of home and family, has not been prominent, or strong. The home and family situation has been more or less stable. But this will change in the year ahead, from May 26, as Jupiter moves into your 4th house and brings happy changes in the family situation. Many of you will move, others will renovate the existing home, others will buy second homes, and some will find that they have access to other homes. The family circle will expand, and this will go on well into next year. The expansion of the family circle generally happens through birth or marriage, but not always. Sometimes you meet people who are like family to you, who fulfil that role in your life. As we mentioned earlier, women of child-bearing age are more fertile than usual.

Jupiter is your career planet and his position in your 4th house gives many readings. The most obvious is that you pursue your career from home. Family and family connections are involved in your career. Another way to read this transit is that home, family and your emotional well-being *are* the career this year, the actual mission for the year ahead. The home base must be secure and happy before real career expansion can happen.

Those of you involved in formal psychological therapies will make great progress this year. But this will happen for many of you even if you are not in formal therapy. The cosmos has its own way of providing therapy. Memories will arise of people and situations from the past that could be affecting the present. It is good to look at these things from your present state of consciousness, and this will in many cases bring healing and resolution.

A parent or parent figure has love this year. It seems happy. But a move is not likely, nor is it advisable. Siblings and sibling figures have had many changes in recent years. This year things seem to be settling down in a happier way. The year ahead is happy for them, but a move is not likely and the home and family situation tends to the status quo.

Children and children figures in your life are having a very spiritual kind of year, but again a move is not likely, though there is nothing against it. Grandchildren, if you have them, or those who play that role in your life, seem to be making important renovations in the home. Also, they seem to be embarking on long-term psychological projects or therapies. These will go on for many more years.

If you're planning renovations in the home, and many of you are, July 21 to September 4 would be a good time. If you're thinking of redecorating or otherwise beautifying the home, May 24 to June 17 would be a good time.

Finance and Career

Last year was an excellent financial year for you, and the year ahead also seems prosperous. Though your money house is not strong this year the fact that the north node of the Moon will be in the 2nd house all year shows that there is much happiness and fulfilment to be found in pursuing financial goals. Sometimes the north node of the Moon creates excess. Your problem this year could be too much rather than too little money. But this is a good problem to have.

Mars is your financial planet. He is relatively fast moving. During the course of a year he will move through eight signs and houses of your Horoscope. Thus, there are many short-term trends in finance depending on where Mars is at any given time and the kind of aspects he receives. These are best dealt with in the monthly reports.

Mars will make one of his rare retrogrades in 2024, from December 6 to the end of the year. This is the time to exercise more caution in financial affairs. If possible, avoid major purchases or investments during this time. If these things have to happen, if it is not in your control, give them serious scrutiny.

While you are enjoying finance this year the opposite is true for the spouse, partner or current love. He or she seems bored with money and probably will pay less attention to it. Two eclipses in his or her financial house this year will shake up the finances and force needed changes.

A sibling or sibling figure will have a banner financial year.

Children, or children figures, are living the high life, but finances seem stable. The same is true for a parent or parent figure. He or she is living the high life but finances tend to the status quo. For them prosperity will be happening next year and the year after.

Grandchildren, or those who play that role in your life, have excellent job opportunities this year. These seem lucrative and happy.

With your 10th house of career basically empty in the year ahead (only short-term planets will move through there), career doesn't seem a major focus this year. It will more or less be status quo.

Until May 26 you can further your career with good communication skills. Good sales and marketing activities will boost the career. More education and 'up-skilling' will also boost the career.

After May 26, as we mentioned, the focus should be on home and family and getting into the right emotional state. Interior activities seem more important for the career than overt outer actions. I would also read this as preparing the home and family foundations that will allow for the expansion of the career later on. It seems more about constructing the infrastructure upon which a successful career is built rather than the superstructure this year.

Love and Social Life

With most of your planets in the Eastern sector of your chart, the sector of self, and with your own house ultra-powerful and your 7th house practically empty, this is not an especially strong love and social year. You seem more focused on yourself and your own personal path to happiness than on other people.

This is one complication. But there is another, stronger complication. Saturn is in your sign all year. While this gives great management skills and a healthy down-to-earth attitude to life, this transit is not especially good for love and romance. Perhaps, unconsciously, you present a dour and forbidding kind of demeanour. People can see you as cold, aloof, separate and distant. Now, this is not your real nature. You Pisceans are basically warm and friendly kinds of people. But this Saturn energy comes out subconsciously.

Happily, there is much you can do to improve the situation. First off, lighten up a bit. One can be a good manager without being overbearing. Secondly, make it a spiritual project to project love and warmth to others. Do this every day and you'll see dramatic changes in your love life.

The area of friendships, Platonic kinds of relationships, seems much happier this year. Existing friends seem very devoted to you, and opportunities for new friendships and to be involved in group activities will find you as you just go about your daily business. You are attracting spiritual kinds of friends and perhaps are more involved in spiritual and charitable organizations.

Mercury is your love planet. As our regular readers know, he is a very fast-moving planet and his movements tend to be erratic too. Sometimes he moves very fast, sometimes he moves slowly and sometimes he goes backwards. This tends to describe your love life and the kinds of love attitudes that you have. They can be erratic and constantly changing. There are many short-term trends in love that depend on where Mercury is at any given time, his speed of movement or lack thereof, and the kinds of aspects he receives. These short-term trends are best dealt with in the monthly reports.

Mercury as your love planet shows that you're attracted to people who are easy to talk to and smart. Ease of communication, ease of intellectual sharing, is a romantic turn-on. Thus, you would be attracted to intellectual types of people – writers, teachers, bloggers, etc. You would find romantic opportunity at lectures, seminars, school functions, the library or bookstore.

However, Mercury does double duty in your Horoscope. He is both your love planet and your family planet. So, in addition to the importance of intellectual sharing, emotional sharing is also important. You gravitate to people with strong family values, and family and family connections can play an important role in your love and social life.

Self-improvement

Neptune, the generic spiritual planet, has been occupying your own house for many years now. This enhances your already strong spirituality. More importantly this is an extended period of time in which you are learning about and experiencing the power of spirit over the physical body. In relation to spirit the body is like clay in the hands of the potter. Spirit, through your mind and will, shapes and forms the body as it wills. The body has no will of its own. It has appetites, habits and passions but no will of its own. It must, eventually, take on the form assigned to it by spirit. So, this year continues to be a good year to shape your body through spiritual means. It is good to hold a positive body image in your mind. I would choose an image of a time in your life when you were happy with your appearance. Hold on to this image, focus on it as much as possible, and eventually it will start to manifest in your physical body. A good affirmation to assist this is: 'I am created in the image and likeness of the divine, and this is my image now.'

Pluto, as we've said, begins a long, 30-year transit through your spiritual 12th house this year. This year is only the beginnings of the transit but next year it will be more permanent. The whole spiritual life is going to be transformed. We all hold a lot of mental, intellectual rubbish about this subject, and Pluto, who is very good at his job and very thorough, is going to eliminate this. Generally, if the erroneous concepts are not that deep the elimination can proceed harmoniously and easily. However, if the concepts are deep rooted and held with very fervent conviction, the elimination can be quite dramatic.

With Pluto now beginning to move through your 12th house, spiritual growth is not about reading more books and acquiring more knowledge. It is more about removing the concepts, thoughts and patterns that obstruct the spiritual flow. It's more about getting rid of obstructions than about adding anything.

For more information on astrology, healing and spiritual topics, please visit my blog at www.spiritual-stories.com.

Month-by-month Forecasts

January

Best Days Overall: 6, 7, 14, 15, 23, 24
Most Stressful Days Overall: 1, 2, 8, 9, 21, 22, 28, 29
Best Days for Love: 1, 2, 8, 9, 18, 19, 27, 28, 29, 30, 31
Best Days for Money: 1, 2, 9, 10, 11, 16, 17, 18, 19, 28, 29
Best Days for Career: 1, 2, 8, 9, 10, 11, 18, 19, 28, 29

Basically a happy month ahead, Pisces. Enjoy. The main headline is the incredible power in the beneficent 11th house – 60 per cent of the planets are either there or moving through there, signalling that the month ahead is unusually social. You are meeting all kinds of new people and making new friends. You are active online and on social media. Children and children figures in your life also have active social lives, and depending on their age there are many romantic opportunities for them. This is a month where you expand your knowledge of science, astrology, astronomy and technology. Many people have their Horoscopes done under these kinds of aspects.

Your financial planet Mars enters your 11th house on the 5th and will stay there for the rest of the month. This is a good aspect for buying high-tech equipment and gadgetry. It also shows that you can earn from these things. Your knowledge of science and the tech world will also increase this month.

The spiritual life is always important for Pisces but this month even more so. On the 20th the Sun moves into your 12th house of spirituality and the spiritual focus becomes more intense. Pisceans always have supernatural kinds of experiences, more so than other signs, but during this period they start to increase. You know how to handle this, however.

Health is good this month, but keep in mind that Saturn is still in your sign and so energy is probably not up to its usual levels. But the short-term planets are supporting you and making up the difference. Enhance the health in the ways mentioned in the yearly report and until the 20th give more attention to the back, knees and bones. Back and knee massage is very beneficial. After the 20th give more attention to the ankles and calves; they should be regularly massaged.

Love is free-wheeling until the 14th. Singles find love and romantic opportunity as they focus on their career. There are romantic opportunities with people involved in your career. On the 14th your love planet Mercury moves into your 11th house and romance can be found online, via social media, or as you get more involved with friends, groups and organizations. You are, however, more cautious in love from the 14th onwards.

Finances should also be good. With Mars in conservative Capricorn from the 5th onwards, the financial judgement is sound. You might take risks, but they will be well hedged and well thought out.

February

Best Days Overall: 1, 2, 3, 10, 11, 19, 20, 29
Most Stressful Days Overall: 4, 5, 17, 18, 24, 25
Best Days for Love: 6, 7, 8, 9, 17, 18, 24, 25, 26, 27, 29
Best Days for Money: 6, 7, 12, 13, 14, 15, 17, 24, 25, 26, 27
Best Days for Career: 4, 5, 6, 7, 14, 15, 24, 25

With your 12th house of spirituality super strong this month (60 per cent of the planets are either there or moving through there – a huge amount of planetary power) your challenge will be to keep your feet on the ground and deal with the mundane matters of the physical plane. The invisible world is so much more interesting than the visible! The dream life is so active and interesting that one wonders why you bother waking up. Nothing on earth matches it. Yet, in spite of all this, you should handle your earthly responsibilities. You were put here for a reason. All these spiritual truths you are seeing lose their value if they are not translated to the physical plane. They are given to make our life here on Earth better and more elevated.

The new Moon of the 9th occurs in your spiritual 12th house and is a particularly creative and fun kind of day. More importantly, it will clarify your spiritual insights, visions and dreams as the days go by.

On the 19th as the Sun moves into your own sign it becomes easier for you to deal with earthly, so-called, reality. You begin a yearly personal pleasure peak. Spiritual pleasures are wonderful, but so are the pleasures of the five senses. Your body was given to you for a reason, and it is time to pamper it and give it what it needs. It is good to get the body in the shape that you want.

Health and energy are still good this month. You can enhance the health further with ankle and calf massage until the 19th and with foot massage from the 19th onwards. Spiritual-healing techniques are always beneficial for you, and you always respond well to them, but after the 19th even more so. Your ability to heal others will also increase from the 19th.

Your health planet travels with Saturn from the 24th to the 26th. On those days enhance the health with back and knee massage. Hands-on healing will be stronger those days than metaphysical kinds of healing.

Finances are good this month, and get even better in March. Mars in your 11th house until the 13th shows that your fondest financial hopes and wishes are coming true. On the 13th your money planet enters your 12th house and signals excellent financial intuition. The spiritual world is very interested in your financial well-being.

You are in a strong cycle of personal independence at the moment. The month ahead, especially from the 19th onwards, is about you attaining your personal path of happiness. This is not selfishness. This is just a cycle that you're in. Others are important and should always be respected, but your way is best for you. Make the changes that need to be made to enhance your personal happiness. Others will support this, especially from the 23rd onwards. The time will come to put others first, but that time is not yet.

March

Best Days Overall: 1, 9, 10, 17, 18, 27, 28
Most Stressful Days Overall: 2, 3, 15, 16, 22, 23, 29, 30
Best Days for Love: 2, 7, 8, 9, 11, 17, 18, 19, 20, 27, 28, 29, 30
Best Days for Money: 4, 5, 7, 8, 11, 12, 13, 14, 15, 16, 22, 23, 27, 28
Best Days for Career: 2, 3, 4, 5, 13, 14, 22, 23, 29, 30

Another happy and prosperous month ahead, Pisces. You absorbed your fill of spirituality last month and this month it is time to get back into your body. You're still in a yearly personal pleasure peak, so enjoy the physical delights of the five senses. It is good to pamper the body and thank it for the selfless service it gives to you.

Like last month, the month ahead is about following your bliss, following your personal path of happiness. How can you be useful to others if you are not physically well or happy? Instinctively you understand this and are probably acting on it. The personal appearance shines. There is much beauty, grace and glamour to the image, especially from the 11th onwards. Love pursues you this month and you seem to have it on your own terms. This is a month for having your way in life.

A lunar eclipse on the 25th, while strong in its effects on children or children figures in your life, is relatively mild on you. However, keep in mind that if this eclipse hits something sensitive in your personal Horoscope, the one cast especially for you, it can be powerful indeed. So it won't hurt to take a more relaxed, easy kind of schedule while this eclipse is in effect. This also goes for the children or children figures. They should stay out of harm's way.

The eclipse occurs in your 8th house of regeneration and causes the spouse, partner or current love to make important financial changes. These can be disruptive while they are happening, but the end result is usually good.

More importantly, this eclipse brings psychological encounters with death. Generally, this is not physical death, only psychological encounters. You or someone close to you can have a near-death kind of experience, a close call. Perhaps you read of the death of some celebrity, or you hear of the death of someone that you know. Perhaps you have dreams of death. The dark angel has his ways of letting you know that he is around. Basically, these are messages to get more serious about life and to fulfil the function that you were born to fulfil. After all, life is short and can end at any time.

Many Pisceans are involved in the creative arts. This eclipse will produce changes in their personal creativity. Perhaps a new insight comes, or perhaps flaws are seen in their approach and changes become necessary.

A parent or parent figure is forced to make important financial changes.

April

Best Days Overall: 5, 6, 13, 14, 15, 23, 24, 25
Most Stressful Days Overall: 11, 12, 18, 19, 20, 26, 27
Best Days for Love: 7, 8, 16, 17, 18, 19, 20, 26, 27, 28
Best Days for Money: 1, 2, 5, 6, 7, 8, 9, 10, 13, 14, 18, 19, 23, 24
Best Days for Career: 1, 2, 9, 10, 18, 19, 26, 27

A monster solar eclipse on the 8th is the main headline this month. This is the strongest eclipse we will have this year. It is not only a total eclipse, but it impacts many other important planets in your chart, so it strongly affects several different areas and various important people in your life.

There is no need to panic, as this never helps, but it would be good to take common-sense precautions. Unnecessary driving should be avoided. If you must drive, be more mindful and careful about it. Spend more quiet time at home, read a book, watch a movie and, best of all, meditate. This advice is also good for the spouse, partner or current love as well.

The eclipse occurs in your money house and shows the need to make important financial changes. The events of the eclipse will show where your thinking, planning and financial strategies have been amiss. The changes you make are likely to be good ones, as you are also in the midst of a yearly financial peak. Still, it is not usually pleasant while the changes are happening.

Mercury, your love planet, is directly impacted by this eclipse and thus your current relationship will get tested. Probably, there are shake-ups in your social circle as well. The beloved is likely to be having personal dramas, and perhaps near-death experiences or psychological encounters with death. Be more patient with him or her. Sometimes long-repressed grievances arise in the relationship and now they must be dealt with.

Mercury is also your home and family planet, and rules one of your parents or parent figures. There are dramas in the life of this parent or parent figure and in the lives of family members. Often some hidden flaw in the home that you knew nothing about surfaces and must be dealt with.

Venus is also directly impacted by this eclipse. Thus, the spouse, partner or current love experiences financial dramas and needs to make important financial changes, too.

The impact of the eclipse on Venus, the ruler of your 8th house, signals more psychological encounters with death. Like last month there are many ways that this can happen. You, or people you know, have near-death experiences, or you can hear of the death of someone you know. Sometimes people dream of death. The cosmos is never punitive, only educational, and is giving you a deeper understanding of death. While we should love life, we should also understand what death is all about. The cosmos has its own unique ways of teaching us about this.

May

Best Days Overall: 2, 3, 4, 11, 12, 20, 21, 22, 30, 31
Most Stressful Days Overall: 4, 9, 10, 15, 16, 23, 24
Best Days for Love: 5, 6, 7, 8, 14, 15, 16, 25, 26, 27, 28
Best Days for Money: 5, 6, 8, 13, 14, 15, 16, 24, 26, 27, 28
Best Days for Career: 8, 15, 16, 23, 24, 26, 27, 28

Health is good until the 20th, but afterwards will need more attention. Until the 20th enhance the health with neck and throat massage; after the 20th make sure to get enough rest. Enhance the health with arm and shoulder massage, massage of the lung reflex and fresh air and breathing exercises. Diet and emotional harmony also become more important from the 20th onwards. The good news is that you will have emotional happiness from the 26th onwards.

The Sun, your health planet, travels with Uranus on the 13th and 14th. This signals changes in your health regime and positive results from spiritual-healing methods. The Sun travels with Jupiter from the 18th to the 20th, showing a happy job opportunity, a career boost and happy health news.

The main headline of the month is the power in your 4th house from the 20th onwards. Your 4th house of home and family is chock-full of planets, and good ones to boot. Beneficent planets. There is great pleasure and happiness and dealings with the home and hearth this month. Even your career planet Jupiter moves into your 4th house on the 26th. Home and family are actually your mission, your real career, this month – and for the rest of the year ahead with Jupiter taking up long-term residence in your 4th house. Many of you will pursue external types of careers but perhaps from home.

Jupiter's move into your 4th house can bring a move, if not this month, then in future months, or the fortunate purchase or sale of a home. Jupiter can bring the enlargement of the present home or the acquiring of additional homes. All these scenarios fit the symbolism of Jupiter moving through your 4th house. Women of childbearing age are much more fertile than usual, as we mentioned in the yearly report. This tendency will go on well into next year.

You're in a great month for making psychological progress, Pisces, and for gaining psychological knowledge. Those of you involved in formal therapy situations will make great progress. But even if you're not in any formal type of therapy, much psychological healing will happen. The cosmos in its infinite wisdom has its ways of doing this.

June

Best Days Overall: 7, 8, 17, 18, 26, 27
Most Stressful Days Overall: 5, 6, 12, 13, 19, 20
Best Days for Love: 5, 6, 12, 13, 15, 16, 17, 26, 27
Best Days for Money: 1, 2, 5, 12, 13, 14, 21, 22, 24, 28, 29, 30
Best Days for Career: 5, 14, 19, 20, 24

Health still needs watching until the 20th. The good news is that you will see a big improvement from the 20th onwards. In the meantime, make sure to get enough rest. If you're exercising be aware of what is going on in the body and try not to push it beyond its limits. Enhance the health in the ways mentioned in the yearly report, but also give more attention to the arms, shoulders and lungs. Arm and shoulder massage, as well as massage of the lung reflex point, will be beneficial. Diet also seems important this month.

Your 4th house of home and family is still very powerful, and happy, this month. So, continue to pay attention here. If you have an external, outer career it would be helpful to pursue it from home and in meditative, inward kinds of ways.

Finances seem good this month as Mars, your financial planet, is in your money house and in his own sign until the 9th. Thus, he is more powerful on your behalf and this spells extra earnings. On the 9th Mars enters your 3rd house and stays there for the rest of the month. This shows earnings from buying, selling and trading. Also, it shows that whatever you are doing, good sales, marketing and good use of the media are important. Until the 9th you need to be careful about taking risks and overspending. After the 9th, as Mars moves into Taurus, the financial judgement becomes more stable and conservative.

Love seems happy this month. Your love planet Mercury is moving forward speedily, indicating confidence and fast progress towards your social goals. Mercury travels with Jupiter on the 3rd and 4th and this brings a happy romantic opportunity for singles. On the 17th Mercury moves into your 5th house of fun and creativity. This aspect favours love affairs and flings rather than serious committed love. For those already in a relationship this shows a need to have more fun with the beloved.

On the 20th the Sun enters your 5th house and you begin a yearly personal pleasure peak. It's time to have fun and enjoy some leisure. Having fun is excellent therapy for your health as well. A carefree, joyous attitude will heal or alleviate many health problems.

July

Best Days Overall: 4, 5, 6, 14, 15, 16, 23, 24
Most Stressful Days Overall: 2, 3, 9, 10, 11, 17, 18, 29, 30, 31
Best Days for Love: 5, 6, 7, 8, 9, 10, 11, 17, 18, 25, 26, 27, 28
Best Days for Money: 1, 2, 3, 9, 10, 12, 13, 21, 22, 24, 26, 29, 30
Best Days for Career: 2, 3, 12, 13, 17, 18, 21, 22, 29, 30

A happy month, Pisces. You're still in the midst of a yearly personal pleasure peak until the 20th. This is a time for pursuing leisure activities and for expressing your personal creativity. There is much involvement with children and children figures in your life, which is also a good thing. It is the child that knows how to be happy, and we can learn this from them.

Mars, your financial planet, is in your 3rd house until the 20th. So, like last month, you earn through buying, selling, trading, and through good marketing and PR skills. On the 13th and 14th Mars travels with Uranus. This brings sudden and unexpected money or financial opportunities to you. It also brings a sharp financial intuition. On the 20th Mars moves on into your 4th house and stays there for the rest of the month. This transit shows you spending more on the home and the family, and perhaps earning through them too. Family and family connections seem important in the financial life.

The family as a whole seems more prosperous in the month ahead – especially one of the parents or parent figures.

Health is good this month. You can enhance it further with right diet, massage of the abdomen and the abdominal reflex, and in the ways mentioned in the yearly report.

On the 22nd the party slows down and you enter a more serious kind of time. You're in the mood for work and service. Your 6th house of health and work becomes very powerful on the 22nd. Because health is basically good, I presume the focus will be more on work than on health. Job-seekers have many job opportunities, and good ones. Those who hire others will find good workers. Even those of you who are already employed will have opportunities for overtime and for side jobs.

On the 22nd your health planet the Sun moves into his own sign and house. Thus, he is powerful on your behalf. After the 22nd enhance the health with chest massage, massage of the heart reflex point and in the ways mentioned in the yearly report.

Neptune, the ruler of your Horoscope, begins to retrograde on the 2nd and will be moving backwards for many months. Along with this, the planetary power overall is moving to the Western, social sector of your Horoscope. So, self-will, personal initiative, is becoming less and less important while social skills and other people are becoming more important. The timing is very nice. Your good comes to you through the good graces of others. Your social skills are more important than your personal abilities. Let others have their way, so long as it isn't destructive.

Children and children figures prosper from the 22nd onwards.

August

Best Days Overall: 1, 2, 11, 12, 19, 20, 28, 29
Most Stressful Days Overall: 5, 6, 7, 13, 14, 26, 27
Best Days for Love: 5, 6, 7, 8, 17, 18, 21, 22, 29, 30, 31
Best Days for Money: 8, 9, 17, 18, 19, 20, 21, 22, 26, 27
Best Days for Career: 8, 9, 13, 14, 17, 18, 27

Health is reasonable until the 22nd. But after then it needs more watching. In fact, it won't hurt to pay more attention to health all month. As always, don't let yourself get overtired. Enhance the health with massage of the heart reflex and chest massage until the 22nd and afterwards with abdominal massage and massage of the small intestine reflex.

The new Moon of the 4th occurs in your 6th house of health and this should be a good healing day. But, more important than any temporary relief it gives is that the new Moon will clarify health issues as the days progress. This will go on well into next month. All the information that you need will come to you naturally and normally. It will also clarify questions that you have about your job situation.

Until the 22nd it is good to do all those boring, detail-oriented tasks that you keep putting off – your accounts, filing, etc. They will be easier because you're more in the mood for such work.

Love is active, but very complicated. On the one hand you begin a yearly love and social peak on the 22nd, so there are many romantic opportunities for singles. The problem is that Mercury, your love planet, is retrograde from the 4th to the 25th. In addition, Neptune (you) will be retrograde all month. So, neither you nor the people that you meet are sure of what you want, and there are many doubts and uncertainties about love. This is so in existing relationships as well. You and the beloved are beset with doubts. The only solution is time. Enjoy the love opportunities that will surely come but there is no need to rush into anything or make any important decisions.

Mars, your financial planet, spends the month in your 4th house. You are spending more on the home and family and probably are earning through them as well. Family and family connections are very important in your financial life.

Mars will travel with Jupiter from the 11th to the 14th and this signals financial increase, a nice pay day. This can come from a pay rise, official or unofficial, through a parent of parent figure, or through the increase in the value of assets that you already own.

September

Best Days Overall: 7, 8, 16, 17, 24, 25
Most Stressful Days Overall: 2, 3, 9, 10, 22, 23, 29, 30
Best Days for Love: 2, 3, 4, 5, 12, 13, 14, 15, 21, 23, 24, 29, 30
Best Days for Money: 4, 5, 7, 8, 14, 15, 16, 17, 18, 19, 22, 23, 24, 25
Best Days for Career: 4, 5, 9, 10, 14, 15, 22, 23

A lunar eclipse on the 18th has a powerful impact on you, so be sure to take it nice and easy while it is in effect. It is powerful for two reasons: one, because it occurs in your own sign; and two, because it impacts Neptune, the ruler of your Horoscope and a very important planet in your chart.

All of you will feel this to some degree but those of you born later in Pisces, March 14–18, will feel it the strongest. This eclipse produces a need to re-evaluate yourself, your image, your self-concept, your opinion of yourself and the way that you want others to see you. This is generally a healthy thing to do from time to time but now the events of the eclipse force it. Either you define yourself for yourself, or others will do it for you, and this will not be so pleasant. In the coming months these inner changes will naturally be reflected in your outer appearance, wardrobe and image. You will present a different image; people will see you differently.

If you haven't been careful in dietary matters, this eclipse can produce a detox of the physical body. While the symptoms of this detox often seem similar to the symptoms of sickness, it's really not the same thing. This is merely the body getting rid of what doesn't belong there.

Children and children figures in your life experience personal dramas and should also reduce their schedules over the eclipse. This doesn't mean that they avoid things that need to be done, only that unimportant diary dates are rescheduled for another time. Friends, a parent or parent figure are forced to make important financial changes. Friends can have personal dramas happening. There are important financial changes in spiritual or charitable organizations that you are involved with.

Every lunar eclipse will agitate the dream life. A lunar eclipse in Pisces even more so. Disturbing dreams during this time should not be given too much attention. Most of it is just psychic rubbish stirred up by the eclipse.

October

Best Days Overall: 4, 5, 13, 14, 21, 22, 23, 31
Most Stressful Days Overall: 6, 7, 8, 19, 20, 26, 27, 28
Best Days for Love: 1, 4, 5, 12, 13, 14, 21, 22, 24, 25, 26, 27, 28, 31
Best Days for Money: 2, 4, 5, 11, 12, 13, 14, 15, 16, 19, 20, 22, 23, 29, 30, 31
Best Days for Career: 2, 6, 7, 8, 11, 12, 19, 20, 29, 30

A solar eclipse on the 2nd shakes up the world and different parts of your life. This eclipse is not as strong as the last solar eclipse in April, but it is still very strong. So it would be a good idea for you, parents, parent figures and family members to take a nice easy, relaxed schedule. Do whatever needs to be done but reschedule anything else. This advice is also important for the spouse, partner or current love. There's no need to be involved in stressful or daredevil type activities. Stay out of harm's way as much as possible. Stay close to home, read a book, watch an interesting movie, or meditate.

This eclipse occurs in your 8th house and shows that the spouse, partner or current love is forced to make dramatic kinds of financial changes. It could be that these involve important career changes as well, and can cause personal dramas in his or her life. Be more patient with the beloved while the eclipse is in effect – and even afterwards.

Once again, the dark angel is letting you know that he is around, bringing psychological encounters with death. The dark angel will never take anyone before their time, but we rarely know when that time is. So, death will be brought to your attention one way or another – sometimes through a near-death experience, sometimes through the death of someone you know, sometimes by dreams of death – in order that you can understand death on a deeper level. This will help you live your life better.

Because Mercury is directly impacted by the eclipse, your current relationship is being tested. The beloved is having all kinds of personal dramas – financial, career and perhaps physical dramas. Be more patient with him or her this month.

Much of what we have said above also applies to a parent or parent figure.

Because Mars is directly impacted by this eclipse as well, you, too, are having financial dramas and need to make dramatic financial changes. These financial dramas are affecting both you and the beloved.

This eclipse causes dramas in the home. Perhaps repairs are needed in the home. With Jupiter in your 4th house these dramas can actually be good things, but good things can be just as disruptive as bad things. Perhaps family members are having multiple births, and these, though happy, require a lot of reshuffling in the home life. But there are other scenarios as well.

November

Best Days Overall: 1, 2, 10, 11, 18, 19, 28, 29
Most Stressful Days Overall: 3, 4, 16, 17, 22, 23, 24, 29, 30
Best Days for Love: 3, 4, 12, 13, 20, 21, 22, 23, 24, 29, 30
Best Days for Money: 2, 8, 9, 12, 13, 16, 17, 20, 21, 26, 27, 29, 30
Best Days for Career: 3, 4, 8, 9, 16, 17, 26, 27, 29, 30

Health and energy look good this month, especially until the 21st. After that, health will need keeping more of an eye on. This month the health is enhanced with detox regimes until the 21st and with massage of the liver reflex and thighs from the 21st onwards. As always, when energy is low, especially after the 21st, make sure to get enough rest.

Until the 21st your 9th house is very powerful. This is a beneficent house and any planet that occupies it automatically becomes more beneficent. So, your health planet in the 9th house until the 21st is a wonderful health signal. Even if you have pre-existing conditions, there should be good news about them while the Sun is in this house.

This is a great transit for college-level students or for those applying to college. There is success here. If you are involved in legal issues, these go well too. This is a good month to pursue religious, philosophical and theological studies. The mind is more attuned to these subjects and you should get good results. Foreign lands often call under these kinds of transits, but with Jupiter retrograde this is a better time to plan these things than for making the trip.

Though energy is lower after the 21st, nice things are still happening. You begin a yearly career peak and there is much career progress happening. You have a good work ethic, which is noticed by superiors. The family as a whole, and especially a parent or parent figure, is very supportive of the career. The love life, too, seems centred around the career. With Mercury, your love planet, near the top of your Horoscope, it shows that love is high on your list of priorities and tends to success. Singles gravitate to powerful and successful people: power and position are romantic turn-ons. But love is complicated this month. Your ruling planet Neptune is still retrograde this month, and Mercury starts to retrograde on the 26th. So, neither you nor those you attract are sure about things. Both of you have doubts and reservations that only time can work out. Best to enjoy love for what it is without trying to project too far into the future. There is no rush.

The love planet in your 10th house gives other messages as well. It is good to pursue career objectives through social means. Your social skills and general likeability are probably just as important as your professional skills. It would be good to attend or host the right kind of parties and gatherings. A good part of your socializing seems career related.

December

Best Days Overall: 7, 8, 15, 16, 25, 26
Most Stressful Days Overall: 1, 13, 14, 20, 21, 27, 28, 29
Best Days for Love: 2, 3, 4, 9, 10, 13, 14, 17, 18, 19, 20, 21, 22, 23, 24, 31
Best Days for Money: 6, 9, 10, 14, 17, 18, 19, 23, 24
Best Days for Career: 1, 6, 14, 23, 24, 27, 28, 29

Continue to watch your health until the 21st. If you're exercising, be aware of what's happening in the body. If you feel pain or discomfort, take a break. Avoid pushing the body beyond its limits. Health should improve after the 21st. In the meantime enhance the health with massage of the liver reflex and the thighs until the 21st. After the 21st enhance the health with back and knee massage. Massage of the gall-bladder reflex would also be good after the 21st.

Though overall energy could be a lot better, the career is successful. You're still in the midst of a yearly career peak and much progress is happening. The family as a whole seems more successful and, like last month, they seem supportive of your career. You don't have the usual conflicts between home and career these days. The love life is starting to straighten out, too. Neptune (you) starts to move forward on the 7th and Mercury (the beloved) starts to move forward on the 15th. There is more clarity and better judgement in love and social matters.

Your love attractions are pretty much as they were last month. Singles are attracted to people of position and power. Power and position are still strong romantic turn-ons and you are meeting and mingling with these kinds of people this month. Pursuing your career by social means still seems important in the month ahead. Much of your socializing is career related. By all means attend, or host, the right kind of parties and gatherings. Your professional skills are very important, but your social skills might be just as important in furthering your career this month. Singles have romantic opportunities as they pursue their career goals and most likely with people who are involved in their career. The problem with this is a tendency to relationships of convenience rather than of real love.

Mars will spend the month in your 6th house, which indicates you are earning from your hard work, the old-fashioned way. Mars makes one of his rare retrogrades this month, on the 6th. He only goes retrograde once every two years, so it is a relatively unusual event. Major purchases or investments are best put on hold after the 6th. They need more due diligence. There is a need now to clarify the financial thinking and goals. Earnings will still come, but perhaps with some delays. Your financial planet in the sign of Leo can make you even more speculative and risk-taking than usual. But this should be avoided this month, especially from the 6th.

The new Moon of the 1st occurs in your 10th house and prospers the career. It is also a good career day for children and children figures in your life. More importantly, career issues are going to be clarified as the days progress. This will go on until the next new Moon on the 30th. This second new Moon of the month – a pretty rare event – occurs in your 11th house, making it an excellent social day. It seems more festive than usual.